THROUGH THE YEAR WITH THE IRISH SAINTS

THROUGH THE YEAR WITH THE IRISH SAINTS

Stella Durand

VERITAS

Published 2020 by
Veritas Publications
7–8 Lower Abbey Street
Dublin 1
Ireland
www.veritas.ie

ISBN 978 1 84730 917 4

Copyright © Stella Durand, 2020

10 9 8 7 6 5 4 3 2 1

A catalogue record for this book is available from the British Library.

Designed by Jeannie Swan, Veritas Publications
Cover design and art direction by Lir Mac Cárthaigh
Printed in the Republic of Ireland by SPRINT-print Ltd, Dublin

Veritas books are printed on paper made from the wood pulp of managed forests. For every tree felled, at least one tree is planted, thereby renewing natural resources.

Dedicated to Ray Simpson, who first inspired my enthusiasm for the early Irish saints, and who continues to inspire.

With sincere thanks to: Ned Kennedy, Monsignor Brendan Byrne, Bishop Kevin Doran, Dr Susan Hood, Chris Potylycki, Síne Quinn, Daragh Reddin, Pamela McLoughlin, Leeann Gallagher and the staff at Veritas Publications.

CONTENTS

INTRODUCTION	11
JANUARY	13
FEBRUARY	35
MARCH	57
APRIL	79
MAY	101
JUNE	125
JULY	147
AUGUST	171
SEPTEMBER	193
OCTOBER	215
NOVEMBER	237
DECEMBER	259
BIBLIOGRAPHY	281
INDEX OF SAINTS	285

INTRODUCTION

My interest in the Irish saints was initially sparked by several contacts in my youth with the erudite Archbishop George Simms. In 1995, when I was about to start training for ordination in the Church of Ireland, I came across a new dispersed ecumenical community that was starting up based on Lindisfarne, the Holy Island off the coast of Northumberland in north-east England. I became a member of this community in 1997, inspired by Revd Ray Simpson, to whom this book is dedicated and who inspired me to find out more about the saints and to write a book about St Columba. The community is international – with three hundred and fifty members at least. The Irish branch is called Cairde an Anama.

This book features saints who were born in Ireland and who spent their ministry there. It also includes saints who were born elsewhere but spent their ministry in Ireland – for how could we omit St Patrick? This category will include the recently canonised St John Henry Newman, who is considered by many to be an honorary Irishman. Saints who were born and often educated in Ireland and who went to other countries as missionaries are also included. How could we miss out Columbanus, Fursey and Kilian? Those not yet canonised are listed with 'blessed' or 'venerable' as appropriate rather than 'saint' before their name. There are about a thousand Irish saints to choose from, so naturally the choice was dictated by how much was known about the saint's life.

Saints often had several names: their Irish name, the anglicised version of their Irish name, a Latin name and sometimes also a pet name. The best-known name has been chosen where possible, but the other ones have been listed as well. Where possible, the feast days will be the traditional one for the saint, but very often there are two or three saints commemorated on the same day. When this occurs then some have been referred to the nearest available date.

Hagiography, writing about saints, is quite ancient. Irish hagiography was a definite literary genre, whereby each saint had attributed to him or her a conventional and predictable set of miracles, many of them in imitation of Jesus Christ, such as turning water into wine, having twelve disciples and raising the dead to life. Some of these stories have been included, for their spiritual meaning, for what we can learn from them to help our own Christian pilgrimages, especially in the cases where the legends are all we know about the saint in question. One can imagine how they arose when we think of the legend of St Kevin and the blackbird: local people would have said something like, 'Kevin prays so long a bird could have hatched her eggs in the time', and this would have been embroidered as it was passed on, in a kind of Chinese whispers. The intention has been to be as historically accurate as possible while including the miracles attributed to each saint in order to reflect on the inner meaning of some stories – this is a devotional book rather than a history book per se. The stories of some of the saints are priceless, full of humour and often quirky. Although these men and women were strict and ascetic, one senses that there was also a strong strain of joy running through their lives.

It is suggested that after reading the mini-biography, you go on to read the reflection and spend time thinking it through. Then you can make up your own prayer or collect thanking God for the saint and what you have learnt or we all can learn from reflecting on his or her life, and possibly even affirming a resolution based on that.

May God bless you in your working through of this book.

JANUARY

1 JANUARY
St Fanchea/Faine/Garbh

D.585. FEAST DAY: *1 January or 20 January*

St Fanchea, born at Clogher, was an abbess who founded Rossory Convent on Lough Erne. She was the sister of the famous St Enda of Aran, warrior-prince of Oriel. Once Enda's soldiers passed by her house singing a song of victory. Fanchea told them not to approach as they were contaminated by blood. It was she who urged Enda to abandon his life of violence. He agreed on condition she give him one of her nuns as a bride. She granted his request, but the young woman died on the eve of the wedding, and Enda took this as a sign that he should join the Christian Church. His fellow soldiers tried to dissuade him, but thanks to Fanchea's prayers their feet became rooted to the ground enabling Enda's escape. Fanchea later left the convent to join Enda on Inis Mór, Aran Islands, Co. Galway.

REFLECTION

Have I ever considered how the influence of a family member could sway a person to a better life? Have I ever used my loving persuasion to help a family member as Fanchea did?

2 JANUARY
St Munchin/Manchen/Muncius/Manchianus

D. SEVENTH CENTURY. FEAST DAY: *2 January*

The patron saint of Limerick was affectionately known as Munchin the Wise. His name actually means 'the little monk'. He was abbot of a very large monastery at Mungret near Limerick, which may have been founded by St Patrick. Munchin is also credited with founding a church (Cill Mainchín) on the island of Inis Sibhton. When the community was challenged to a test of intellect by a neighbouring monastery, they dressed some young monks up as women and set them to washing clothes in the river that the opposing team had to cross. When the visiting team heard the washerwomen conversing in Latin and Greek, so daunted were they by the display of erudition that they turned tail and fled. This led to the saying: 'As wise as the women of Mungret'.

REFLECTION

Do I, like the little monk, use my sense of humour to help me unwind in difficult times and to see the funny side of challenging situations?

3 JANUARY

St Fionnlugh/Finlugh/Finnly

D. SIXTH CENTURY. FEAST DAY: *3 January*

St Columba founded the abbey of Tamlachtfinlagan near Lough Foyle in Co. Derry, where he instated Fionnlugh as its first abbot. Fionnlugh joined St Columba on the island of Iona, off the Scottish coast. Once, when Columba's life was in danger on the island of Hinba near Iona, Fionnlugh donned his master's clothes and was pierced with a spear in an assault intended for Columba. Miraculously, Fionnlugh remained unhurt. He was the brother of Fintan of Dooen and Coona, Co. Limerick, who was a distinguished missionary. According to legend, Fionnlugh lived until the grand old age of two hundred and sixty.

REFLECTION

Who would I go out of my way to protect at all costs? Could I trust God to protect me in dangerous circumstances?

4 JANUARY
St Dabeoc

D. FIFTH OR SIXTH CENTURY. FEAST DAY: *1 January or 24 July*

St Dabeoc was the founder of the monastery on Saints' Island on Lough Derg, near Pettigo in Co. Donegal. Dabeoc was half Irish. He came to Donegal from Wales in the fifth or sixth century. He was said to be the youngest of ten sons, who all became priests, and seven sisters, who all became nuns. Dabeoc is regarded as the patron saint of Saint Patrick's Purgatory on Station Island. People who have visited the cave through the centuries have spoken of grievous pains endured but also of beholding ineffable glory. It is a popular place of pilgrimage today for both Christians and non-Christians.

REFLECTION
Have I visited any of the pilgrimage sites in my own country? Or abroad? Could I enrich my spiritual life by visiting any of the country's many Christian monuments?

5 JANUARY
St Scuthin/Scothinus/Schotin/Scolan

D. SIXTH CENTURY. FEAST DAY: *2 January*

St Scuthin, son of Sedne from Slieve Margy in Ossory, crossed the Irish Sea to be educated by St David, patron saint of Wales. He returned to Ireland and founded a monastery at Tascoffin, Co. Kilkenny, near the River Barrow. He was a learned man and wrought many miracles. He lived a particularly ascetic life, being ever cautious of the danger of 'inner warfare', of the flesh rebelling against the spirit. Scuthin developed the habit of plunging into a tub of cold water as a penance. The story goes that he became so spiritual from his asceticism that he could walk on water. On one occasion, according to the legend, Scuthin was doing just that when he met St Finbar sailing by in a boat and he tossed a scuthin flower to Finbar – the flower after which he is named.

REFLECTION

Scuthin was very concerned about inner warfare and the danger of giving in to temptation. What are the major temptations in my life and how can I wage battle against them?

6 JANUARY

St Dimma/Dioma/Dime/Domaingert

D.658. FEAST DAY: *6 January*

A member of the ruling family of Munster, Dimma became a monk at an early age under St Colman Elo at Lynally, Co. Offaly. Colman made him eat well while young to prepare himself for the rigours of monastic life once he came of age. Dimma is reputed to have copied out a book of Gospels for St Cronan of Roscrea in forty days without eating or sleeping. (Although many scholars are understandably sceptical about this because of the timescale!) The book, known as *The Book of Dimma*, is now in the Old Library, Trinity College Dublin. Dimma became Bishop of Connor.

REFLECTION

Even allowing for some embellishment, St Dimma's achievement in creating *The Book of Dimma* is quite remarkable. Have I the patience for tasks that take a long time to complete? Can I apply myself to cultivating a greater sense of the spiritual without losing patience?

7 JANUARY
St Kentigerna/Cennitghearna

D.734. FEAST DAY: *7 January*

Kentigerna was the daughter of the seventh century King Cellach of Leinster, and sister to St Comgan. After the death of her husband, Feredach, she went to Ross in Scotland as a missionary. She travelled with her family, to join her son Foillan, who had been living as a hermit there for several years. She laboured alongside her brother, and was particularly supportive of families facing difficulties. Having founded several churches, Kentigerna became a recluse on a small island on Loch Lomond known as Nun's Island, Inchelroide, Royal Island or Inch Cailleach (Island of the old woman). She is known as the Mother of Saints, and as 'Loch Lomond's Lady of Grace'. She is regarded as the patron saint of Loch Lomond.

REFLECTION
Not many people are willing to work with dysfunctional families, but those who do make an invaluable contribution to society. Could I pray for God to send workers into that particular harvest field, and pray for families known to me who are experiencing difficulties?

8 JANUARY
St Albert

D. SEVENTH CENTURY. FEAST DAY: *8 January*

Albert was the patron saint of Cashel, and possibly Bishop of Emly, since Cashel was not then a bishopric. Albert resigned his see and went into exile for Christ, wandering as far as Rome and the Holy Land. Along with his brother Erhard, who resigned his see of Ardagh to go abroad to evangelise, Albert preached throughout Bavaria. He was a bishop at Ratisbon. He died at the end of the seventh century. His other brother or companion Hiddulp became Archbishop of Treves. Albert and and his brother Erhard are buried in Ratisbon, near to Oberammagau. He is much venerated still in Ratisbon, where an order of nuns called the *Erardinonnen* in memory of his brother were founded after their deaths.

REFLECTION

To have been called away from a comfortable position to go and serve God abroad, takes courage. Am I willing to move out of my comfort zone if God calls me to?

9 JANUARY

St Fillan/Foillan/Phillane

D.755. FEAST DAY: *9 January*

Fillan was the son of St Kentigerna and Feredach, who entered St Munna's monastery in Wexford. He went to Scotland before his mother and uncle St Comgan did. He became a hermit at Strathfillan near St Andrew's, later joining his mother and uncle in Ross. To distinguish him from other Fillans, he is known as Fillan of Loch Earn. His bell and crozier are still preserved. Legend says that he had a light that shone out of his arm and enabled him to write in the dark. Robert the Bruce venerated Fillan and attributed his victory at Bannockburn to his intervention. His festival was kept in Killin as a holiday for mill workers as they believed he started the first market and the first mill. His handbell is in the National Museum of Antiquities in Edinburgh.

REFLECTION

Becoming a hermit showed that Fillan put prayer as his number one priority. How much do I prioritise prayer? How important is it to me?

10 JANUARY
St Diarmaid/'Diarmaid the Just'

D.540. FEAST DAY: *10 January*

Diarmaid was a prince from Connaught, a friend of St Senan, who founded a monastery on Inis Clothrann on Lough Ree, where he had retired for solitude. He is said to have been the brother of St Feidlimidh and St Femia. Diarmaid is thought to have fostered the carpenter Beoaidh's sons, Ciarán and Donnan, and to actually have started the practice of choosing church men for their natural abilities. He was St Ciarán's confessor. He is often known as 'Diarmaid the Just'. Ruins of six churches have been found on Inis Clothrann. He is buried on the island, which is a site of pilgrimage. Diarmaid's burial place is supposed to be protected against women, female children or pagans, none of whom are allowed to touch it. A woman who violated this is said to have met with instant death.

REFLECTION
Diarmaid was soul-friend or confessor to Ciarán who did him credit. Am I the material that a soul-friend could be made of? Do I give advice lovingly and after prayer? How could I improve as a Christian friend?

11 JANUARY
St Ernan

D. SIXTH OR SEVENTH CENTURY. FEAST DAY: *11 January*

Ernan was a monk who was probably a hermit on Tory Island. The records are extremely vague about this saint. Columba is said to have founded a monastery on Tory Island, leaving a 'venerable local man' in charge – Ernan. There was an Ernan among the twelve disciples who went to Iona with Columba. That

Ernan was probably Columba's uncle. We will never know for certain if this was the same man.

REFLECTION

Whether the venerable man put in charge of Tory Island was Columba's uncle or not, we can learn from his example. 'Venerable' might not necessarily imply an old age – the important thing is that he was considered trustworthy and suitable to be in charge. Am I considered as a person worthy of being put in charge of an enterprise or project? Am I trustworthy and honest? Am I hardworking? Am I a person who others could work well with and whose authority they would respect?

12 JANUARY

St Loichene the Silent

D.694. FEAST DAYS: *12 January and 12 June*

St Loichene was the Abbot of Kildare, several hundred years after the time of its founding by St Brigid. He was best known as Loichene the Silent, but also occasionally dubbed Loichene the Wise. Not much else is known about him, but that he met with a violent death. According to *The Annals of Tigernach* he was murdered.

REFLECTION

Silence and wisdom – one can learn something from the merging of these two attributes in one person! Sometimes it is wise to be silent. It is certainly wise to cultivate a silence in which deep prayer can happen, so we can have a loving communion with God. Do I use silence in this way? Do I use the silences provided in the Church's liturgy to good effect? Remembering that it is said that all the answers we need are within us, do I remain silent before giving advice or sorting out problems in order to reach the deep springs of wisdom and the Holy Spirit within me?

13 JANUARY
St Kessog/Makkesagius

D. SIXTH CENTURY. FEAST DAY: *13 January or 10 March*

Kessog was a son of the King of Cashel. As a child he was playing with two other princes when they all fell into a lake. His two companions were tragically drowned. Kessog prayed all night with the result that his two companions were restored to life. He went as a missionary to Scotland, and ministered around the Loch Lomond area, where he is remembered at Monk's Island and Luss. He became a bishop known as Makkesagius around 520. He was said to have been martyred abroad and his body returned wrapped in herbs. He is buried in the village of Luss, whose name means 'herb'.

REFLECTION
Kessog prayed all night for his two little companions. When prayer for healing is needed, do I give up too quickly? Perseverance in prayer can be necessary sometimes. How good is my perseverance? Or am I yielding to the modern age's demand for instant answers?

14 JANUARY
St Dubhthach of Iona/Duach/Duffy

D.938. FEAST DAY: *5 February*

Dubhthach was the son of Dubhán, from a family who were members of the Conall clan, as was St Columba. There are several holy wells recalling him by name in Co. Donegal, at Annagry in the parish of Templecrone and on the island of Inishdooey in the parish of Tullaghobegly. He became Abbot of Iona in 927. During his abbacy, which lasted twelve years, it is thought that the Iona community relocated to Kells in Co. Meath.

REFLECTION

When we come to a place that is totally new to us, do we ever think of claiming it for God or of praying for its people? Are there any places you find it particularly hard to pray for, or are reluctant to pray for? Ask God to show you the reason for this.

15 JANUARY

St Ita/Íte/Mida/Íde/Deirdre

D.570. FEAST DAY: 15 *January*

Ita is the most famous Irish female saint after Brigid and is dubbed 'foster mother of the saints of Ireland'. From the Decies in Co. Waterford, she founded and became the first abbess of a convent in Killeady in Co. Limerick with a boys' school attached. She became spiritual director to Enda, Brendan and Colman. She restored a carpenter, Beohan, to life so he could rear his son – later St Mochaemog. She advised Brendan he would never reach the New World in a boat for which blood had been spilt and should choose a wooden boat rather than one made of skins. She is credited with saying: 'Three things that please God most are: faith in God with a pure heart, a simple heart with a grateful spirit, generosity inspired by love. The three things that displease God most are: a mouth that hates people, a heart harbouring resentments and trusting in wealth.'

REFLECTION

How well do I match up to Ita's list? If I fall down on any of them could I make a resolution to do something about them with God's help?

16 JANUARY
St Fursey/Fursa/Furcy of Peronne

D.649. FEAST DAY: *16 January*

Fursey was born on the shores of Lough Corrib in Co. Galway. He was cured of a serious illness following a near-death experience, from which he returned full of joy. During the incident he saw two angels who told him that his mission was to preach. He founded a monastery at Killarsagh, preached in Ireland for twelve years then England where he founded the monastery of Burghcastle (possibly Cnobbersburgh) in Suffolk in 631. He was a hermit for a period before moving to France, where he founded the abbeys of Lagny-sur-Marne, Peronne (ever since known as 'Peronne of the Scots'), and St Quentin. He was very holy, had visions which were highly regarded, written about fully by St Bede, 'the Father of English History', and he brought about many conversions. He died at Mazerolles but was buried at Peronne at the insistence of the inhabitants.

REFLECTION
Fursey was used by God as he gave himself to God joyfully and was always available and open to God. Do I offer my availability to God? Joyfully?

17 JANUARY
St Ninnidh

D. SIXTH CENTURY. FEAST DAY: *18 January*

Listed among the Twelve Apostles of Ireland, he was known as St *Ninnidh Láimdearg* (of the red hand), not to be confused with the earlier St Nennid, a contemporary of St Brigid, known as St *Nennid Láimhiodhan* (of the pure or clean hand). While being educated under St Finian of Clonard it was he to whom St Ciarán lent his Gospel book as he had none, causing Ciarán to be called 'half-Matthew'. He also trained with Enda of Aran. He founded his monastery on the island of Inismacsaint on Lower Lough Erne, and also had a hermitage near Derrylin, where his holy well can be found at Knockninny, a steep hill where he spent Lent. He founded many churches and was an abbot, a teacher and a bishop, his diocese stretching all the way to Donegal Bay.

REFLECTION

In his eagerness to spread the Christian church far and wide Ninnidh must have envisaged all the land around him as potentially part of the Kingdom of God. Do I see such potential around me in my locality? Could I visualise and pray for this?

18 JANUARY

St Aedamair

D. FIFTH CENTURY. FEAST DAY: *18 January*

Aedamair was one of the early holy women of Ireland and was reputed to be the first woman to take the veil from St Patrick. She belonged to a community of women at Clogher, again one of the earliest. She was originally from Galway or Mayo and was said to have supported Columba at the Battle of Cooldrevny (popularly known as 'The Battle of the Books') late in her life; however, this would only be possible if she lived a very long life! Maybe this should be seen as a tribute to her zeal for fighting for just causes; or it could refer to a different Aedamair. (The law exonerating women from fighting in battles – the *Cain Adamnain* – was only enacted in 697, and until then it was common for women to participate in battle.)

REFLECTION

Aedamair obviously felt passionate in her support for Columba. Do I feel passionate enough about anything to fight for it? What non-violent methods can I use for righting this wrong or forwarding this just cause? Could I list them and then pray about how to help?

19 JANUARY
St Blathmac

D.825. FEAST DAY: *19 January*

Blathmac was one of the most celebrated of the Irish monks of Iona. From a royal Irish family, he was a monk and abbot in Ireland before going to Iona. There is a St Blathmac's church and holy well near Corofin, Co. Clare. He had a prophetic warning that a viking attack was imminent and he and others buried the reliquary containing Columba's bones as a result. He is said to have warned his monks of the attack, saying: 'Make up your minds. Those of you who can face death stay here with me; let the others save themselves while they can.' He was offered his life if he told of the whereabouts of the reliquary; he refused and was hacked to death.

REFLECTION
Blathmac knew the viking invaders would not revere the memory of Columba, so he was firm and loyal, paying for it with his death. Where do my strong loyalties even unto death lie? Blathmac gave his monks the choice of staying or fleeing, reluctant to force martyrdom on those not ready for it. Do I make allowances for the weaknesses of others?

20 JANUARY
St Fechin of Fore/Mo-Fecha/Vigean

D.665. FEAST DAY: *20 January*

Fechin was from Bile Feichín in Co. Sligo. He trained in Achonry under St Nathy, who urged him to be ordained, 'to offer the King of Heaven and Earth to the people'. Fechin baptised the whole population of Omey Island. He was the Abbot of Fore, Co. Westmeath, and the Abbot of Cong, Co. Mayo, from which the beautiful Cross of Cong later came. He founded abbeys at Ballisodare, Imaid Island, Omey and Ardoileán, and Tullach Fobhair near Naas. The remains of beehive huts on Omey Island can be seen today. He healed people and prayed for Ireland to be free of famine. He was described in the *Felire of Oengus* as 'holy-worded' and 'fair-worded'. After his death a friend witnessed a light so bright that it was believed all Ireland's demons fled for a time.

REFLECTION
Do I pray blessings on Ireland? What particular blessings would I want to pray for her today?

21 JANUARY

St Briga of Annaghdown

D. SIXTH CENTURY. FEAST DAY: *not known*

Briga was the sister of St Brendan. She is said to have been educated by Bishop Erc at Tralee. She became Abbess of Annaghdown in Galway. She had a monastery built there for her by her brother, as she could not bear to be separated from him. This was where her brother Brendan ended his days, nursed by Briga.

REFLECTION
These female saints led a very simple life free of luxuries, but still managed to be very hospitable, giving from their hearts out of their poverty rather than from their abundance. Can I appreciate the simplicity of giving a small gift from my poverty? Caring for her brother too was an act of loving giving. Could I maybe share the caring that others do, even in a small way, such as visits, a beautiful letter or card, or helpful gift of a small comfort, cooking or feeding or washing, ironing or mending clothes?

22 JANUARY
St Cuman of Aharney

D. FIFTH CENTURY. FEAST DAY: *not known*

Cuman was one of five female saints who shared the same name. She was the sister of Briochsech, St Brigid's mother. She was associated with a church at Aharney in the townland of Ballyconra in the barony of Galmoy, Co. Kilkenny. The legend about her recounts that when she was pregnant, St Patrick met her and blessed her and the cross he made with his crozier remained imprinted on her forehead. Patrick also prophesied that Cuman would give birth to many saints both male and female. In fact, she also gave birth to Tuathal Malgharbh who became High King of Ireland and her firstborn son became a bishop, Bishop Maine of Aghanagh.

REFLECTION
Cuman's influence on her children meant they chose Christian careers. Could I increase my influence on my children or other relatives? Maybe by prayer as well as loving actions? Could writing letters or sending emails be a good way of encouraging the young people in my life?

23 JANUARY
St Maimbod

D. 880. FEAST DAY: *23 January*

Maimbod was an Irish monk who took a vow of poverty and went on a mission scantily clothed but with a heart aflame for God. During his journeys, Maimbod preached in Northern Italy and Gaul, and visited the tombs of many saints. He was welcomed by a nobleman in Burgundy, who pressed on him a pair of gloves as a reminder to pray for him. Unfortunately, Maimbod was attacked and killed by robbers who stole his gloves. The attack occurred near Besançon, where he had been praying at the local church. He was buried at Besançon and miracles occurred at his tomb. While his relics were being transferred, the bishop carrying them was cured of blindness. The bishop instituted the feast day in Maimbod's honour.

REFLECTION
Would I like to be described as having a heart aflame for God? If so could I pray for the Holy Spirit's help in making this true of me?

24 JANUARY

St Guasacht

D. FIFTH CENTURY. FEAST DAY: 24 January

Guasacht was possibly the very first of St Patrick's disciples to be given a church. He was the son of Miluic, under whom Patrick had worked as a slave. When Patrick returned to Ireland as bishop he set off to visit Miluic, but Miluic locked himself in his house and then set it on fire. Miluic carried out this dramatic act to avoid meeting his former slave. But Guasacht welcomed St Patrick, who had nurtured the young boy for the seven years of his slavery. Patrick educated him and ordained him at Granard, and possibly also consecrated Guasacht as Bishop of Granard, Co. Longford. Two of his sisters became possibly the very first nuns consecrated to the religious life by St Patrick, both of them were named Emer and both are buried at Clonbroney. They are said to have been very fond of Patrick and brought him food when he was out watching the flock. Guasacht is described as a foster brother of Patrick's. (Fosterage might explain the fact that there were two Emers.)

REFLECTION
Have I influenced for good those who have had an opportunity to live close beside me? Do I still pray for them?

25 JANUARY
St Fincheall

DATE UKNOWN, POSSIBLY FIFTH CENTURY. FEAST DAY: 25 January

Fincheall was from Slieve Guaire, near the present-day parish of Drung, Co. Cavan. Her hermitage was in the parish of Kildrumsheridan. Knockbride parish was dedicated to the female saints Fincheall and Brigid. *Disert Fincheall* was a dependency of Fore, and is probably the modern Drumhurt, near Cootehill. No details of Fincheall's life have survived, but scholars think she was a contemporary of St Brigid as their names are together in dedications locally.

REFLECTION

The asceticism of saints like Fincheall might sound harsh, but what it really meant was simply that she was giving up things that did not aid her soul's growth and did not help her to love others more and be a better Christian. Are there things that are hindering my soul's growth and militating against my growth into being a better Christian and a more loving person? Is there something that I have allowed myself to depend on or become addicted to, that I could try giving up?

26 JANUARY
St Bride/Briga of Kilbride

D. FIFTH CENTURY. FEAST DAY: 7 or 2 January

Bride was Abbess of Kilbride, Co. Waterford. She is celebrated along with her seven sisters. She is famous for having met St Patrick in the plain of the Liffey and warned him of a plot against his life. She was visited by St Brigid of Kildare and received that saint with great joy and washed her feet. The water in which they were washed was used by another nun to apply to her crippled feet and her feet were healed. On another occasion she is said to have seen the devil as a monster when St Brigid signed her eyes with the sign of the cross.

REFLECTION

Bride would hardly have been privy to the conspiracy against Patrick; she more likely was told about it by God in what is called by St Paul 'the gift of knowledge'. This was common among early Irish saints. Do I regard such spiritual gifts as for another time or do I see the need for them in today's world?

27 JANUARY

St Attracta/Taraghata/Araght

D. FIFTH CENTURY. FEAST DAY: 11 August or 6 January

Attracta was received into the religious life by St Patrick, and legend recounts that during the ceremony a veil fell from heaven. She was a robust pioneer. When St Patrick sent her to a place of his choice she met one disaster after another, adapting to that austere life – killing a wild animal herself, raising the drowned local bard to life, using deer to drag the timber in lieu of horses, and using her hair for the cords to pull the timber for lack of ropes. She was the founder of the Convent of Killaraght in Sligo and of another in Roscommon, and is patroness of the Diocese of Achonry. Skilled in herbal medicine and famous for her hospitality and charity, Attracta founded a hospice on the shores of Lough Gara near Boyle in Co. Sligo. She was half sister to St Conall, who refused to let her settle near him because he was eschewing the company of women.

REFLECTION

When things go wrong for me do I sulk or complain or adapt as this feisty, resilient and self-sufficient saint did? How could I do this in a difficult situation I am facing now?

28 JANUARY
St Cannera/Canair

D.530. FEAST DAY: *28 January*

For many years a recluse living at Bantry, Cannera had a vision of all the churches in Ireland sending forth bright fiery flames, but St Senan's church's flames on Scattery Island were the brightest of all. So she travelled there to spend her final days, wishing to receive the last sacraments there. But St Senan had a rule that no woman should ever enter the enclosure, so he refused her entry. She replied, 'Christ came to redeem woman no less than to redeem man. He suffered for the sake of women as much as for the sake of men. Women as well as men can enter the heavenly kingdom.' Senan then relented enough to give her a place on the brink of the waves and brought her the Eucharist as she lay dying on the shore. She was buried on the coast and became a patroness of sailors, who to this day salute her resting place.

REFLECTION
How bright a blaze is my local church making? How bright a blaze am I making? Could I see myself being as outspoken as Cannera about an injustice in my own time? If not, what is stopping me?

29 JANUARY
St Dallan Forgaill/Eochaid

D. C.598. FEAST DAY: *29 January*

Eochaid from Breiffne became known as Dallan ('blind man') as he became blind in later years, and Forgaill because his mother's name was Forchella. He was a great scholar who wrote many books, going on to become the chief bard of Ireland. He wrote a eulogy on St Columba after Columba had saved the Bardic order at the Synod of Druimceatt. Columba refused to allow Dallan to read it out at the synod believing a man should not be praised in his lifetime. When an angel informed Dallan of Colmcille's death, he immediately set about publishing the eulogy. Miraculously his sight also returned at that point. He was martyred following a pirate attack on his way to visit the island monastery of Iniskeel in Co. Donegal. Dallan's church at Kildallan was situated within a rath.

REFLECTION
Dallan is a good example of someone who did not let his disability hold him back from living a full life. Do I overcome my own disabilities, however small, in a similar way?

30 JANUARY

Blessed Dom Columba Marmion

1858–1923. FEAST DAY: 30 January

Columba was a Benedictine abbot who had been ordained at The Irish College in Rome, and taught Philosophy at Clonliffe College, Dublin. He joined the Benedictines at Maredsous in Belgium and became of Prior of the Abbey of Mont César in Louvain. As well as being a professor of Dogmatic Theology at Louvain, he had a huge workload, including preaching inspiring retreats and hearing confessions, and an enormous correspondence. He became Abbot of Maredsous, and when the First World War broke out he managed to bring the community to Ireland, which helped establish the order there. A master of the spiritual life, his books are translated into many languages. He prayed unfailingly for Ireland. Two Benedictine abbeys have been placed under his patronage: Aurora in Illinois and Glenstal in Co. Limerick.

REFLECTION
Dom Columba Marmion's prayers could have made quite a difference to Ireland. Do I pray for my country? A little or a lot?

31 JANUARY

St Aedan of Ferns/Edan/Mogue/Maedoc

555–632. FEAST DAY: *31 January*

Aedan was born on what is now St Mogue's island on Templeport Lough, Co. Cavan. He founded monasteries at Rossinver, Co. Leitrim, Ferns, Co. Wexford, Drumlane and Killeshandra, Co. Cavan. He was the first Bishop of Ferns. He had a close spiritual relationship with St David of Wales, having been trained by him in his austere tradition, which he kept up. Aedan performed many miracles, which display his kindness and generosity. Once when away from his monastery in Ferns he had a vision of one of the monks ploughing and slipping in front of the sharp plough as the oxen turned; in the vision he raised his hand and stopped the oxen; and this did indeed save the monk's life. He is said to have lived for seven years on barley bread and water.

REFLECTION

Aedan would have survived on barley bread and water because he had other sustenance – prayers, scripture reading and the sacrament of Holy Communion. Have I discovered this 'other bread' that Jesus spoke of? How could I get more of it?

FEBRUARY

1 FEBRUARY
St Brigid

452–524. FEAST DAY: 1 *February*

One of the three patron saints of Ireland, Brigid was born in Faughart, Co. Louth, her mother was Briocsech and her father Dubhtach was a chieftain in Leinster. Brigid is said to have pulled out her eye rather than agree to an arranged marriage. She took the veil as a nun under St Mel of Longford, who is said to have read the wrong service over her, that for the making of a bishop. When Mel's mistake was pointed out he attributed it to the intervention of the Holy Spirit. Brigid was a bishop in all but name, and is always depicted with a crozier, to which she would have been entitled as abbess of the double monastery in Kildare that she oversaw with the aid of Conleth. She had a wonderful way with animals, and was known for healing miracles, prayer and great generosity. It was said that Brigid was constantly meditating and thinking of the Lord in her heart and mind, and using her time on the roads for prayer. She was wise and her advice was sought by church leaders in many parts of Ireland. A fire tended by her nuns was said to have been kept alight continuously for a thousand years.

REFLECTION
Could I use my travelling time for prayer? Which attribute of the saint speaks most loudly to me?

2 FEBRUARY
St Columban of Ghent

D.969. FEAST DAY: 2 *February*

Columban is regarded as the patron saint of Belgium. He was an Irish Abbot and leader of a missionary band who travelled to Belgium, probably to escape the Danes. Columban acquired a wide reputation for sanctity as he lived out his life in a cell in a cemetery near St Bavo's church in Ghent, spending his time in prayer and austere penances. He is buried in St Bavo's Cathedral. His name is invoked by the Belgian people in times of calamity.

REFLECTION

The word 'austerity' can make a modern person shiver. The Irish saints were enthusiastic about their discipline as their actions brought them closer to God. Could I simplify my life in any way? Could I see the Way of Life I have chosen as a gift to Jesus? Could I think on this for a while and examine what my own austerities could fruitfully be, maybe in the next penitential period, for example, in Lent or in the forty days after Pentecost, which were traditionally penitential days for the early Irish Christians?

3 FEBRUARY

St Anatolius

D. ELEVENTH CENTURY. FEAST DAY: *3 February*

Anatolius was a bishop in Ireland, whose Irish name is unknown. When returning from a pilgrimage to Rome, he founded an oratory near Salins in Burgundy, which he dedicated to St Symphorian. He lived the rest of his life there in a mountainside retreat overlooking the valley called *Pagus Scotengorum*, a favourite stopover for Irish pilgrims. (However, some say he died only a few days after settling there.) Anatolius is credited with a large number of miracles. A church at Salins was built in his honour.

REFLECTION

The early Irish Christians had a strong conviction that they would be shown their place of resurrection. Like Anatolius, have I ever found a place where I felt peaceful and happy? Places where the veil is particularly thin between earth and heaven appeal to a lot of people, such as Lindisfarne, Iona and Glendalough. Maybe I could spend some time at one of these or find another special place?

4 FEBRUARY
St Loman of Trim

D. C.450. FEAST DAY: *4 February or 11 October*

Loman was a nephew of St Patrick, who accompanied him on his mission to Ireland. They travelled to Trim on a boat, Loman singing psalms as they went. The son of the Lord of Trim, Fortchern, was so enchanted by Loman's singing that he converted to Christianity. Crowds then came to be baptised. Patrick set up a diocese in Trim with Loman as its first bishop – the first diocesan bishop in Ireland, twenty-five years before Armagh. Loman loved books and had an extensive library of which he was very proud. It is said that when he died all the book-satchels in Ireland fell off their pegs to honour Ireland's greatest bibliophile.

REFLECTION
Loman's voice enchanted others. Can I bring joy to others by singing hymns or uplifting songs? Why not make the effort for God if it brings people to faith? It is good to learn some by heart too.

5 FEBRUARY
St Buo

C.900. FEAST DAY: *5 February*

Throughout the seventh and eighth centuries Irish monks were sailing to the Faroe Islands and Iceland. Buo and Ernulph were Irish holy men who travelled to Iceland. Their bells, books and staffs were found by the Norwegians when they 'discovered' the island. Buo and Ernulph became distinguished missionaries.

They built a Christian church at Esinberg on a site formerly used by pagans for human sacrifice. Buo was a champion of social justice for all and helped to end the practice of human sacrifice on Iceland.

REFLECTION ❧

Buo was not content only with preaching the Gospel but fought to bring justice and humanity to Iceland. Opposing human sacrifice cannot have been easy. Have I the courage to stand up against any practice I know is unjust? Could I ask God's help with standing against practices that pollute, discriminate, sell humans into slavery or widen the gap between the rich and the poor?

6 FEBRUARY

St Mel/Melus

D. C.487. FEAST DAY: *6 February*

Mel was from a family of seventeen sons and two daughters, all of whom entered monasteries or convents. He was the first abbot-bishop of Ardagh in Co. Longford. He was quite a family-minded man, and was a nephew of St Patrick, and taught his Aunt Lupita. Mel was a zealous preacher and missionary. During his profession of St Brigid, he read the wrong service over her – that of consecrating a bishop. He took this as the Holy Spirit's guidance. His kindness was seen when, at the Synod of Tailtu, Mel intervened with a king on behalf of a supposed transgressor. The cathedral dedicated to him in Longford town was destroyed by a fire in 2009, in which his crozier was also damaged, but has been completely refurbished and reconsecrated.

REFLECTION ❧

Would I be as confident of the rightness of a once-off breach of convention if I felt it was God's guidance? Would I have the courage to speak up if I found someone was being wrongly accused?

7 FEBRUARY
St Loman of Lough Owel

D. SIXTH OR SEVENTH CENTURY. FEAST DAY: *7 February*

Loman had two hermitages: one on an island in Lough Owel, Co. Westmeath, called *Inis Mor* or Church Island; the other at *Port Lomáin* near Multyfarnham. In the first place he lived on 'Alexandric herbs' (*smyrnium olus-atrum*, or 'Alexanders') which grew abundantly there. In Port Lomáin he was visited by Bishop Eidchéan of Clonfad on the night that Colman of Lynn was born, when marvellous kinds of music were heard around the church. Two townlands are named after him in the Diocese of Ardagh: Drumlomain North and Drumlomain South. The psychiatric hospital in Mullingar is dedicated to him, which would suggest that he healed people suffering mental illnesses.

REFLECTION

Like Jesus in the desert, the Irish hermits survived on very little as they nourished themselves with Biblical literature, especially the psalms. How well do I absorb this spiritual nourishment? Have I learned how to really feed on the word of God?

8 FEBRUARY
St Onchu/Oncho/Onchuo

D. C.600. FEAST DAY: *8 February*

Like his father before him, Onchu was a poet from Connaught. It was said of him that 'his speech was of Christ'. After a career as an antiquary in Connaught, he became a monk under St Mogue at Clonmore. Onchu was a friend of St Finan the Leper, who, because of his condition, declined Onchu's invitation to join him in travelling around Ireland collecting relics, in order to preserve memory and increase devotion. Clonmore became a place of pilgrimage because of all the relics Onchu had collected. Saints Finan, Mogue and Onchu are reputed to be buried at the foot of St Mogue's Cross in the church yard at Clonmore Co. Carlow.

REFLECTION

In what way am I preserving the memory of saintly people who have inspired me? Have I ever made a list of the people who have helped me on my spiritual journey or my favourite saints?

9 FEBRUARY

St Marianus Scotus of Ratisbon

D.1088. FEAST DAY: *9 February*

Marianus' Irish name was Muiredach MacRobartaigh. He came from a prominent Donegal family, who were the hereditary keepers of *The Cathach*, Colmcille's Psalter known as 'The Battler' because the Battle of Cooldrevny had been fought partly on account of it. He made a pilgrimage to Rome. He was a gifted and very swift scribe and lived in St Peter's Church. He was later given the church and a layman built a monastery for him there, which became an Irish monastery that flourished and expanded after his death. He had a reputation for holiness and being filled with the Holy Spirit. The tradition of using the name 'Scotus' or 'Scot' for Irishmen continued on in Europe long after Scotland became established.

REFLECTION

Do I think that holiness is something reserved for saints or do I feel that we all should be aiming at becoming holy? Do I realise it is often a very slow process, a thing that the Holy Spirit does in us if we allow him? Do I allow him? If not, what is stopping me?

10 FEBRUARY
St Erhard

D.686. FEAST DAY: *8 January*

Erhard was a missionary bishop. He resigned his see of Ardagh to go to the Continent. At first he spent time with his brother St Hidulph in the Vosges district, and then went to Bavaria to preach the Gospel. A woman born blind, Odilia, a future saint, was baptised by Erhard and recovered her sight as a result. In mediaeval times there was a community of religious women called *Erardinonnen* who kept up a vigil of prayer at the saint's crypt in Ratisbon – this order was sanctioned by Pope Leo IX. Many other miracles were attributed to him as well.

REFLECTION
Do I experience miracles happening through me? If not, could it be that I wander too far from God each day and neglect to keep in touch with him, and fail to fill my heart each day at the fountain of love He pours upon us? How could I rectify this?

11 FEBRUARY
St Gobnait/Gobinety/Abigail/Abina

D. SIXTH CENTURY. FEAST DAY: *11 February*

Gobnait left her home in Co. Clare to escape a family feud. She settled in the Aran Islands, where an angel told her that this was not to be her final home but rather a place where she would see nine white deer grazing. She located this place near Ballyvourney, Co. Cork. She founded a nunnery there with the help of St Abban. She was renowned for her skill as a beekeeper. Among other miracles her prayers stayed the course of the plague; in early Irish style she marked off the area around Ballyvourney as consecrated ground across which the plague would not dare to pass. When her sister was ill, St Abban died, and Gobnait prayed that her sister wouldn't hear the keening. According to legend to this day people do not hear things in that spot, even the loudest thunder!

REFLECTION ✦

Could I become more thoughtful of other people's comfort as a way of caring for them? Or as a way of 'washing the feet' of those who have no faith?

12 FEBRUARY

Mono/Monon

D. SEVENTH CENTURY. *FEAST DAY: 16 January*

Mono from Killeavy became a hermit in the Ardennes, where he preached the Gospel. He then set out for Rome to ask the intercession of Sts Peter and Paul for his mission. On the way over the Alps, he met a bishop who had left his pallium behind. Mono fetched it for him. Mono was rewarded with a place to be a hermit at Nassogne, in today's Belgium. He fasted frequently and spent nights in prayer, giving alms generously and defending the rights of his neighbours which were deeply important to him. Following an imprudent criticism of a certain person's moral conduct, Mono was martyred, slain by a hired assassin. A flood of light was seen around the spot of his martyrdom, and the locals grieved him sincerely and came in great crowds to his funeral.

REFLECTION ✦

Do I criticise others? A salutary exercise is to divide a page in half and write in the top other people's faults as you perceive them and in the bottom your own; there will be more duplication than you might have expected!

February

13 FEBRUARY
St Modomnoc/Domnoc/Dominic

D. C.550. FEAST DAY: *13 February*

Modomnoc was an Irish monk who became a pupil of St David in Menevia. He was a gardener as well as beekeeper in Wales. When he returned to Ireland the bees followed him. He tried to usher them back to Wales, but they swarmed again, prompting St David to allow him keep the bees with his blessing. Back in Ireland the bees were installed in hives in Modomnoc's monastery in Fingall, *Lann Beachare* or Church of the Beekeeper, near Balbriggan. He later settled in Co. Kilkenny at Tiobradh Fachtna near the River Suir, in the Barony of Iverk. This, it is believed, was the start of beekeeping in Ireland.

REFLECTION
St David's blessing on the first swarm of bees could have had a very good effect on beekeeping in Ireland. Do I ever think to pray for bees and other pollinators who are suffering today as a result of the use of pesticides and global warming?

14 FEBRUARY
St Manchán of Mohill

D.538. FEAST DAY: *14 February*

St Manchán was the soul-friend and advisor of St Caillin and his designated successor as Abbot of Fenagh. He became abbot of Fenagh for seven years after burying St Caillin, according to his instructions, in Reilig Mochaomhog. The correct full Gaelic name of Mohill is *Maothail Manchain*. He is said to have founded seven churches, including the monastery at Mohill which continued throughout the Middle Ages as an Augustinian House. A local fair was named Manchán's Feast after him.

REFLECTION ~

St Caillin had left very explicit and complex instructions for his burial. Manchán was a loyal friend. A friend is someone who can be relied on and who will be understanding about our idiosyncrasies. Am I such a loyal friend?

15 FEBRUARY

St Farnan/Forannan/Farannan

D. C.590. FEAST DAY: *15 February*

A follower of St Columba at Iona, Farnan later returned to Ireland and became a hermit at Alternan near Dromore West, Co. Sligo. He is also associated with Downings, Co. Kildare, in the parish of Caragh. There is a holy well near the village of Prosperous, Co. Kildare, called St Farnan's well. It was told that whoever drank of it would lose all enjoyment of alcohol. He was given to extreme ascetical practice that included standing up to his armpits in cold water, sleeping outdoors on a stone pillow and listening to the sounds of the sea and wildlife. Farnan's relics were said to have healing properties and his cell at Alternan was the site of an annual Garland Sunday Pilgrimage.

REFLECTION ~

It sounds as if the saint had a great deal of compassion for those afflicted with alcohol addiction. Today with alcohol readily available, do I pray for people with this and other addictions?

16 FEBRUARY
St Dicuil/Desle of Bosham

D.625. FEAST DAY: *18 April or 18 January*

This Irish monk accompanied St Fursey to East Anglia. When they were later obliged to flee due to persecution, Dicuil and six other Irish monks were the first to bring the Gospel to the Sussex coast. They founded a monastery at Bosham, nearly five kilometres from Chichester. Bede records that they lived a life of service to God in poverty and humility, and did not gather many people to hear them preach. In spite of that, one of Dicuil's disciples became Bishop of Rochester, and the King of Sussex was among those who became baptised. Dicuil's work was continued by Wilfred.

REFLECTION

The quality of the few converts Dicuil had would have made up for the lack of quantity. It is so easy to get hung up on numbers. Do I tend to do worry about quantity rather than quality in my own life? Dicuil and his companions were obviously dedicated to building the Kingdom of God slowly but surely. Is my life serving God's kingdom?

17 FEBRUARY
St Fintan of Clonenagh

D.603. FEAST DAY: *17 February or 15 November*

Fintan of Clonenagh was the most famous of the seventy-four saints of this name. A bishop and an abbot, he was described by St Columba as 'a handsome holy-looking man with ruddy cheeks and shining eyes, his hair flecked with white'. He and his monks lived on a diet of barley bread and water. He was warned in a dream that he would receive advice about how to deal with his critics from a person the following morning. The next day he met a blind and dumb man who was miraculously given the power of speech for just long enough to advise that while the strict diet was fine for Fintan himself, the monks were to be treated more leniently. He mitigated the severity of the routine following the encounter.

REFLECTION
Do I make this mistake of expecting others to follow the same strict regime as myself? Do I have enough respect for difference and diversity in people? Fintan prayed for those who had no one else to pray for them; could I pray for the forgotten people of the world?

18 FEBRUARY

St Colman of Lindisfarne and Inishboffin

D.676. FEAST DAY: *18 February*

Colman was an Irish monk from Iona, who became the third Abbot of Lindisfarne in 661. At the Synod of Whitby, he vigorously defended the Irish dating for Easter and traditional tonsure, using Columba's authority. He was defeated by Wilfred, who said Peter not Columba had been given the keys of the Kingdom. Colman returned to Ireland with a number of monks who carried the relics of Iona. They founded a new monastery on the island of Inishboffin. The Saxon monks among them became unhappy at their treatment. Colman helped them set up their own monastery at Mayo, called 'Mayo of the Saxons', which flourished for nine hundred years.

REFLECTION
Colman found a satisfactory solution to the problem of the Saxon monks and thereby created another successful monastery. His support ensured that good came of the bad situation. Could I come up with a similarly creative solution to a difficult problem in my own life? After prayer?

19 FEBRUARY
Blessed Mary Aikenhead

1787–1858. Feast day: 19 January

Mary Aikenhead was the founder of the Irish Sisters of Charity. The order was a non-cloistered order dedicated to works of charity and religious instruction as well as caring for the elderly, infirm and orphans. The sisters also visited hospitals and prisons. The daughter of a Protestant doctor in Cork, Mary's father converted to Catholicism on his deathbed. She asked Bishop Murray of Dublin could she become a Sister of Charity. She went eagerly up to Dublin to meet the others, only to find she was the only one! So she trained in New York, returning three years later to be professed by Bishop Murray. The sisters were ministering angels during the cholera epidemic. She regarded the poor as God's nobility. It was said of her that she found God in all things and loved Him in all people. Many congregations were founded in Ireland and elsewhere.

REFLECTION
Mary's eagerness to be a sister – yet her disappointment that she was alone – is understandable; yet could this prompt me to realise that often God is calling me to be the first to do something, not merely to follow others?

20 FEBRUARY
St Olcan/Bolcan/Volcanus

D. c.480. Feast day: 20 February

When Olcan's pregnant British mother heard news of her Irish husband's death, she went into a deep coma and was buried. A week later a passer-by heard a baby wailing, and the tomb was opened. His mother was dead, but Olcan survived. He was baptised by St Patrick, trained in France and made a bishop after which he went on to found his own monastery at Armoy. He is also said to have taught MacNisse. A local chieftain, Saran, was tyrannising the whole countryside, and in order to save Saran's many captives, Olcan promised eternal life to him. Saint Patrick's annoyance with Olcan for this led to Patrick cursing Armoy. It was in fact sacked by a Dalriadan king and later burnt. According to *The Book of Armagh*, Olcan became Bishop of Armagh in 474.

REFLECTION

Where Olcan's disagreement with Patrick is concerned, we don't know all the facts so can't judge. Saran may have been repentant. It would be a shame if criminals were not offered the chance to repent and believe. Do I pray for the work of prison chaplains and warders?

21 FEBRUARY

St Molagga/Molacca/Laicin

D. C.655. FEAST DAY: *20 January*

Molagga was venerated around Fermoy, Co. Cork. He was born of humble and pious parents, who lived in celibacy until St Cummian the Tall prophesied they would have a son who would become a great saint. He was born after a seven-month pregnancy and people flocked to see this miracle child. His parents were bringing him to be baptised by an anchorite, Mochnall, but met Cummian the Tall on the way, who agreed to baptise their son. There was no water, but suddenly a choir of angels appeared and water sprang from the ground. Molagga founded monasteries in Wales; Tullamain, Co. Tipperary; Balbriggan, Co. Dublin and Timoleague (*Tech Molagga* – Molagga's house) in West Cork. He played an active part in stopping local wars, brought a woman who died in childbirth back to life, stopped a wildfire, healed a tumour and restrained bees.

REFLECTION ❧

Molagga seems to have been able to turn his hand to anything which was needed, from ceasing civil unrest to quenching fires, from healing a growth on a King's face to restraining bees. He must have realised that no subject is too small to be prayed over. Have I realised this yet?

22 FEBRUARY

Mael-Brigid/Maol Brighde/Maelbrithus MacDurnan

D.927. FEAST DAY: *22 February*

The son of Tornan and Saorlaith, Mael-Brigid means devotee of Brigid. He was a saintly abbot who held two posts: Archishop of Armagh *circa* 883 and Abbot of Iona in 891. He was said to have been elected to these posts because of his great wisdom and virtue. He was reputed to be 'the head of religion in Ireland and the greater part of Europe'. *The Gospel Book of Macdurnan* was named after him (now in Lambeth Palace). He calmed a riot in Armagh, inducing both parties to abstain from violence. Three times during his incumbency the Danes sacked Armagh.

REFLECTION ❧

Mael-Brigid's gentleness and calming influence can be seen in his calming of the rioters. Have I qualities which would be able to calm a riot, even in my own home? Could I cultivate this sense of peacefulness even while other people are engaged in emotional scenes and violence?

23 FEBRUARY

Sts Fingar and Piala

D. FIFTH CENTURY. FEAST DAY: *14 December*

Fingar and his sister Piala were King Clyto's children. This king received St Patrick graciously and was one of St Patrick's earliest converts. King Clyto wanted Fingar to expel paganism from the area by military force, but he refused. Fingar and Piala along with a group of companions sailed to Brittany. There Fingar was converted by an experience of the beauty of nature. The story goes that while washing himself, he caught sight of his reflection and was struck by his beauty. Fingar understood immediately that beauty came from God. He resolved to consecrate himself to the service of his creator as a hermit. An angel later warned him to leave the area, so the group sailed to Cornwall. They were all martyred at the mouth of the River Hayle near Penzance, by the local chief who resented their preaching the Gospel.

REFLECTION

Being in nature and aware of its beauty and its creator drew Fingar closer to God. Can I take inspiration from Fingar's experience and find beauty in nature and the presence of God there?

24 FEBRUARY

Cummeen the Fair / Cuimine Fionn / Cummineus Albus

D.688. FEAST DAY: *24 February*

Cummeen was a very erudite and scholarly man, who founded a church at Disert Chumin in Leinster. Then later, from 657 to 669, he was called out of solitary life to become Abbot of Iona. He wrote a life of Columba, now lost but maybe used by Adamnan as a source. His abbacy coincided with the Synod of Whitby. He tried unsuccessfully to introduce the Roman Paschal

Rite to Ireland, which made him unpopular in Iona. *The Book of Mulling* in Trinity College Library contains some verses of a hymn he wrote. Some Scottish sites were dedicated to him, including Fort Augustus whose previous name was *Cille Chuimein*.

REFLECTION ~
Cille Chuimein was probably Cummeen's private retreat away from Iona. It can be a relief to have some solitude. Have I somewhere I can retreat to privately when I feel the need to spend time alone? If not, could I create somewhere?

25 FEBRUARY
Ciannan

D.489. FEAST DAY: *25 February*

Legend has it that when St Patrick was escaping from his early slavery in Ireland, Ciannan sold him to some merchants for a copper cauldron before repenting and converting to Christianity. He eventually became bishop and abbot at Duleek. He and Patrick exchanged rules. Ciannan's rule might have been stern at the beginning but by mediaeval times it had been modified. Saint Mochua of Timahoe consecrated Ciannan's stone church at Duleek, which was unusual for the time. Most churches were built with wood. His good health was attributed to bathing in a bottomless vessel. Many legends have become attached to Ciannan, scholars even think he might have been a Christianisation of a pre-Christian God, Lugh, who was also associated with a remarkable vessel.

REFLECTION ~
Do I see Christ as the fulfilment of all that was true in the pre-Christian culture of Ireland? The God *Lugh* was the God of Light, and the aim of every Christian is to open to God to allow more of his light into our lives. What darkness in the world now do I feel particularly called to shine God's light into?

26 FEBRUARY

Sts Ethna and Fidelma

D.433. FEAST DAY: *11 January or 26 February*

King Laoghaire of Connaught had two beautiful daughters: Ethna and Fidelma. Ethna was fair-haired and Fidelma had red hair. The sisters were fostered and educated by two Druids, Coplait and Maol, in Co. Roscommon, near Tulsk. They met St Patrick by chance while at Ogulla well, where Patrick preached to them. They were filled with enthusiasm and asked many interested questions, including, 'When can we see Christ's face?' Eventually Patrick baptised them and gave them Holy Communion. They both left their bodies and went to heaven immediately. Coplait and Maol were angry, but eventually they too were baptised and became monks, tonsured by Patrick's hand.

REFLECTION

When did I find a chance meeting turned into something really special? Do I help other people's chance meetings with me to become special? Have I any interested and enthusiastic questions to ask about the faith?

27 FEBRUARY

St Saran

D.661. FEAST DAY: *20 January*

There are at least twelve saint Sarans, but this one is Saran of Ferbane where he started a house to provide shelter for pilgrims on the way to Clonmacnoise. There is a holy well dedicated to him in Co. Offaly, near Shannonbridge, at the edge of Moystown Demesne. *Tisaran*, meaning Saran's house, is present-day Ferbane. He is thought to have once been *erenach* – a high office holder, similar to an archdeacon – in St Maedoc's monastery in Templeshanbo, and Bede lists him as a teacher.

February

REFLECTION ✺

Saran met a need of the day by providing shelter for the pilgrims. What need of today could I meet? Could I write a list and then pray carefully about this? I might be pleasantly surprised!

28 FEBRUARY
Aedh Mac Bruic

D.589. FEAST DAY: *28 February or 10 November*

Aedh was born into a royal Ulster family, but was treated badly, being put to work as a swineherd. He was helped by Christians to find the pigs when they went astray. Their help had a lasting impression on him. When he was denied a share of his inheritance by his brothers, he chose to become a monk, remembering the Christians' kindness. He founded a church in Killare – now called Rathugh – at Rathconrath, Co. Westmeath, near the base of the Hill of Usneagh. He later became a hermit at Slieve League. His cell and holy well can still be seen. Aedh was skilled in medicine and also performed many miracles. He was known as a healer especially of headaches. Saint Columba was said to have been aware of the moment of that holy man's death.

REFLECTION ✺

Have I found that when things go against me, a higher power is helping me? Has my life showed – as Aedh's did – how in spite of misfortune we can forge through to a fulfilled life? What misfortunes do I feel are still dogging me? Could I cast these cares on God?

29 FEBRUARY

During a Leap Year this can be a day for remembering all those Irish saints whose lives have become obscure, although their names are known. Maybe there is a saint on the list from your own locality. Thank God for these quietly holy people and make up your own prayer. A selection of some of their names follows: Aodh, Aodhan, Beagán, Beag, Bearchan, Beccan the Blind, Bran of Clane, Ciaráns, Colga, Colm, Colman, Coman, Comman, Corpre, Criotan, Cronan, Cummaneth, Curcach, Dinertach the Bashful, Dubhliti, Eriad, Ernan, Faolan the Stammerer, Fionnbarr, Fionan, Foila, Id, Iladan, Imar, Ingheana, Laserian, Lonan, MacTail, Manchán, Mobiu, Mochaemóg, Mochaoimhe, Mochonóg, Mochua, Moloca, Muadan, Nuadha, Patrick, Riaghail, Rioch, Rioghnach, Ronan, Sacar, Saran, Scire, Siadhal, Sillan, Sineach, Sylvester, Ternog, Tida, Tola, Tighearnach, Tochumracht, Trean, Trenan, Ultan.

REFLECTION

What made these people saints? Openness to God and a deep love for Him, self-denial, loving and compassionate service to others, prayer which continued all day long and two attributes which are rare today – commitment and enthusiasm. Perhaps we should say of them as Saint Ignatius of Loyola is reported to have said: 'They were as human as I am. So I could be as saintly as they were.'

MARCH

1 MARCH
St Marnock of Portmarnock/Eirnin/Erneneus/Mearnóg

D.589. FEAST DAY: *1 March*

Marnock was the affectionate name for Ernan (*'Mo-Ern-Óg'*). Saint Columba found Marnock as a child at Clonmacnoise hiding under a procession canopy where he was trying to touch the hem of Columba's robe. Columba blessed his tongue, prophesying it would be given great eloquence by God. He became an assiduous preacher of the Gospel, founding churches at *Cluain Deochra*, Co. Longford, Rathnew, Co. Wicklow, Dunleckney, Co. Carlow, and Portmarnock, Co. Dublin.

REFLECTION

Have I ever thought of having the tools of my trade or profession blessed, whether tongue or hands or implements? Do I try to keep sacred and secular things apart or do I merge the two as the Irish saints did? Have I ever thought of doing as St Columba did and give a special blessing to those children who are 'naughty', helping to bring out their good qualities?

2 MARCH
St Ciara/Ciar

D.679. FEAST DAY: *5 January or 16 October*

Ciara was a descendant of a High King, born in Tipperary, who established a religious community at Kilkeary, Co. Tipperary. It attracted so many followers that she asked St Fintan Munnu to assist her obtain land for a second convent, which was built at Tehelly in Co. Offaly. Her prayers are reported to have put out a fire in the region by request of St Brendan of Clonfert.

REFLECTION

Ciara was resourceful and asked for support and assistance in order to build a second convent. Are there situations in which I can reach out to others for support? Also a situation can change because an individual has been receptive to allowing God in to transform it. Do I complain about difficult situations or do I relinquish them to God? Those Christians who have accepted Jesus' offer of friendship thus know his help in times of trouble, fear and anxiety even in the bleakest of situations. Have I found this to be true?

3 MARCH

St Christicola/Cele Chriost

D.731. FEAST DAY: 3 March

Christicola was from a distinguished family in Ulster. He went to Leinster in order to live a contemplative life. He built a cell at Templeogue in Dublin by the River Dodder. He tried hard to reject all ecclesiastical preferment, but succumbed eventually and became Bishop of Kilteel. He was known for his wise counsel – so much so that in fact 'wise counsel' became his epithet. He made a pilgrimage to Rome with some companions and saved their lives when they were given hospitality by evil-minded men who tried to steal their purses.

REFLECTION

The pattern of withdrawal from the world and then becoming a leader is common among the Irish saints. Would I consider it a good idea for all leaders to have periods of withdrawal and prayer? Could withdrawing regularly become part of my life if it is not already? Hermits often attracted crowds because of the power of their holiness and love. As a familiar saying goes: 'Think love and love surrounds you and all of whom you think.'

4 MARCH
St Ciarán of Saighir

D. FIFTH CENTURY. FEAST DAY: *4 or 5 March*

Ciarán was one of the four pre-patrician bishops along with Ibar, Declan and Ailbhe. He was born on Clear Island, Co. Cork, around 375. Possibly he was trained by St Martin of Tours, in Rome and Lérins. After founding a monastery near the Fastnet Rock, Ciarán settled at Saighir, Co. Offaly, living in caves, clad in skins, with a wild boar and a wolf as his first 'monks'. People thronged to him from near and far, both women and men. His mother Liadáin gathered the women into a convent, pre-dating Brigid's foundation. His early biographer states: 'By the shining light of his example… he drove away the shadows from peoples' minds'. Among his many miracles he prevented a local battle, healed a woman by using blackberries growing in the snow and caused the cuckoo to be heard on a winter's day to save a woman.

REFLECTION

How wonderful to be the sort of person who drives away the shadows from people's minds by my example, as Ciarán was described. What sort of example am I giving by my life? How could it be improved?

5 MARCH
St Piran

D.480. FEAST DAY: *5 March*

Piran left his home in Ireland to share his faith in Cornwall. Many places there are named after him. He had a hermitage at Perranporth where an oratory buried beneath the sands was excavated in 1858. His life inspired many working men through the centuries. When he founded a monastery at Perranzabuloe, many of his converts joined him there under his abbacy. He is credited with rediscovering the method of smelting tin, and that the tin ore in the stone rose to the surface in the shape of a white cross. The Cornish tin miners made him their patron and the Cornish flag is known as St Piran's cross – a white cross on a black background, symbolising the power of God's light overcoming the darkness of evil. On St Piran's Day the Cornish people wear the flag on their bodies and march in the street.

REFLECTION

Do I believe that the power of God's light will overcome every darkness eventually? Has it overcome the darkness in my own life?

6 MARCH

St Aglenn/Aiglend

D. SIXTH CENTURY. FEAST DAY: *6 March*

Aglenn was a daughter of Leinin and sister of St Colman of Cloyne. The church she and her five sisters founded was called the Church of the Daughters of Leinin, *Cill Inghean Leinin*, hence present day Killiney, in south Dublin. There is a ruined church on the spot with a Greek cross in relief on the west doorway. Unlike her sisters, who remained virgins, she is said to have given birth to three sons, all of whom became saints – St Fintan of Slanore, St Colum of Myshall and St Lughaidhe of Tiernacreeve.

REFLECTION

Bringing up a Christian family is a valuable way of serving God. No doubt Aglenn's sons were also influenced for good by their godly aunts and uncle. Whichever of these roles are my own, do I see it as a task from God? Do I pray for my charges as much as care for them physically? St Monica prayed her famous son St Augustine into the faith as well as leading by her example. Could I be inspired by this?

7 MARCH
St Naile/Nadal/Natalis/Notan/Nael

D.564. FEAST DAY: *27 January*

Naile founded the monastery of Kilmanagh, Co. Kilkenny, thirteen kilometres west of the town. He went on to be Abbot of Kinawley (*Kill Naile* in Irish) and Devenish, the successor to St Laserian there. He had a reputation for learning and sanctity. He is said to have had one hundred and fifty monks there and Senan, later of Scattery Island, was one of his first pupils. He required his monks to take turns in watching the flocks and herds. Naile prophesied Senan's greatness and once encouraged him to pray for a dead prince, the only son of a chieftain, who was then restored to life.

REFLECTION

The incident of raising the boy to life shows Naile's strength as a mentor. He did not immediately heal the boy himself although no doubt he could have done, but he was eager to encourage others to learn and so asked Senan to do it. Do I encourage others to use their gifts?

8 MARCH
St Senan/Priscianus

D.544. FEAST DAY: *8 March*

Formerly a soldier, Senan heard a wave crashing at his feet while he was watching cattle and felt called to the spiritual life. He broke his spear and made it into a cross. Saint Raphael told him God had put a monster on Scattery Island to keep humans away until Senan was ready to make it a holy place. He founded a school and a bishopric there, having first gotten rid of the island's monster and thoroughly blessed the island. He welcomed many monks to the island, which had a great reputation for learning and holiness. Senan was said to convert everything he read into a treasure to draw upon. He undertook the most menial tasks in the monastery, reading a book while grinding corn. He also created several other foundations in the Shannon Estuary area.

REFLECTION

Do I treasure the things I read? Have I some means of remembering these precious lessons I am learning? Some people use a journal to record such things; while others like to underline or highlight passages of Scripture they felt have spoken to them.

9 MARCH

Lughaidh/Lugadius/Luach

D.589. FEAST DAY: 24 March

Lughaidh was one of several St Lughaidhs. The name is pronounced 'Lewy'. He was from a family living on the east side of the Inishowen peninsula, and the church at Clonleigh in Raphoe North was under his patronage. His two brothers were also saints, St Dochonna of Boyle, Co. Roscommon, and St Cormac, the latter also a bishop of Upper Moville, in Inishowen. Little is known of Lughaidh's life.

REFLECTION

These early Irish saints lived in a God-filled world, seeing him in every part of His creation, all of it indwelt by him. Have I come to realise the indwelling of God in all of his creation, in addition to his holiness and greatness beyond our imagining? These saints lived and moved and had their being in God, which gave them the ability to pray continuously. Could knowing that help me to make efforts in that direction?

10 MARCH

Finan Lobur/Finan the Leper

D.680. FEAST DAY: *1 March*

Finan's name means that he suffered from chronic ill health; the word *lobhar* was used for ulcerative skin conditions as well as leprosy. The story is that in order to heal a boy who was blind, unable to speak and a leper, God told Finan that he had to be willing to take the leprosy on himself. Finan is said to have agreed cheerfully and joyfully, and immediately became covered with ulcers – thus healing the boy. A penitent wanted to share his leprosy, Finan warned him that he would be unable to bear the pain. The penitent was duly afflicted with the leprosy and was unable to bear such agony and asked to be healed of it, and was. In spite of his pain, Finan became Abbot of Swords and then for the last thirty years of his life Abbot of Clonmore, Co. Carlow, where he is buried.

REFLECTION ∾

How cheerfully and joyfully do I do what I can to help others even if it costs me? Do I persevere in spite of pain?

11 MARCH

Aengus the Culdee

D.824. FEAST DAY: *11 March*

Aengus was co-founder of the *Céili Dé* (spouses of God) movement with St Maelruain. He once saw angels ascending and descending upon a grave, and asked who was buried there. It was a poor old man who used to recount and invoke all the saints of the world before going to bed and again on rising. Aengus began his own poem on the spot that became the *Feilire Aonghusa*. Aengus was a monk at Clonenagh and went on to become

Bishop of Tallaght, where he wrote the second martyrology, *The Martyrology of Tallaght*, after a decree had gone out that a reading from a martyrology should be done daily in all monasteries. He described himself as a poor man of Jesus' family and a mendicant. As a hermit, he was extremely ascetic, neglecting his appearance. He always took on the most menial tasks; while doing his tasks Aengus raised his heart and thoughts towards heaven.

REFLECTION

Have you any tasks which are repetitive that you could use as opportunities to do as Aengus did and raise your heart and thoughts to heaven while doing them?

12 MARCH

Mura/Murrol/Muirol/Murus/Muirdhealach

D.645. FEAST DAY: *12 March*

Mura was a disciple of St Columba, who appointed him Abbot of Othan Mór Monastery near Fahan in Inishowen West, on the shore of Lough Swilly, Co. Donegal. A tall cross now marks the site. Mura wrote a life of St Columba in verse form which is quoted in *The Martyrology of Donegal*. He was the patron saint of the Uí Neill who swore on his staff. He was said to have subdued wild beasts. (One less savoury legend says he was held in such high regard that visitors would drink from the stream he used as a privy.)

REFLECTION

Subduing wild beasts could mean Mura was so strong he fought with them and won; or it could mean that he was so gentle and holy they lay down at his feet. It could also be symbolic, meaning that he overcame the wild beasts in his own nature. The best way to overcome the wild beast in us is not to fight it but to subdue and transform it by the holiness and gentleness of Christ. What are my wild beasts?

13 MARCH
St Gerald/Giraldus/Gerailt

D.727. FEAST DAY: *13 March*

Gerald was an Englishman who became Abbot of Mayo, which was near present-day Claremorris. It became known as 'Mayo of the Saxons'. Colman of Inishboffin had founded the monastery on land given by a local king. Gerald established several other monasteries. He was credited with having 3,300 monks around him at Mayo and a further fifty at Leyney, Co. Sligo. He was miraculously healed of the plague and helped other plague victims by putting the hood of his cloak over them. He was said to have raised someone from the dead. He also miraculously removed a very large stone from the River Moy that had been obstructing the fishermen's nets.

REFLECTION

Gerald's gifts were extremely practical. What practical problems could I ask God to provide a solution for through me? To be concerned with other people's practical problems is a sign that we care. Could I spend time thinking through what practical help is needed by the people I know?

14 MARCH
St Anmchadh

D.1043. FEAST DAY: *30 January*

Anmchadh was a monk at Abbot Corcoran's monastery at Iniscaltra on the River Shannon. The Abbot banished him from Ireland for being too generous to visitors because he had provided second helpings of refreshments after a meal. Anmchadh wandered around Europe until he came to the monastery of Fulda in Germany where he became a recluse. Marianus Scotus, his contemporary, wrote of how when he celebrated mass over Anmchadh's tomb, supernatural light was visible and heavenly psalmody could be heard.

REFLECTION

Irish people have tended to encourage guests to enjoy just one more drink for the road, or pushed too much food onto people who have had enough. Have I learned yet that the offer of friendship, a listening ear, going for a walk together, or a chance to relax, are also ways of showing hospitality and that alcohol is not the only way to socialise? Could I teach this to the young people I have contact with?

15 MARCH

St Dichull of Inis-mac-Nessa (Ireland's Eye)

D. SEVENTH CENTURY. FEAST DAY: 15 *March*

Dichull was one of the seven sons of St Nessan of Lambay Island all of whom became distinguished ecclesiastics. He was also known as Dichull Dearg (Dichull the Red) because of his hair. He studied under Maedoc of Ferns and also spent some time at Clonmore. He and his brothers built an oratory on Ireland's Eye, and transcribed the four Gospels. The manuscript is extant and is called *The Garland of Howth*. He shares a feast day with two of his brothers, Beoán and Colmán. There were many raids on the island by Danes, and it had to be rebuilt in the eleventh century.

REFLECTION

What would my dream island be like? Would I be happy there all the time or would I need to get to the mainland occasionally? Does this say to me that I am a well-rounded person, keeping the contemplative and active dimensions in balance? If not which quality needs developing?

16 MARCH
St Eusebius of St Gall

D.884. FEAST DAY: *30 January*

Eusebius went from Ireland to St Gall in the ninth century and became a hermit on Mount St Victor, spending thirty years there in solitude and prayer, edifying all who knew him from peasants to kings. The year before his death the king erected a monastery on Mount St Victor for Eusebius, endowing it handsomely so that a hospice could be built for pilgrims on their way to Rome. Eusebius was killed by some local people whom he had admonished. He is venerated as a martyr.

REFLECTION

St Eusebius showed great courage, even at the cost of his death. Am I fearful of confronting a person in case they take offence? Can I find a way of framing criticism in an encouraging and constructive way?

17 MARCH
St Patrick

385–461. FEAST DAY: *17 March*

Born in a Roman colony in either Britain or Brittany, at the young age of sixteen, Patrick was captured and brought to Ireland as a slave. He used the hours watching flocks to pray and he developed a great love for God. He was rescued miraculously and travelled to France, where he trained for the priesthood at Lérins. In 432 he returned to Ireland as a missionary bishop. He established an indigenous church and integrated the Christian faith with the Irish culture. Patrick travelled with a large team – including smiths, woodworkers, a judge, a charioteer, a bell-ringer and embroiderers – to set up churches, ordain priests and consecrate bishops. He had dramatic contests at Tara with a chief Druid, and on the top of Croagh Patrick with a crowd of demons after his pre-Easter fast. A friendly and greatly beloved man. Two of his writings have survived: *Confessio* and *Letter to Coroticus*. In his autobiographical *Confessio*, he claims not to be a scholar but gives testimony to his deep personal faith and divine vocation to serve God in Ireland. In *Letter to Coroticus*, he complains about nominally Christian soldiers of Coroticus, who were raiding and who had even killed some newly baptised Christians. It was said of him: 'St Patrick brought the love of God and the light of Christ to an island even the calloused Romans considered too savage to conquer.'

REFLECTION
Patrick's time herding was put to good advantage to develop his prayer life. Do I use half-idle times in good ways? Can I learn this from St Patrick, or to work in a team, or respect for places deemed holy by others?

18 MARCH

Fridian/Frediano/Frigidian

D.588. FEAST DAY: *18 March*

Fridian trained for the priesthood in Ireland before going on a pilgrimage to Italy. At Monte Pisano near Lucca, he became fascinated with the lifestyle of holy hermits. Fridian was inspired and was determined to live the rest of his life there. However, his holiness and good works came to the attention of authorities. As a result he was called to be Bishop of Lucca in 560. He had twenty-eight years of arduous labour, much of it taken up with the fight against the heresy of Arianism and the constant Lombard invasions. His own cathedral was destroyed – it is now restored and renamed San Frediano's. Many miracles are attributed to him, including changing the course of the River Aiser in order to save crops at risk of flooding.

REFLECTION
Fridian's holiness attracted the townspeople to make him Bishop of Lucca. Do we similarly value holiness today? Do I do my bit in praying for my own spiritual teachers, priests, pastors and leaders, and for the wider Church leaders?

19 MARCH

St Lachtain/Lactanus/Lachtean/Lachlan/Lachtiniu

D.672. FEAST DAY: *19 March*

Lachtain was educated at Bangor. Saint Molua had foretold his birth, and according to legend he did not smile until Lachtain was born and later looked after and educated him. Lachtain became Abbot of Achadh Ur (now Freshford), Co. Kilkenny. He once paid a visit to St Carthage at Lismore, and, having compassion on the monks of the extremely austere St Carthage, brought a very generous gift in the form of thirty cows and a bull. He hid his gift and went ahead and asked for a drink of milk. The monks, having no cows, drew some water instead; Carthage blessed it, turning it into milk. Lachtain blessed it back into water and told the servant to tell Carthage that he had asked for milk not for water, and he would not partake of food until Carthage had accepted his gift! He is credited with many miracles. A bronze reliquary that contained his arm is in the National Museum. His arm is the symbol of the town of Freshford, where St Lachtain's well is reported to cure eye ailments.

REFLECTION
Healing was Lachtain's gift; also compassion. Have I the compassion to want to support and pray for people who are suffering?

20 MARCH

Adamnan of Coldingham

D. C.680. FEAST DAY: *31 January*

Adamnan was an Irish monk who undertook some penitential pilgrimages and met St Ebba on one of them en route to Scotland. He became a monk at the double monastery at Coldingham, near Berwick, founded by Ebba. He was remarkable for long periods of fasting and prolonged vigils. He is also reputed to have had the gift of prophecy. His rule was extremely rigorous. He learned in a vision that Coldingham would be destroyed by fire because of the senseless gossip and other frivolities of the monks. This did happen, but after Ebba's death, as Adamnan predicted. (Not to be confused with St Adamnan of Iona, Columba's biographer.)

REFLECTION

Fasting for religious reasons has gone out of fashion today, but health-enthusiasts often fast. The practice does bring many benefits, including greater spiritual awareness. Health permitting, would I consider fasting for a period perhaps? Or give up a daily treat, for instance a takeaway coffee, and donate the money to charity?

21 MARCH

St Enda/Eanna/Einne of Aran

D. C.530–535. FEAST DAY: *21 March*

Enda was originally a warrior, who was advised to become a monk by his sister, the nun Fanchea, when his bride-to-be died. Fanchea helped him overcome his tendency towards violence and exhorted him to go to Whithorn on a pilgrimage of penance. In spite of his character defects, Fanchea knew her brother to be chivalrous and pure. He then went to Rome and founded a monastery there called 'Place of Joy'. He sought a place where he could have uninterrupted communion with God and nature, and finally settled on Inis Mór in the Aran Islands. He had the ability to interpret dreams and did so for novice Ciarán of Clonmacnoise, prophesying that his influence would spread from the banks of the Shannon to all of Ireland. His monastery was a model of excellence for many others, and many sought him out as a mentor, including Ciarán and Brendan.

REFLECTION
We all need such times of withdrawal and self-examination in our Christian pilgrimage. Do I take such a need seriously? When did I last have a time of penance?

22 MARCH
St Darerca

D. FIFTH CENTURY. FEAST DAY: *22 March*

Sometimes called St Darerca of Valentia Island (to distinguish her from St Moninna, who was often called Darerca). She was a mother and a widow, known as the 'sister' of St Patrick. She was the mother of seven sons, including St Mel of Ardagh and St Rioch of Inishboffin, and two daughters. It is supposed that she followed her brother St Patrick to Ireland with her family and later became a nun. She worked at first as St Patrick's embroideress, making altar cloths and chasubles for him. She is credited with co-authoring a hymn with St Seachnall.

REFLECTION
To have authored even half a hymn shows that Darerca's thoughts were under the Holy Spirit's control and that she did not spend her time as an embroideress idly daydreaming but praising God. Can I see some potential here for growth? Do I pray for my family in the moments when my mind does not need to be occupied with the present task?

23 MARCH

St Ive/Ia

D.450. FEAST DAY: *3 February*

Ive was the daughter of a Munster ruler, who became a nun in Ireland. She sailed to Cornwall with a group of Irish missionaries. Legend has it that she sailed to Cornwall on a leaf – that's likely to have been a poetic description of the curragh she sailed in. Ive built her cell at the mouth of the River Hale, now called St Ives. A community sprang up around her. She was protected by a powerful local chieftain called Dinna, who at her request built a church at present day St Ive's. According to some, she was martyred in Brittany where she had gone with seven hundred and seventy seven disciples.

REFLECTION

We can learn something from Ive's boldness in persuading a local ruler to build a church. People who have that sort of 'boldness' and courage can make things happen! It was not Ive's personal powers that won him over, it was God in her. I need to have confidence that through me God can persuade people to do good. Do I need to learn to let God give me the words in such circumstances?

24 MARCH

St Macartan/Aidus

D. C.505. FEAST DAY: *24 March*

Macartan was baptised by St Patrick in Calry, North Sligo. He was appointed as the first Bishop of Clogher in 454, and spread the Gospel in Tyrone and Fermanagh. Macartan was St Patrick's companion and bodyguard when he travelled to pagan areas to preach the Gospel. He is described in the *Annals of the Four Masters* as St Patrick's 'champion', or the 'strong man', as he used to carry St Patrick across rivers and rough terrain. His symbol is the rowan tree as his original name was Aidus the Son of Carthen (which means Rowan-tree). He was a great preacher and once preached a twenty-four-hour sermon! A beam of supernatural light is believed to have illuminated his book while reading in near darkness.

REFLECTION
Could I carry Jesus over rough territory in the same way? Could I be a champion for him? What is rough territory today? What would this entail for me? Could I make up my own prayer about this? Do I ever pray for 'supernatural light' to mentally illumine my reading of scripture?

25 MARCH
St Caimin

D.653. FEAST DAY: *24 or 25 March*

Caimin was a distinguished scholar, whose commentary on Psalm 119 is still extant. (*St Caimin's Psalter* in Killiney is of a later date.) A hundred years later than St Colm of Terryglass, Caimin became head of the monastery at Iniscaltra, on Lough Derg and is said to be the reason why that island is called 'Holy Island'. When the seventh-century church was being built there, Caimin asked his friends King Guaire and Cummian the Tall what they would like the church to be filled with. Guaire said gold and silver; Cummian said books for the students; Caimin said the diseased and infirm of every class so that he could bear their infirmities in his own body for the Saviour's love. All three wishes are reputed to have been granted.

REFLECTION
Caimin's answer shows us what the man was made of. What would my answer to the question have been? Would I change it in the light of Caimin's answer? How well do I do on the compassion scale? How could I improve here?

26 MARCH

St Lappan

D.687. FEAST DAY: *26 March*

Lappan was a disciple of St Finbar who later headed a monastery founded by St Carthage on the island of *Inis Pic* in Cork Harbour, now anglicised to Spike Island. The island housed a prison for many years, known as Ireland's Alcatraz, and later a correctional facility. Lappan also had a monastery on Little Island. He became the third Bishop of Cork, overseeing much of Cork Harbour. He died in 687. It is thought by some that Ruisne MacLappan (another saint) was his son. This would make sense of the claim that Lappan studied under Nessan, the successor to Finbarr.

REFLECTION
We cannot tell how the places we now live in will develop in the future, but we can do our best to make them beautiful, happy and holy places while we are alive. Do I pray for the area I live in? Have I had my house blessed? Do I ever think of praying for those who will live here after I have moved on?

27 MARCH

St Gelasius/Giolla MacLiag/Giolla Iosa

D.1174. FEAST DAY: *27 March*

Gelasius was the son of the foremost Irish Bard of his time, and was educated at Derry. He started off as *erenach* or archdeacon of the Columban community in Derry, then abbot there for sixteen years. He became Archbishop of Armagh in succession to St Malachy. He was an indefatigable worker, reforming and reorganising monasteries throughout Ireland. Derry became an episcopal see under him. In 1135 he saw the whole city of Derry burn to ashes. He spent much time on his visitations reconciling opposing parties. He had the cathedral rebuilt in stone on a grander scale. Gelasius experienced great grief over the taking of Ireland by Henry II of England. On his death he was mourned as a saint by the entire population of Ireland. He was said to have depended on only one cow for his sustenance.

REFLECTION
Is peacemaking needed near to me, even in the family? Could I pray about being used as a peacemaker? Or could I pray that difficult family members find peace in themselves?

28 MARCH
St Tuathal/Tutilo

D. C.915. FEAST DAY: *28 March*

Tuathal was a younger member of the party who arrived at St Gall under the Irish Bishop Marcus and his nephew Moengal in the ninth century on his return from Rome. He was trained by Moengal at the music school there, and he was reported to be eloquent, quick-witted and handsome. A true renaissance man, he was regarded as a talented musician, sculptor, painter, poet, builder, goldsmith, teacher and composer of music for stringed instruments. He was also the head of the cloister school. Paintings signed by him can be found in St Gall and in other European towns. The chapel of St Catherine in which he was buried was renamed St Tutilo after him.

REFLECTION
Multitalented Tuathal used his gifts to serve God. What talents or skills could I dedicate to God, whether small or big, practical or artistic? Have I a deep-down desire to develop some talent that I could give time to in order to serve God, even something simple like selling knitting in aid of refugees or painting an old person's house?

29 MARCH

St Lassair

D. SIXTH CENTURY. FEAST DAY: *29 March*

Lassair was a niece of St Fortchern, who studied under Finnian of Clonard and Ciarán of Clonmacnoise. Legend has it that at Clonard neither of them looked at each other during the instruction. An angel is said to have carried Lassair to the convent of Finnian's sister, Riognach. Lassair lived up to her name, which means light, and was said to be full of divine ardour. She built a church at Doire mac Aedh and wrought many miracles there.

REFLECTION

By studying with Finnian and Ciarán, Lassair was doing something that was 'not done' by women in those days. Would I have the courage to do something that was 'not done' if I thought it was right and God's will for me? Not looking at each other meant that they were avoiding any occasion of temptation. Do I refuse to put myself into situations where temptation will be unavoidable? To avoid occasions of such temptation is sensible.

30 MARCH

St Cronan/Mochis of Balla

D.637. FEAST DAY: *30 March*

Cronan's parents had a low estimate of his mental abilities, so they made him a shepherd. God had other plans. Saint Comgall found Cronan as he saw angels flying over the house. Comgall educated Cronan at Bangor to become a shepherd of souls. Comgall sent him to found his own monastery. When Cronan asked where, Comgall said a well would lead him to the spot. Sure enough a well appeared overhead in the guise of bright vapour that led them to Balla, Co. Mayo. Cronan was known for miracles, which included curing a crowd of some 2,500 people who had been afflicted with yellow fever.

REFLECTION
Have I ever felt held back by others' low estimate of my capabilities? Do I realise God's estimate of me is the best one, and that I have unlimited potential? The story of the well means there is a right place and time for my fulfilment, and God will point me to it some way or other, maybe in unexpected ways.

31 MARCH
St Melle/Mella

D.787. FEAST DAY: *31 March*

Melle was the mother of two sons, one a priest and the other an abbot, St Tigernach, who built a church for her on the shores of Lough Melvin, Co. Leitrim – known as Daire Melle. She is one of several saints connected with the district of Rossinver. There is an island on the lake called the Island of the Saints. Melle was Abbess of the convent there and awakened the love of God in the souls of her nuns – as she had done for her two sons. This she did with gentleness, forbearance and true charity.

REFLECTION
A firm faith in and love for God is the greatest gift a mother can give her children. Have I passed my own faith on to my family, my nieces and nephews and godchildren? It is a happy thing that Melle awakened the love of God gently in them, as evangelism that is brash and aggressive can have the opposite effect. How gently and lovingly do I share my faith with others?

APRIL

1 APRIL
St Caidoc

D.649. FEAST DAY: *1 April*

With his fellow Irish monk Fricor, Caidoc landed in France in 622. They took the Roman road and preached as they went. Their preaching in the highly pagan Picardy led to the conversion of a nobleman called Riquier, who had come to their defence when they met with violence. He showed them kindness and courtesy whereas the people they were working among, the Morini tribe, ill-used them most ignominiously. Riquier took orders and founded the monastery of Centule in Picardy (now called St Riquier), according to St Columbanus' Rule. Caidoc and Fricor both became monks under him. The relics of Fricor, Caidoc and Maugille are all resting at St Riquier's church.

REFLECTION
Have I often misjudged the success of what I am doing? Do I value nobility of character – that Riquier showed – as better than nobility of birth or social status? Or do I still see these things as the world does?

2 APRIL
St Bronach

D. SIXTH CENTURY. FEAST DAY: *2 April*

Bronach was a female saint who gave her name to Kilbroney, Co. Down, half a mile from Rostrevor, where she founded a church in the sixth century. For years an invisible bell would be heard ringing in the graveyard of Kilbroney Church. Many people dismissed this as a ghost story, but in 1885 during a storm a great oak tree in the graveyard fell and when it was chopped up St Bronach's bronze bell was found in the fork of two branches. It was probably hidden at the time of the Reformation to prevent it being removed. The bell is preserved as a relic in the nearby church of Rostrevor. *The Martyrology of Donegal* describes Bronach as 'The virgin of Glenshesk and of Kilbroney'.

REFLECTION

We know very little about St Bronach as a person, but we do know that the area of Rostrevor has continued to be a place of prayer and even holiness down the centuries. What a wonderful legacy to leave! What kind of legacy would I want to leave behind even if I am not remembered as a person?

3 APRIL

St Keelin/Caolainn

Date unknown. Feast day: 3 February

A number of saints known as Keelin have been recorded. The main one was from Connaught. Her feast day was the day for gathering red seaweed in Connemara. One of her churches was near St MacDara's Island in present day Moyrus parish near Roundstone. Keelin became noted for her piety. Her biographer said of her: 'She won the esteem and affection of her sister nuns by her exactness to every authority and also by her sweet temper and tender disposition.' She also was known as one of three maidens who 'never took offence or demanded goods in reparation for outrage'.

REFLECTION

In these days when people are urged to be assertive, could I also be sweet-tempered? Could I also be a person who never takes offence? Do I realise that such a disposition does not mean one is a weak person – just a humble person rather than a proud person?

4 APRIL
St Tigernach

D.548. FEAST DAY: *4 April*

Tigernach was baptised by St Brigid who became his godmother. His legend claims that he was captured by Welsh raiders, brought to Britain, escaped and went to Candida Casa in Scotland for education for the priesthood. Brigid urged him to become a bishop but he became a hermit first. He later became the abbot of Galloon Island on Upper Lough Erne, then Bishop of Clones in Co. Monaghan. He was very holy and ascetical, and raised several people from the dead, including an Archbishop of Armagh. He once baptised a whole locality of people who had been worshipping an idol. They turned to God when Tigernach made the sign of the cross revealing a large demon, which he banished. He was blind for the last thirty years of his life, and lived alone given to prayer and contemplation.

REFLECTION
Tigernach's decision to be a hermit first before he became a bishop reminds us of Thomas Merton's saying that the saints can love everybody because they love God first. Is my first love reserved for God?

5 APRIL
St Beagán of Emlagh/Beccan

D. SIXTH CENTURY. FEAST DAY: *5 April*

Beagán of Emlagh, Lower Kells, Co. Meath, is included in one of the lists of Ireland's twelve apostles. He was said to have been one of Ireland's three *athlaoich*, laymen who became monks at a late age. It seems that Diarmuid Mac Caearball, the High King, drowned his son Breasal in punishment for stealing a nun's cow. The King felt remorseful and begged Beagán to restore his son back to life. Beagán was reluctant at first, but St Columba joined his voice to the request and Beagán's prayers restored the boy to life.

REFLECTION

Beagán can only have held back from restoring the boy to life out of humility, but Columba knew that he had the faith to do it. Irish saints were often humble, becoming nothing so that God could be everything in them. God in him healed the boy. Could I, like Beagán, have a late vocation to be a channel of God's healing to people?

6 APRIL

St Cellach/Celestine/Celsus

D.1128. FEAST DAY: *6 April*

Cellach became Archbishop of Armagh as a layman, as had become the custom. He was a reforming Archbishop, who decided to put an end to this irregularity, so he took holy orders, restoring Armagh to its primacy. He named St Malachy O'Morgair as his successor, sending him his crozier as death approached, thus ending the custom of hereditary abbots and archbishops. Cellach had given Malachy extra training in the reform methods of St Carthage at Lismore. He was indefatigable in discharging his duties, and very given to fasting and prayer. His skill gained a truce between two warring kings. During his time, Armagh Cathedral burned down and he had it repaired. Cellach presided over the reforming Synod of Rathbreasil in 1111. He is still remembered and celebrated in Armagh.

REFLECTION

Mediation skills are very much in demand today and the extra dimension of Christian love and prayer would make them even more effective. Could I be such a mediator? Would I be willing to train for it?

7 APRIL
St Finan Cam

D. SIXTH CENTURY. FEAST DAY: *7 April*

Finan was from West Cork. He was known as 'Finan Cam' (Finan the crooked) because he had a stoop. He had a particular gift at stopping rain and even when his mother was expecting him, her garments would remain dry no matter how heavy the rain. Later as Abbot of Kinnity, Finan made sure no rain fell on the harvesters. He is also credited with: stopping time to help a person in a hurry; restoring a calf to life that a poor man had killed; healing a paralysed boy; and stopping a probable battle by making the attackers 'see' their villages on fire. Finan had the gift of healing from childhood – it is said that he healed some of his young friends from an early age. Once his monks ran to put out flames emerging from his dwelling, and witnessed him walking out unharmed. Finan explained it was the Holy Spirit's power that protected him. He may have had a church on the island of Inisfallen.

REFLECTION
Sometimes we forget that children too need and can receive divine healing. Is there a child I should be praying for now?

8 APRIL
St Tigernan

D. FIFTH CENTURY. FEAST DAY: *8 April*

Tigernan founded a church at Errew on the shores of Lough Conn, Co. Mayo. It later became a large abbey. There is also a holy well there, *Tobar Tigernan*. His dish was preserved by the O'Flynns, the *erenachs*, or hereditary wardens of Errew. In 1413 the abbey was profaned by Robert MacWattin who brought a prisoner there forcefully. Saint Tigernan appeared to MacWattin in a vision every night until he released the prisoner. MacWattin then presented some land to the abbey for ever.

REFLECTION
Whether we put it down to a dream or an actual vision, MacWattin's conscience was being bothered. A modern equivalent is not being able to sleep properly because of a deed we have done that we regret. Have I ever thought of asking the Holy Spirit's help in deciphering the meaning of a dream that seems to be important and which remains with me during the day?

9 APRIL

St Cuanna

D.650. FEAST DAY: *4 February*

Cuanna was from Annadown near Tuam, Co. Galway. He may have been a half-brother to St Carthage, by whom he was educated. He was a compiler of annals and a hermit, and was said to recite the psalter while standing in a stream of water. People from all over Ireland visited him for his miracles, his absolution, his guidance and soul-friendship which influenced them to a life of holiness. At a conference near his cell Cuanna saw a bell take shape overhead. He said it represented their brother Fursey, who was then at Peronne, but wanted to join the confraternity. When he heard his brothers were about to fight a battle he warned their opponents to flee. He could tame wild animals and had a pet deer.

REFLECTION
What kind of influence do I have on other people? Would I warn people of potential violence? Would I make a suitable soul-friend? How about reciting psalms by heart – could I learn one or two favourites?

10 APRIL
St Paternus

D.1058. FEAST DAY: *10 April*

Paternus was an Irishman who became an anchorite at St Meinwerk's Monastery in Paderborn, Lower Saxony. He asked to be bricked up in a cell adjoining the Abbey for his life. He preached against the evil that was rampant in Paderborn. He prophesied that the city would be destroyed by fire within a month. The people of Paderborn jeered at him. But in 1058 this did come to pass, and Paternus was the only monk not to survive as he kept to his vow of enclosure and died in his cell. The mat on which he died, which somehow survived, became an object of veneration by the people who had scoffed. Marianus Scotus was one who visited and prayed upon the mat and wrote the story of Paternus.

REFLECTION

Paternus was an example of one hundred per cent commitment. How committed am I to following Jesus? Paternus was willing to shine God's light into dark places instead of staying comfortably at home. Is God calling me to leave my comfort zone? What dark places are calling out to me for help and rescue?

11 APRIL
St Mogue/Aidan of Clonmore

D. SIXTH CENTURY. FEAST DAY: *11 April*

Aidan was better known by his affectionate name Mogue (Mo-Aedh-Óg: My little Hugh). Saint Moling called him 'The Golden Vessel', a very complimentary nickname. He founded the monastery in Clonmore, Co. Carlow (*Cluain Mór Maedóc*) in 560, with five thousand monks at one time. Mogue is reputed to have lived until the age of a hundred. There were a total of nine sainted Abbots of Clonmore. Locals today say that the holy well of St Mogue cures warts if approached solely for that purpose. Once an army started to descend upon Clonmore and Mogue went out alone to meet it, drew a line with his staff and told no one to tread beyond it. One soldier did so and died, and the army retreated.

REFLECTION
If we take saints in a wide meaning, not just those officially beatified, who do I know today who would be called a saint. How could I imitate them? We are all called to be saints at the far end of our process of sanctification by the Holy Spirit; what does the Holy Spirit need to work in me most at present?

12 APRIL

St Erkenbode

D. EIGHTH CENTURY. FEAST DAY: *12 April*

Erkenbode and two companions, Luglius and Luglianus, left Ireland to be missionaries in France. The two companions were killed by robbers. Erkenbode buried them and continued on to join a monastery at St Omer, eventually becoming the abbot there. In 720 he became bishop of Therouanne for twenty years while continuing to oversee the community at St Omer. Erkenbode built many churches and monasteries, and the monks were devoted to him. He was known to have prayed incessantly and consoled the poor and afflicted. People certainly flocked to him.

REFLECTION
In those days people would flock to a holy man who radiated the love of God and was filled with the Holy Spirit. Have I anyone in mind that I could visit like this when I have some free time? Erkenbode's being full of the Holy Spirit was in all probablilty the secret of how he managed continual prayer. Do I see continual prayer as just for saints or should all Christians aim for this?

13 APRIL
St Elwyn

SIXTH CENTURY. FEAST DAY: *22 February*

Elwyn was an Irish monk who went to Cornwall with a group of Christians which included St Breaca, who had been a nun at Kildare. He is remembered at Portleven – at the mouth of the Hayle River – which is derived from his name. So he must have started his work immediately in that area where he first landed. The fact that a town is still called after him is testimony to the enduring influence he had.

REFLECTION

Influence is a subtle thing and not something we can easily measure. What sort of influence would I like to have on the neighbourhood where I live? How would I like to be known and remembered there – for what qualities? We exert some sort of influence wherever we go, even if not intending to. Saint Paul likens Christians to letters from God; what would I like my life to be saying to the world?

14 APRIL
St Tressan

D. SIXTH CENTURY. FEAST DAY: *7 February*

Tressan, a disciple of St Fursey, heard a voice telling him to leave Ireland. In France Remigius Archbishop of Rheims gave him and his brothers protection so that they could spread the Christian faith. Tressan was illiterate and started off in his new country as a pig-herd, driving his pigs to the door of the church so that he could hear Mass. Tressan received instruction from the priest, studying while faithfully doing his herding job. He was ordained and ministered at Mareuil on the Marne. Once he fell asleep on a journey and the staff he had stuck into the ground opened up a spring with the property of curing the ague. He died at Avenay, where he is patron. Pope Clement authorised the printing of an office for him. Devotion to Tressan is very strong in the Rheims area.

REFLECTION
Do I feel that God calls us all to serve him in some special way that only we can? What thing is God calling me to do for him now? Could I persevere in spite of an inauspicious start?

15 APRIL

St Ruadhan

D.584. FEAST DAY: *15 April*

Ruadhan was seven feet tall and counted among the Twelve Apostles of Ireland. His community was at Lorrha by Lough Derg, Co. Tipperary, and lasted for several centuries. *The Stowe Missal* was written there in the ninth century. There is little evidence for his cursing of Tara but the story does witness to the great respect Irish people had for the spoken word and its power. Ruadhan is said to have protected a chieftain who came for sanctuary, by hiding him in the cellar. When the High King asked where the man was, Ruadhan replied truthfully: 'I don't know where he is unless he is under your feet'. Some lepers asked him for alms so he gave them the horses that were pulling his chariot; immediately two deer leapt out of the forest to replace the horses. He also healed lepers. They said Ruadhan was filled with the love of God since infancy, and although royal was more noble within.

REFLECTION
Do I judge people by what is within them rather than their outside appearance or status?

16 APRIL
St Etchen

D.577. FEAST DAY: 11 *February*

Etchen's parents were very pious. His mother was barren for many years and is reputed to have conceived thanks to the prayers of St Brigid. Etchen was a Bishop of Clonfad, near Killucan, Co. Meath, and was a friend of Kevin of Glendalough. He also had a part to play in St Columba's life, possibly ordaining him a priest. The legend claims that he was supposed to be ordaining Columba as a bishop, but ordained him in error as a priest and Columba declared himself content to remain a priest all his life. Etchen founded a church at Clonfad in the parish of present-day Killucan. He is listed as both Bishop and Abbot of Clonfad.

REFLECTION

Etchen's 'mistake' could have been the will of God, guided by the Spirit, given Columba's personality. Etchen, as all those early saints, was filled with the Holy Spirit as his normal state. Am I limiting the influence of the Holy Spirit in my life by keeping it for special occasions and not for everyday life? Could I invite the help of the Holy Spirit for what I have to face today? Tomorrow? Next week?

17 APRIL
St Donán/Donnan

D.618. FEAST DAY: 17 *April*

Donán was an Irish saint from the Cruithne race who went to Scotland. He laboured for the conversion of the pagan tribes in the west and the Western Isles, and settled at Eigg. He was martyred for the faith with his companions. Columba had refused to be his soul-friend, saying it was not fitting to be soul-friend of one destined for red martyrdom (death for the faith). In 618 Donán and fifty-two monks were brutally murdered by the pirates of Eigg on Easter Sunday. The pirates were said to have been called in by a rich woman who kept three sheep on the island and objected to the monks using the place as well. The pirates broke in during Mass, but Donán asked for a respite until after Mass; the deed was done in the refectory. The names of St Donán's fifty-two companion martyrs are recorded in *The Martyrology of Tallaght*.

REFLECTION

Donán was uniquely qualified to labour in Scotland because his Cruithnian language was similar to Pictish. We all have something special or unique about us. Could I use my uniqueness to help others?

18 APRIL

St Laserian/Molaise of Leighlin

D.639. FEAST DAY: *18 April*

Laserian healed his nurse of a snakebite. His tutor Abbot Murin was healed of blindness by washing his face with water the infant Laserian had touched. He studied in Killeshin, Iona and in Ireland under Fintan-Munnu. He refused a kingship, preferring to withdraw as a hermit to a Holy Island off the coast of Arran Island in Scotland. He was taught for fourteen years under Pope Gregory the Great, who ordained him. Laserian presided at a synod in Leighlin in 630, and two years later St Gobban invited him to take over the Abbacy of Leighlin, where he became the first Bishop of Leighlin. It is said that once he restored a man to life whose mother had carried him to the monastery gate with his severed head. *The Feilire of Aengus* says of him: 'Laisren of burning virtues; Abbot of bright-shining Leighlin'. He combined the active and the contemplative life very successfully.

REFLECTION ←
How successfully do I combine the active and contemplative aspects of being a Christian?

19 APRIL
St Cognat

DATE UNKNOWN. FEAST DAY: *11 February*

A virgin, of Urney on the north bank of the River Erne. The name Urney comes from the *Earnaidhe*, a tribe that gave its name to Lough Erne. Two cells attached to the now ruined church there were once used as a school. No record remains of Cognat's dates or her life.

REFLECTION ←
Cognat must have been an anchorite, living on her own in a relatively safe place, the church. In these hectic times, one has sympathy with this act of solitude. Do I ever feel the need for more peace, quiet and isolation? How could I come by these? Withdrawing is a way of fostering the Christian pilgrimage, of becoming what God intends us to be. It is a long process, and rarely happens overnight! This is what Cognat was facilitating. Do I see any signs that the process is continuing and taking shape in my life? What more is needed?

20 APRIL
St Monessan

D.456. FEAST DAY: *20 April or 4 September*

Monessan was a Saxon princess who became filled with the Spirit. She resisted entering into an arranged marriage – even when drenched in cold water she would not relent. She asked her parents who was the maker of the 'wheel by which the world was illuminated?' They took her to Ireland to see St Patrick, explaining to him that her desire to see God was very passionate. She went to Kill-na-ningen near Armagh to be instructed by Patrick. Monessan was very beautiful and many princes desired to marry her. She loved God with all her heart and all her soul and disregarded riches. Patrick baptised her in the three-fold name and her legend tells that she died straight after this.

REFLECTION

Monessan's faith was so strong that she was committed to a spiritual life. Her relationship was one of faith. She adored God and took to heart His offer of a deep relationship or friendship with Him. How seriously do I take this offer of God's to all His children? Even if accepted at one time of my life, do I cultivate and nourish this relationship and treat Him even better than I treat my best friends?

21 APRIL

St Nennid

D. FIFTH CENTURY. FEAST DAY: *2 or 21 April or 13 November*

Known as *Nennid Láimhiodhan* (Nennid of the clean hand), Nennid was a priest who was St Brigid's personal chaplain. She encouraged him in the faith since meeting him as a giddy youth racing around the Curragh. They prayed for each other; she prophesied that he would administer the last rites to her. Nennid placed a locked brass gauntlet over his hand so that it would not be defiled before administering the sacrament to Brigid. Although he was in Rome when Brigid was dying, he hastened back to do that, having been warned of the event by an angel. He lived a century earlier than Ninnidh of Inismacsaint.

REFLECTION

It could be that 'giddy youths' are worth trying to win over for Christ, as well as the steadier, conscientious ones, for they would have the potential of being leaders. Brigid was a good mentor and role model. She saw Nennid's potential. We all need encouragement on our spiritual journey. Who gives me encouragement? And who can I encourage?

22 APRIL
St Berach/Barry

D. SIXTH CENTURY. FEAST DAY: 15 *February*

Berach from Gortnaluachra near Mohill, Co. Leitrim, was tutored and fostered by his great-uncle St Fraoch, who had seen a luminous halo surrounding Berach's parents' house. At baptism Fraoch changed his nephew's name from Fintan to Berach, which means 'one who takes direct aim with the point of a sword', or 'acute', because of his nephew's acuteness, wisdom and miracles. Berach was a friend and fellow monk of St Kevin, from whom he drove out demons with his special bell. He went out with a stag attached to his chariot, to found a monastery where the stag lay down. This turned out to be in Cluain Coirpthe, now called after him Kilbarry, Co. Roscommon. Berach is said to have prayed incessantly and shone with the light of wisdom. He dissuaded a fellow monk from going to Rome by showing him a vision of Rome that satisfied him.

REFLECTION

Am I acute and straight or do I prevaricate? Does my name mean something which could indicate my character? If not which name would I choose? What could I learn from the meaning of that chosen name? Could I profitably use unallotted times to pray or reflect, like Berach?

23 APRIL

St Ibar/Ivor/Iberius/Iborus

D.499 OR 500. FEAST DAY: *23 April*

Ibar was one of the four pre-Patrician bishops along with St Declan of Ardmore, St Ailbhe of Emly and St Ciarán of Saighir. He directed St Darerca/Moninna for some time, as she had gone south to his monastery because her own was too distracting because of visits from relatives. Ibar is listed in *The Book of Armagh* as one of St Patrick's bishops, but this was after a long period of not accepting Patrick's authority as he was not Irish. After many quarrels with Patrick, an angel made peace and harmony between them, and they then lived in brotherhood. While going to greet Patrick with Ailbhe, Ibar went ahead as the master, until an angel blinded his eyes, telling him Ailbhe had precedence. When Ibar accepted this his eyes were healed. His monastery was in the area of Wexford harbour on what was once Beggary Island, now silted up.

REFLECTION
Peace and harmony after a long period of quarrelling can happen to any of us. How open am I to reconciliation with someone I have been quarrelling with for years?

24 APRIL

St Fortchern

D. FIFTH CENTURY. FEAST DAY: *17 February or 11 October*

When Loman came in a boat up the river Boyne to Trim, Fortchern heard Loman singing the psalms. He was so enchanted by the sound that he came to the boat to receive the faith. Fortchern's father, the chieftain Feidlimidh, gave Trim to Loman who became its first bishop. Near his death Loman named Fortchern as his successor, refusing to bless Fortchern unless he

April 95

took on the task. After three days as bishop, Fortchern handed over his see to Cathlaid the Pilgrim. Fortchern felt that if he were bishop, it would be like taking back the gift his father had given to God. He founded monasteries at Killoughternane and Tullow, which became a centre of learning. Fortchern was St Finnian of Clonard's first tutor.

REFLECTION
St Fortchern must have put himself into other people's shoes and thought what the critics and gossips among them would say, acting according to the principle of St Paul that we should avoid actions that would offend the weaker brethren. Does this principle apply to anything in my life?

25 APRIL

St Macaille of Croghan/Machuleus

D. C.489. FEAST DAY: *25 April*

Macaille was the first Bishop of Croghan in Offaly. He took part with St Mel in St Brigid's ordination, placing the veil on her head. The tradition is that it was also he who protested strongly that Mel had used the wrong rite – that for a bishop rather than a nun. He was traditionally a son of Darerca, St Patrick's sister, which would make him possibly a younger brother of St Mel's. He was described as 'a great bishop, a rod of gold, a vast bar'. He may have become the Bishop of Longford later. His name means 'man of the veil', so his fame came from his association with St Brigid.

REFLECTION
Did Macaille protest as 'a stickler for the rules', or did he realise that this was a prophetic act? Maybe he knew that Brigid was their equal. We see this progression in some denominations, especially with female bishops in the Anglican church now. Maybe he foresaw that coming to all churches in time? What progression would I like to witness in society or a particular faith?

26 APRIL

St Trudpert

D.607. FEAST DAY: *26 April*

Trudpert was an Irish pilgrim who decided to build his hermitage in the Black Forest. He met Othbert, Lord of Alsace, near the River Rhone, who tried to modify Trudpert's asceticism, and gave him two workmen to help him to build a monastery at Bresgau. Trudpert was always hard at work whenever they arrived and also still at work when they left. Three years later he was murdered by being struck on the head with an axe while he was resting from his labours. This was done by some different workmen – for trying to build another church at Krozingen, on the German side of the Rhine. His monastery in the Black Forest was considered the first of its kind on the east bank of the River Rhine. It continued for twelve hundred years.

REFLECTION
Trudpert provided a good example to his workmen by joining in himself and being the last to clock off. Do I give leadership in this way to those I ask to work for me?

27 APRIL

St Aenghus of Burt

D. FIFTH CENTURY. FEAST DAY: *18 February*

Aenghus was from Inishown West, the son of Oillil son of Eighan. He was ordained by St Patrick and probably became a bishop.

REFLECTION
Not much is known about Aenghus' life, but he was obviously a man with a strong vocation. Do I have a strong belief? Are there

April 97

ways I can strengthen my faith? Aenghus was certainly a person whose heart was no longer restless as he had found his rest in God. Is my heart still restless or have I found my rest in God? Does this rest in Him withstand the trials and temptations of modern life? Does it give me peace? Does my disposition to God need renewing and deepening now?

28 APRIL
St Cronan/Mochus of Roscrea

D.626. FEAST DAY: *28 April*

Cronan founded fifty religious houses, of which Roscrea, Co. Tipperary, was the most famous. He chose this spot because he saw the gates of heaven open there and multitudes of angels approaching it. His first monastery was in an inaccessible spot, so he moved to a main road to be more accessible for the poor and needy. He was renowned for his hospitality, even in old age when he became blind. One legend says he transformed water into ale for some weary travellers, making them drunk in the process. He was Abbot of Roscrea, and it is believed that *The Book of Dimma* was written by one of the monks there. A legend claims that Cronan was distressed over losing a copy of the Gospels in a nearby lake. It remained in the water for forty days. When the book was found, not a single letter of the text had been destroyed.

REFLECTION
Have I ever felt about a certain spot that this was the gate of heaven, as Jacob and also Cronan did? Could many spots on earth be such gates if we were willing to open our eyes to them?

29 APRIL

St Hymelin

D. EIGHTH CENTURY. FEAST DAY: *10 March*

Hymelin was the brother of St Rumold of Malines. The brothers were Irish monks who went on pilgrimage to Rome. Hymelin was seized by a fever at Vissenacken, and asked a girl passing with a pitcher of water to give him a drink. There was plague in the locality and the girl had been told not to let anyone touch the pitcher. After initially refusing, she eventually gave in and allowed him to drink. When she got to her master's house those who drank the water said it was wine. So the local priest fetched Hymelin, who refused a bed and slept in the barn for three days before he died. When he died a radiant light was seen around the body and all the local bells started ringing of their own accord.

REFLECTION

This saint unselfishly refused a bed so as not to contaminate other people with the plague. How would I have reacted in the same circumstances? Do I consider others and the impact of my actions or decisions, even when I'm ill? Have I thanked those that have cared for me when I was sick? When life delivers hard knocks, what is within tends to come out. How attentive am I to cultivate the love of God for all my fellow creatures deep within me?

30 APRIL

St Pellegrinus/Peregrinus

D.643. FEAST DAY: *1 August*

Pellegrinus was an unnamed Irish *peregrinus* or pilgrim, who went, as many Irish did, on a *peregrinatio pro Christi* with no intention of returning. Mount Pellegrino in the Italian Alps is named after him. He lived for some time in a hollow tree. He is honoured at Modena and Lucca. He had a little chapel at the top of the mountain, which later became a hospice for pilgrims. A tradition there is to ring a bell on winter evenings in case any travellers in the area had lost their way. They also put long poles along the road to mark the way and kept a dog ready for rescue work. Free board and lodging would be given to the poor for three days. He died at the age of ninety-seven.

REFLECTION

Pellegrinus did much to help the lost to find their way in difficult terrain. Who do I know that seems most lost? Could I pray for them? Love them? Be a friend to them?

MAY

1 MAY
St Cellach/Ceallach/Kellach

B.520. FEAST DAY: *1 May*

Cellach was the elder son of Eoghan, King of Connacht. He was educated by St Ciarán at Clonmacnoise. He renounced his heritage to become a monk, but his father died while the younger son was still a minor and Cellach allowed himself to be persuaded to become king without informing Ciarán. Revolts and political intrigue followed and he rued the day he accepted the kingship. Cellach later upheld his younger brother Muredach's claim, did penance and returned to the monastery. He then became Bishop of Killala, but often retired to a hermitage on Lough Conn, *Oilean Etgais*, where he had seen a vision of angels. His brother Muredach visited him there often to seek his advice. While there he was assassinated by a political rival.

REFLECTION
Cellach put his vocation aside to do right by his family until his brother came of age. Have I been conflicted by family commitments? Like Cellach, can I advise younger people with the benefit of hindsight and the wisdom of experience?

2 MAY
St Germanus/Jarman

D. C.460. FEAST DAY: *2 May or 3 July*

Germanus was from an Irish family who moved to Britain. He met Germanus of Auxerre and was so impressed that he became a disciple and also took the name Germanus for himself. Germanus moved back to Ireland. He became a bishop under St Patrick. He is mentioned in the lives of several saints of that early Patrician period, including St Ciarán. Germanus travelled extensively, preaching the Gospel and helping make peace between warring factions in Wales, Spain, France and the Isle of Man where he was the bishop. He was martyred in Normandy. Germanus is regarded as the Apostle of the Isle of Man, where he converted a robber to Christ.

REFLECTION

Germanus' gift seems to have been preaching. We think of the words of St Teresa: 'Christ has no lips but ours with which to tell the good news to the world'. Are my lips offered to him for his use?

3 MAY

St Colchu/Colgu/Colga/Colgan

D. C.796. FEAST DAY: *20 February*

Colchu was a man of great learning who became Rector of the School at Clonmacnoise, and whose influence spread to the Continent. A remarkable prayer of his is found in *The Yellow Book of Lecan*. He is thought to have taught the famous Alcuin. A letter from Alcuin to him is extant in which Alcuin describes himself as Colchu's son. He is also said to have conversed with St Paul in the flesh. He was very charitable and was said to have prayed to God to light up his soul with charity, mercy and the spirit of forgiveness. He was also known as Colgan the Wise.

REFLECTION

Colchu prayed for charity, mercy and forgiveness. Do I ever think of praying for the characteristics and virtues that I need? What would I pray for?

4 MAY
St Conleth/Mochanna Daire

D.519. FEAST DAY: *3 or 4 May*

Conleth was asked by St Brigid in 490 to be the Abbot and Bishop of Kildare. Brigid was the abbess of the women's monastery and later head of the dual monastery. Conleth was known for his sanctity and for a spirit of prophecy. Previously he had been a hermit in the Newbridge area – Old Connell, where gold had first been smelted in Ireland. He was a skilled metal worker making the liturgical vessels for the monastery. He taught his skilled trade to others. Tragically, he was killed by a pack of wolves on one of his journeys to Rome – which Brigid had advised him against. On a previous journey there, Conleth brought back precious vestments – 'foreign and exotic robes' – which Brigid gave to the poor.

REFLECTION
Conleth used his talents to provide for the monastery and passed on his knowledge. Could I dedicate my talents in some way? Could I pass them on to others? Had he taken St Brigid's advice he would not have been killed. We all need the humility to acknowledge and act on good advice.

5 MAY
Blessed Edmund Rice

D.1844. FEAST DAY: *5 May*

Edmund Ignatius Rice was born to a farming family in Callan, Co. Kilkenny. When he became a widower at the age of twenty-seven, he sold his business and dedicated his life to the education of those who had no money. He was inspired to do this by the Bishop of Waterford who pointed out to him the bands of ragged youths in the streets of Waterford. Edmund gathered other like-minded young men around him and they took religious vows as members of the Congregation of the Brothers of the Christian Schools.

REFLECTION

These Christian Brothers, as they became known, had a way of life that emphasised prayer, study and meditation on the Scriptures. They would have meditated on Scripture really well until it became part of their personality and a continuous source of inspiration and encouragement as well as challenge. Do I use the Scriptures, poems or other forms of literature in that way? Have I discovered the joy of meditating on the words, and of staying with a verse that speaks to me instead of moving on hastily to something else?

6 MAY

St Cera/Ciar/Cior/Ciara/Sarah

D. SEVENTH CENTURY. *FEAST DAY: 6 May*

Cera had a convent at Lisdoonan, Co. Monaghan. Her name means wax, which is suitable as she was skilled at beekeeping, ornamental writing on wax tablets, and also linen-work and making altar-breads. Legend says that she had a flock consisting of one sheep, which she killed to feed St Tigernach on his journey. Tigernach repaid her by miraculously providing a full flock of sheep to feed and clothe her nuns. There is another St Cera, of Kilkeary, Co. Tipperary.

REFLECTION

Cera used her many skills and talents for good; have I done the same with mine? Could I do so more in a small way? Her generosity to Tigernach was amply repaid. The point of giving is not to expect anything in return. Can I give generously without expecting anything in return? Do I fear to give generously because I fear for the future, especially during uncertain times? Could I start depending on God's provision more, remembering the scriptural injunction to cast our bread upon the waters and it will return to us?

7 MAY
St Iserninus/Id/Idus/Fith/Sezin

D.468. FEAST DAY: *6 March, 7 May or 19 September*

Iserninus was a hermit on Clear Island off the coast of Cork. At the age of twenty-five he travelled to Rome, where he met St Patrick, who made him a bishop. In 439 he travelled back to Ireland, along with Secundinus and Auxilius, to help Patrick. A story about him relates that he was reluctant to go back to Ireland but was forced to when the winds blew his boat in that direction! Iserninus founded the church and a seminary for youths at Kilcullen, and another church at Aghade. He helped St Patrick draw up the rules for the new Irish church. A legend about him says that he relit the church lamps by carrying fire in his own hands. Iserninus preached by example as well as words.

REFLECTION
Iserninus' preaching by example shows that he put into practice all he had learnt. Do I put into practice what I am learning day by day or week by week? If more people did this, maybe we would be able to 'light the church lamps' from our own hands, metaphorically.

8 MAY
St Eithne

D. SIXTH CENTURY. FEAST DAY: *8 May*

Eithne was the mother of St Columba, and wife of King Felimidh, a descendant of Niall of the Nine Hostages. She was from the Leinster royalty. While she was pregnant with Columba, she had a dream or vision of a beautiful coloured cloak spreading across the sky. An angel interpreted her dream as meaning that her child would have beauty of character and be a prophet and win countless souls for the Kingdom of Heaven. Eithne prophesied that his teachings would extend throughout Ireland and Britain. One of her serving women also had a dream of parts of Eithne being carried by birds of the earth and air all over *Erin* and *Alba* (Ireland and Scotland). Eithne is said to be buried on a small rugged island near Iona in Scotland, Eilean-na-Naoimh.

REFLECTION

Do I give credence to my own special dreams and visions? If they are hard to understand could I ask angelic help as Eithne did? Do I realise that beauty of character is what other people look for and value in us, rather than outward beauty, style, or other external characteristics?

9 MAY

St Beoadh/Beatus of Ardcarne/Boey

D.524. FEAST DAY: *8 April or 8 March*

Beoadh was Bishop of Ardcarne, Co. Roscommon. He is also known as Beatus – but not to be confused with the ninth-century St Beatus of Lake Thun, the apostle of Switzerland. His real name was Aodh, and the prefix *beo* (bright or living) was added because of his evident holiness. His bell was greatly venerated in Connaught. He was very hospitable and had a house especially for guests. He was also known for his generosity, in particular for giving presents. His name has been anglicised to St Boey. He is also associated with Inishmagrath island on Lough Allen. Beoadh was distinguished for his virtues and for miracles both before and after his death.

REFLECTION

'Beatus' means blessed; but it sounds as if Beoadh was a blesser of others, in his generosity and gift-giving. How much do I bless other people? How do I bless them while giving a gift however small? Do I regard hospitality as a burden or as a chance to bless my friends? How could I improve this situation?

10 MAY
St Comgall

D.603. FEAST DAY: *10 May*

While Comgall was in his mother's womb St Macanisius prophesied that many thousands of monks would obey him. At his baptism by the blind priest Fedelmid, a fountain of water gushed out of the earth that healed Fedelmid's sight. Comgall studied under Finnian at Clonard and under Fintan at Clonenagh. He became a hermit on Lough Erne, where he was so austere, that some other monks there died from starvation. So when Comgall founded the large monastery of Bangor he modified the rule! Bangor had three thousand monks. The monastery was called a 'nursery of saints', and later St Bernard called it 'the vale of angels'. Comgall helped Columba on his visit to Brude King of the Picts as his Cruithnian language was similar to Pictish. He encouraged people to love Christ, to hate wealth, be kind to others, and to advance a step a day. He was described as full of grace and God's love.

REFLECTION

To advance one step a day is good advice, often we attempt too much too soon. Do I try to advance by short daily steps? Do I recognise that achieving a little is manageable and ultimately leads to achieving a lot?

11 MAY
St Lua/Molua/Lugud

D.609. FEAST DAY: *11 May or 4 August*

Molua is the most illustrious of the thirty-seven saints known as Lua or Molua (Molua is the affectionate form of the name). He was a chieftain's son born in Limerick, who was set to herd the cattle. His father did not want him to enter a monastery, but eventually Lua was educated at Bangor and Clonard. He was the teacher of Bishop Flannan, who became his successor as abbot. Conan was another of his pupils. Conan was a poet and loath to do any work. Lua cured him of this gently by presenting one thistle for him to lop off with his sickle; the next day two thistles and so on until Conan was longing to finish the job. It was said of Lua that he was not afraid to reprove a person but always did so with gentleness.

REFLECTION
When reprimanding people am I capable of doing it patiently and gently? Do I love the person even though I'm not comfortable with aspects of their personality, lifestyle or deeds? How can I encourage them towards positive action?

12 MAY
Venerable Edel Mary Quinn

D.1944. FEAST DAY: *12 May*

Edel was a Cork woman who was a member of the Poor Clares for a short while until she fell ill with tuberculosis. She then did Legion of Mary work, and volunteered to go to East Africa to work there for the Legion. She was accepted in spite of her ill health, and there followed seven and a half years of strenuous and enthusiastic work. The Bishop of the Diocese of Nairobi said that after a year of her work the whole atmosphere of the Diocese changed. Edel was nicknamed 'Our Lady's Little Lamp'. She died and is buried in Nairobi.

REFLECTION
Even while suffering from ill health, Edel continued to work enthusiastically and change the whole atmosphere of a diocese. This is no mean feat. Have I adapted in a situation, for example, due to ill health, and found a way to continue to work enthusiastically? Do I avoid enthusiasm or do I realise its literal meaning is 'in-God-ness'? Do I do my work enthusiastically? Could I help to improve an atmosphere somewhere with my cheerfulness and love?

13 MAY
St Abban/Eibbán/Moabba/Abbanus

D.620. FEAST DAY: *13 May*

At the young age of twelve, Abban became a student under St Ibar his uncle. He was known as a holy man and an energetic evangeliser. He was a king's son but chose the religious life. His parents were unimpressed and put him in prison, from which he miraculously escaped. After a hard struggle he won his parents over, convincing them of his true vocation. He is associated with the areas of New Ross and Moyarney, Co. Wexford. He was an abbot and a priest but not a bishop, and many smaller churches also look to him as their founder, including churches in counties Cork and Kerry. His main monasteries were Killabban in Laois and Moyarney/Adamstown in south Co. Wexford. Abban chose Gobnait to preside over the convent he founded at Ballyvourney in Co. Cork.

REFLECTION
Think about the temptation to go in a direction that our family and circumstances are channelling us into. Is this our true calling? Could we ask God to give us the courage Abban had to break away from expectations? How could I show my family or friends that a particular path or decision means a lot to me?

14 MAY

St Davnet/Damnet/Damnait

D. SIXTH CENTURY. FEAST DAY: 14 May

Davnet was a young woman from Co. Monaghan. Her father was St Ronan, a hermit. Her sister was St Lassar of Lough Melagh. She lived and died in the area of Slieve Beagh in the parish of Tydavnet (which means house of Davnet), on the mountain which separates Monaghan from Fermanagh. She founded a church there in the sixth century, with a convent for women. Its location is thought to be in the graveyard of the present Roman Catholic church. Davnet's staff is on display in the National Museum now but formerly was used for testing the truth of oaths. Many criminals confessed while touching this staff or crozier, called the *Bachall Damhnait*. She is often incorrectly identified with St Dymphna who lived a century later.

REFLECTION

The name Davnet means faun and may have described her character. Does my name convey something of myself? Often people have been told by an angel what to call their child, including in the case of Jesus, so it is important. Could I take a new name with a meaning that will inspire me?

15 MAY

St Carthage/Cartach/Mochuda

D.637. FEAST DAY: 15 May

Carthage was tending herds one day when a bishop passed by with his followers, all singing psalms. Carthage was so entranced that he followed them and remained all night outside the monastery listening. He joined the monastery, and spent forty years at Rahan, Co. Offaly, as a hermit. In 636 he went to

Lismore, Co. Waterford, and founded a monastery there in his old age. He died a year later. Carthage rejected the offer of land from the King of Cashel as it was not the place God had chosen. Lismore became a famous monastic school. Carthage did many miracles and healings, including the healing of a king while he was a young man working as a king's pig-herd. Saint Cathal/Cattaldo of Taranto was one of his pupils.

REFLECTION
Singing that is heartfelt and spiritual has a drawing power. Do I sing to God in this way, praying twice as Augustine would have it? Am I capable of refusing a rich gift if it is not God's will? Am I able to know what God's will for me is? Do I listen to Him enough?

16 MAY

St Brendan the Navigator/St Brendan of Clonfert/St Brandon

D.578. FEAST DAY: *16 May*

Brendan was born in Tralee, fostered by St Ita, taught by Bishop Erc then St Finnian of Clonard. He founded the monastery of Clonfert, which became a bishopric in 550 and remained one of the oldest continuous sees in Ireland, with three thousand monks in Brendan's day. Brendan sat on the top of Mount Brandon and looked out to sea to an island where he wondered if God would allow him to become a hermit. He eventually got a positive response and set out for that island in a hide-boat with some companions, to *peregrinare pro Christo* in an attempt to spread the Kingdom of God on earth. Although British explorer Tim Severin duplicated his voyages successfully, many theologians regard the stories as allegorical accounts of the soul's pilgrimage. Brendan was said to be of joyous temperament.

REFLECTION
Am I able to inspire others with my dreams? Has a dream been maturing in me for a long time? Could I pray and await the right

time to start? Might Brendan's joyous temperament be the reason he inspired others?

17 MAY

St Maelduff/Mailduff

D. C.673. FEAST DAY: *17 May*

Maelduff was an Abbot of Durrow who left Ireland to preach to the Anglo-Saxons. He had befriended the French Bishop Agilbert and went over to visit him in Wessex. He stayed on and erected a cell for himself in the woods of Ingleborne. That cell grew into a flourishing monastery, and later became the town of Malmesbury (a corruption of 'Mailduff's burg'). The Venerable Bede wrote that Maelduff was skilled in learning and constant in prayer and would hear the voice of God addressing him. He used rigorous penitential practices, immersing himself up to the shoulders in the stream near his cell, even during winter. His monastery became an important Benedictine Abbey, and his famous pupil the Anglo-Saxon scholar Aldhelm was his immediate successor there.

REFLECTION

How constant am I in prayer? What would help me here? Maybe it was his constancy which helped Maelduff hear the voice of God addressing him: Could I try listening for God's voice as an extension of my daily prayer?

18 MAY

St Cadroe

D. C.975. FEAST DAY: *5 March*

Cadroe was the son of an Irish Prince in Scotland, born as the result of the prayers of St Columbanus. He trained in

Armagh under his foster father Beanus. They preached together throughout Scotland. When Cadroe decided to become a monk some members of his family tried to dissuade him. He went as a missionary to Germany with Malcallan, and became head of the monastery at Waulsort. The King of Germany, Otto I, gave a charter to the monastery stipulating that it was always to be headed by an Irish monk. Cadroe was known as a brilliant monastic organiser and was sent to Metz to restore St Clement's Abbey there which had become decadent. A charter of Emperor Otto III talks of 'Cadroe of blessed memory'. He was remarkable for his humility, healings and miracles. He was said to love all sorts of people and have great compassion for sinners.

REFLECTION

This Christ-like loving of all sorts of people is not easy to cultivate. Can I imitate Cadroe in this? Am I making progress?

19 MAY
St Brunsecha

D. SIXTH CENTURY. *FEAST DAY: 19 May*

Brunsecha was a nun under St Liadain, the mother of St Ciarán of Saighir, in Killyon manastery near Birr, Co. Offaly. Liadain trained Brunsecha in every Christian virtue. Brunsecha was exceedingly beautiful and a chieftain, Dymma, imprisoned her in his castle and raped her. Saint Ciarán came to the castle and tried to remonstrate with Dymma, who said he would only release her if the cuckoo's note awoke him from sleep. It was winter and snowy, but miraculously Dymma did awake to the sound of a cuckoo, so he released the girl. However, Dymma went to the convent and tried to seduce her again. This time she was terrified and died of shock. Dymma's castle went up in flames with him inside it, and Ciarán restored Brunsecha to life.

REFLECTION ✦

This dramatic and horrific story has a hopeful message for many people who suffered a traumatic experience. Do I know anyone recovering from a trauma? If so, how can I support them in their recovery? Would I be open to God's healing power in such a situation?

20 MAY

St Macheanog/Mochaomhog/Pulcherrius

D.655. FEAST DAY: *13 March*

Macheanog was a nephew of St Ita of Killeady, born thanks to her prayers. He was fostered by Ita and studied under her, then under St Comgall in Bangor. The Prior of Bangor reported to Comgall and Macheanog that he had seen the monastery surrounded by devils laying seige to it, but there was only one devil – and him idle – at the king's palace. Macheanog explained that the devil employs all his forces only against those who resist his tyranny. The two saints then cast them out after prayer, commanding them never again to assemble there until the Day of Judgement. He founded a monastery near the present-day village of Kilmacanogue. His main monastery was in Leigh, Co. Tipperary; he is also remembered in Cong.

REFLECTION ✦

Macheanog studying under his foster mother is interesting. It is a fact that our parents, godparents and grandparents often have a lot of precious wisdom they coud pass on to us. Do I ever set out to learn from the older generation? Do I listen to them deeply and draw them out with open-ended questions about their life and what they have learnt?

21 MAY
St Barrind/Barinthus/Barruin/Barrfhionn

D. SIXTH CENTURY. FEAST DAY: 21 May

Barrind was the son of Muredoc and Didhuat, and a relative and colleague of St Columba. He is also credited with having been on a voyage with St Brendan, having inspired that younger man to undertake the voyage with tales of his own previous adventures. Barrind founded two churches: Drumcullen, Co. Offaly, which was on the imaginary line between the northern and southern halves of Ireland and Kilbarron, Co. Donegal, which is where St Columba is credited with miraculously rescuing his staff from the sea.

REFLECTION

Have I any tales to tell that would inspire younger people? We often underestimate the influence we have on other people. What sort of influence would I like to have? How could I achieve that?

22 MAY
St Conall Coel

D. SEVENTH CENTURY. FEAST DAY: 22 May

Conall became Abbot of Iniskeel, a beautiful island off the west coast of Donegal. It can be reached from the mainland on foot at low tide, from Narin Beach. Saint Dallan Forgaill wrote in praise of him. Tragically, it was while on a visit to Conall that St Dallan was murdered by pirates. Miraculously Conall found Dallan's head in the ocean and rejoined it to the body and gave him decent burial. Conall gave his name to a waterfall there, and there is also a holy well which springs from a cavity in a rock.

REFLECTION

Conall must have found the beautiful scenery a continuous reminder of the beauty and presence of God and a help in establishing the habit of continual praise and prayer. Have I ever used solitude and silence for such an endeavour? Praying for others would have been part of his prayer. Have I underestimated the power of prayer for others? Do I do enough of it?

23 MAY

Cassan/Casán

D. FIFTH CENTURY. FEAST DAY: *28 March*

Cassan was the son of Neamhan and a disciple of St Patrick. He founded the Church of Fothairt Airbhreach, Co. Offaly, near Croghan Hill. Saint Finnian of Clonard once was given hospitality by him, during which Cassan complained that the King of the area was demanding gold for his freedom; Finnian provided this miraculously. Saint Patrick prophesied that miracles would abound there after this saint's death, and that many would gain solace from them. This did happen – many miracles were reported as being performed there. A round tower and a Romanesque doorway remain to witness to the spot, now called Temple Finghin.

REFLECTION

Cassan did not let the lack of gold prevent him from starting his Christian pilgrimage. Am I as determined and as single-minded? Has lack of resources ever prevented me starting something? Could I trust that seeking first God's will, these will be provided? Did I notice too that Cassan provided hospitality to Finnian even though he was impoverished?

24 MAY
St Brynach

D. FIFTH CENTURY. FEAST DAY: *7 April*

Brynach left his native Ireland to become a colleague of St David in Wales. He also became a soul-friend to Brychan, the Christian King of Powys. He married Brychan's daughter, Corth, and they had four children. After a pilgrimage to Rome and Brittany, Brynach returned to find that Irish people were no longer welcomed in Wales because of their constant invasions. As a result, he was expelled from various places, placing a strain on the marriage. He eventually settled in Nevern, where the ruler was related to his wife. There the hill where he prayed and communed with angels is called the Mount of Angels – *Mont Ingli* – to this day. He went to Devon later and founded Braunton and other faith communities.

REFLECTION

A soul-friend or *anamchara* is something more intimate and loyal than a spiritual director. Brynach must have been a very special person as he was chosen as a king's soul-friend. Have I been – unofficially or officially – a soul-friend to anyone? How well have I fulfilled this important ministry?

25 MAY
St Malchus/Malachus

D. TWELFTH CENTURY. FEAST DAY: *10 April*

Malchus was a contemporary of Malachy O'Morgair of Armagh, who studied with him and was guided by him. He was a native of Ireland but spent a long time in a Benedictine monastery in Winchester. He restored hearing to a deaf man and intellect to a boy. In 1098 he became a local bishop in Waterford, consecrated by Anselm. With the help of the Ostmen he built a church there. After 1110 he became Bishop of Lismore, Co. Waterford. He was sought out by many for guidance from Ireland and overseas. Under his reign Cormac, the King of Munster became a penitent.

REFLECTION

The time spent in the monastery must have prepared Malchus for his ministry of advising, encouraging and healing. Being a hermit first and then founding a community was very much the pattern for these early Irish saints. Receiving first in order to then give. Do I receive enough, knowing that I cannot give what I do not have?

26 MAY

Libhear

D.619. FEAST DAY: *8 March*

Libhear was a young man who was described as impious and disobedient to his mother. He must have died, for St Canice raised him to life. Libhear repented of his sins. Canice had Libhear's legs fettered, and he followed Canice to Scotland and was taught by him. After seven years of discipleship his fetters were removed. The key had been thrown into the sea at the start, but according to the story it was found miraculously. Canice had directed Libhear to an area near the River Liffey, where a fish some local fishermen caught had the key to unlock his fetters inside it. It is thought that he went on to become Abbot of Aghaboe in Co. Laois, after Canice's death, in succession to his master.

REFLECTION

What fetters might I be wearing that would need supernatural help in unlocking? Could I think and pray about this? Do I believe Jesus Christ wants me to be free? Has following Christ made as big a difference to my life and character as it obviously did to Libhear's?

27 MAY
St Commaigh/Coma

DATE UNKNOWN. FEAST DAY: 19 December

An early Irish female saint about whom practically nothing is known except her name. She shares a feast day with St Samthann, which could well have meant that she had been one of St Samthann's nuns.

REFLECTION
The reason why we know so little about Commaigh could be that she was someone who quietly went about her work without drawing undue attention to herself or seeking credit or acknowledgement for her deeds. The fact that her name is remembered and that she was known as a saint highlights that her work was noted. Can I provide support, care or charity without seeking any recognition in return?

28 MAY
St Molaise of Inishmurray

D. SIXTH CENTURY. FEAST DAY: 18 April

Molaise became the second abbot of the monastery on the island of Inishmurray that had been founded by St Muredach of Killala. He reproved Columba after the Battle of Cooldrevny, suggesting Columba's penance should be going in exile to Scotland to win as many people to Christ as he had caused to die in battle. The windswept and treeless island, now uninhabited, is seven kilometres off the coast of North Sligo. There is an old pre-Christian cashel there and beehive huts. A beautiful old wooden statue of St Molaise showing a saintly face, has survived, and is in the National Museum at Kilmainham in

Dublin. Legend claims he took on diseases at the same time as a penance.

REFLECTION

The penance Molaise gave to Columba was more loving and more appropriate than his fellow abbots' excommunication plans; it had wonderful consequences, as if God had a hand in it. Can I act graciously and forgive someone I feel has let me or a loved one down or disappointed me in some way? Can I find the inner strength to forgive myself for a particular failing?

29 MAY

St Buryan/Briana/Bruniec/Bruinseach

D. FIFTH CENTURY. FEAST DAY: *29 May, but 13 May in the Scilly Isles*

Buryan was an Irish princess who was a friend of St Patrick. She is thought to have gone to Cornwall with St Piran, landing at present day St Ives. She is patron of several parishes in Penzance and the Scilly Isles. She has been described in a poem as a faithful shepherdess, and as 'one glorious within'. Her name means 'Irish Lady' in Cornish.

REFLECTION

This phrase 'all-glorious within' is from Psalm 45. It prompts me to ask am I glorious within or is my inner life not fit for inspection? It must mean thoughts and images and desires, and what goes on in one's mind all the time when nothing else is happening, in 'idle moments'. Am I open and available for letting God's Holy Spirit transform me to being all-glorious within or at least a little more glorious within than at present?

30 MAY
St Maugille/Madelgisilus/Maldegaire/Madelgisel

D. C.685. FEAST DAY: *30 May*

Maugille was an Irishman who went with St Fursey to work beside him in East Anglia. He became Fursey's prior in Lagny after they had gone to the Continent, and was with him at his death and took his funeral. Maugille then went to St Riquiers (now Centule), the monastery founded by the nobleman who Caidoc and Fricor led to faith. He taught and preached there, and lived a solitary life in a little cell near Monstrelet to which he had been led by an angel. A miraculous spring sprang forth nearby that was found to have healing powers after his death. Maugille resisted the offer of becoming Bishop of Canterbury. Vulcan, another hermit, discovered him after he had fled Canterbury. They became hermits together aiming to acquire a new virtue every day.

REFLECTION

If I tried to acquire a new virtue every day – or week, or even month – what virtues would I work on? Fursey was a mentor to Maugille, can I think of a mentor or a friend's virtues that inspire me?

31 MAY
St Sinell/Sinchell/Senchell the Elder/Sincheall of Killeagh

D.549. FEAST DAY: *26 March*

Sinell was one of St Patrick's first converts and recorded as the first that he baptised. He was presented with a cell at Clane by St Ailbhe, where that saint had lived for some time. He later went on to found a community at Killeagh, Co. Offaly, which was only second in importance to St Brigid's foundation in Kildare.

The community survived until the seventeenth century, when the stained-glass windows were removed to the Church of Ireland in Maynooth. Sinell write *Pious Rules and Practices* in the Gaelic tongue. Another Senchell, his kinsman who was a bishop, lived with him there, and they were both noted for holiness. They are both reported to have died of the plague in 549, at a ripe old age.

REFLECTION

Being a hermit gave Sinell time in which to face the darker sides of his character and overcome them. Do I spend enough time in self-examination, acknowledging my darker sides? Are there steps I can take to deal with my darker sides, or am I being tempted to skip the confession of sin and finding forgiveness and concentrate mainly on the more comfortable and comforting aspects of Christian life?

JUNE

1 JUNE
St Ronan/Renan

D. SIXTH CENTURY. FEAST DAY: 1 *June*

St Ronan went from Ireland to Brittany in the sixth century, directed by an angel. He started out in a cave on the coast, ringing a handbell to warn ships of danger, but local beachcombers who depended on shipwrecks for their livelihood chased him away inland to the forest. A wife, jealous that her husband spent so much time listening to Ronan, reported him to the king and accused him of being a werewolf and devouring her daughter. The king set two furious bulldogs onto Ronan; the saint quelled them with the sign of the cross. Meanwhile, the daughter couldn't breathe in the cupboard her mother had locked her into, and had died, but Ronan raised her to life. The route he took over rocky land has been made into a way of penance called the *Grand Troménie* (Breton for 'Tower of Refuge') which takes place every six years. The tradition is that every Breton must perform it at least once in their lifetime.

REFLECTION
St Ronan was persecuted for doing good: am I doing enough good to be worth persecuting?

2 JUNE
St Conall

D. FIFTH CENTURY. FEAST DAY: 2 *June*

Conall was a local saint of Co. Sligo, the son of Domhnall. His holy well at the edge of the north side of Lough Gill is believed to have healing properties. An island in the lake is called after him. He is reported to have been a helper of Saint Patrick, who was having some trouble with the Druids when he was baptising in Co. Sligo. Conall may have gone on to become Bishop of Coleraine. He was a half-brother to St Attracta, and famously forbade her to situate her nunnery too near his hermitage.

REFLECTION ☙

Conall's forbidding Attracta to live too near him with her nuns could be an example of keeping out of temptation's way. Do I put myself in temptation's way when I am not ready, or do I avoid situations where I would be vulnerable?

3 JUNE

St Kevin/Caoimhin

D.618. FEAST DAY: *3 June*

Kevin ('beautiful birth') began his monastic life at Luggala but left when his miracles there made the other monks try to make him abbot. When he made his way to Glendalough an angel cleared the way for him, blessing the trees as they went. His life was one of closeness to nature. He became a hermit first, then others flocked to him and a community grew up around him. He tamed the monster of the Lower Lake, letting it curl around his body while he prayed in the water. Miracles were plentiful. Once a maiden chased him repeatedly so he struck her with a bundle of nettles; she repented and became a nun. He was harried by demons often and banished them from the valley.

REFLECTION ☙

Blessing trees and closeness to nature is not just for New Agers. Could I spend more time outdoors enjoying nature? Could I become a more bless-ing kind of person? Could I do as Kevin did and tame the (metaphorical) monster which is in me, enabling it to work with me instead of against me?

4 JUNE
St Breaca/Breague

D.460. FEAST DAY: *4 June*

Breaca was a nun at St Brigid's monastery in Kildare who travelled to Cornwall with a large group of others. Some Cornwall parishes still bear her name. Some of her companion nuns were also commemorated, including Uni, Germocus, an Irish prince, and Gwinnear, who is known there as Wynnerus. Breaca was martyred in the year 460 at the river Hayle. She founded the Cornish church of Breage, over four kilometres west of Helston.

REFLECTION
St Breaca was obviously guided by her faith to have the courage to leave her home and travel overseas. Her spiritual strength and work is remembered by the church of Breage. Do I allow time to let my inner voice guide me to good deeds? Is there some place I feel drawn to visit?

5 JUNE
St Efflam

D.512. FEAST DAY: *5 June*

Efflam was an Irish prince who went to Brittany. Legend says he came to the aid of King Arthur who was fighting with a dragon. Efflam revived the fainting King and drowned the dragon in the sea. One story relates that he married a woman called Enora, but became a pilgrim for Christ before consummating the marriage. Enora followed him to France and joined him at Plestin-les-Grèves, the two in separate cells. Another old tale tells of how St Efflam solved a dispute peaceably. Jestyn, son of Geraint, went to Brittany from Anglesey and occupied Efflam's hut, which was deserted as he was away on pilgrimage. When Efflam returned he decided to settle the matter peaceably. It was cloudy, so they agreed that whoever's upturned face the sun's rays touched first would live in the hut. The sun's rays touched Efflam first. Jestyn bowed low and returned peaceably to Anglesey.

REFLECTION
Efflam's solution to a potential conflict was imaginative and peaceful. Could I apply imaginative methods to solve any conflicts I am close to at present?

6 JUNE

St Jarlath

D. C.550. FEAST DAY: *6 June*

Jarlath from Co. Down became noted for his extreme poverty and for his teaching skills. He was taught by Benignus at Kilbennad, Co. Galway, who was the man who became Patrick's successor at Armagh. Jarlath is said to have performed thirty genuflections every morning and again every evening. He became Brendan the Navigator's teacher, but Jarlath was very humble and desired to be Brendan's disciple rather than his teacher. Jarlath asked Brendan to choose the site for Jarlath's new monastery where he would end his days; Brendan said it would be where the wheel of the chariot came off. So they drove around in the chariot and the wheel came off in Tuam. Jarlath founded a church in Tuam in 520 that later became one of the four archbishoprics of Ireland. A broken wheel is the symbol of the see.

REFLECTION
Jarlath's humility in wanting to be his pupil's disciple illustrates an important truth: to a certain extent everyone who teaches should be willing to also learn from their pupils. Do I learn from those I teach, if any?

7 JUNE
St Colman of Dromore

D. C.550. FEAST DAY: *7 June*

Colman was the first Bishop of Dromore, and also the titular saint of several other churches, including Inis-Mo-Colmaig in Scotland and Llangolman in Wales. He could well have taught Finnian of Moville. Colman is thought to have been born in Kintyre in Scottish Dalriada, which was seen as almost one country with Ireland at the time. Saint Patrick predicted his birth. He studied under St Caylan at Nendrum and then St Ailbhe of Emly, and was a close friend of St MacNisse of Connor. Legend credits him with restoring to life a woman who had been decapitated and also the future St David of Wales who was stillborn. Another legend states that a fountain sprang from the earth whenever Colman needed to baptise someone.

REFLECTION
St Colman was not afraid to travel and cross frontiers for God. What 'frontiers' can I see that need to be crossed today? In my life? Nationally and internationally? What can I do to forward this?

8 JUNE
St Maelrubha

D.722. FEAST DAY: *21 April or 22 August*

Maelrubha became a monk at Bangor at an early age and was elected abbot there in 668 at the age of twenty-nine. He caught the missionary fervour and begged to be relieved of his abbacy to go to Scotland. His monks were sad to lose him but let him go. He never visited Ireland again. In 671 he founded a monastery at Applecross on the west coast of Scotland, where he caused a great revival of the Christian Church. He travelled throughout the Western Isles and is known as the Apostle of Skye. Holy wells named after him are reputed to be able to cure mental illnesses. Maelrubha went as far north as Skail in Sutherland and died there aged 80 while preaching. Applecross men had to be sent for to carry his coffin home, as the locals could not lift it.

REFLECTION

If I could, would I be keen to die 'in harness' as Maelrubha did, even if it was the harness of a voluntary job or some other kind of Christian service?

9 JUNE

St Columba/Colm/Colmcille

D.597. FEAST DAY: 9 June

Columba, tall, red-haired with a mighty voice, was born at Lough Akibbon near Gartan, Co. Donegal to Felim and Eithne of the Uí Neill royal family. Columba was in the *derbfine*, the group who had the potential for the High Kingship. He was educated by Finnian of Moville, Finnian of Clonard and Mobhí of Glasnevin. A legend claims that when his guardian angel informed him that he could choose his virtues, he chose virginity and wisdom. The angel was so pleased with that choice, he gave prophecy too. He founded around three hundred churches, and monasteries in Derry, Durrow, Kells, Moone, Drumcliffe and Glencolumbkille. He was banished to Scotland as a penance for having caused the Battle of Cooldrevny in 561 in which three thousand and one people were killed, sparked off by complaints against High King Diarmaid, including an unjust judgement concerning his copying of his old teacher's psalter without permission. From Iona, Columba travelled throughout Scotland, preaching among the Picts and founding churches. He had many talents: he was a poet, a member of the Order of Fíli, a prophet and had a wonderful singing voice. He prophesied that the monastery of Iona would be in ruins for many years and then be built up again, which has happened.

REFLECTION
Given the choice of a virtue would I have chosen wisdom? Or something else? Would I have been willing to renounce a possible royal career to serve God instead? What would I be willing to give up for God?

10 JUNE
St Sanctan

D. SIXTH CENTURY. FEAST DAY: 10 June

Sanctan was said to have been the son of a king of Britain. His mother is said to have been a daughter of the King of Ulster. He is thought to have been a brother of St Maedoc of Ferns, but this probably means spiritual brotherhood given the different parentage. He could also have founded a community at Bohernabreena ('road of the Britons') near the river Dodder, Co. Dublin. He became Bishop of Killalesh, Co. Wicklow and Killsantan, Co. Dublin and also was associated with Glenasmole, Co. Dublin. Sanctan composed a celebrated Irish hymn which begins, 'Implore the wonderful King of Angels'. Another poem was written in praise of him; he was described as a saintly sage, soldier and bishop. Because of the similarity of their names many of his churches were renamed St Anne's.

REFLECTION
Sanctan composed a celebrated hymn. Can I find joy and solace in music? Can I also be creative as a way to express my faith? He was described as a sage. Can I find ways to become wiser in my reactions and my daily life?

11 JUNE

St Cuach

D. SIXTH CENTURY. FEAST DAY: *29 April*

Cuach was from Coiningean, Co. Kildare. She was a full sister to St Attracta and half sister to St Kevin of Glendalough, and is associated with a church at Killynee near Arklow, Co. Wicklow. She is credited with having been suckled by a she-wolf. She became a pupil of St McTalius, Bishop of Kilcullen. Bishop McTalius' fellow clergy reviled him because of this, and denounced him. Cuach became abbess of a convent of nuns at Cill Finn Mirghin or Killeen Cormac.

REFLECTION

More power to this woman studying with a bishop! And to him for taking her on! Do I ever feel the desire to study more deeply into any subject, particularly one not usually studied by people of my own gender? Could I find the strength and pray for God to give me the courage of my convictions, and the energy to achieve those dreams either through meditation, prayer or the support of others. What other dreams have I got hidden away and unfulfilled? Could I encourage others to study more deeply or pursue their dreams?

12 JUNE

St Christian/Giolla Criost

D.1139. FEAST DAY: *12 June*

Christian's full name was Christian O'Morgair. He was the brother of Malachy, the great reformer of the church, and was described as a burning and shining light. He became Bishop of Clogher. Saint Bernard of Clairvaux described Christian as: 'a good man, full of grace and virtue, second to his brother in fame, but possibly not inferior to him in sanctity of life and zeal for righteousness'. He was buried in Armagh under the altar, and his relics were venerated. He was also revered on the Continent as a person who shunned ease for the sake of lasting life.

REFLECTION

Could I ever be described as a burning and shining light? Why not? Zeal is not a popular quality today and even regarded with suspicion: could I regain my former zeal or enthusiasm for the Christian message?

13 JUNE
St Ultan of Fosses

D.686. FEAST DAY: 1 *May*

Ultan was the brother of St Fursey and St Foillan, and accompanied them to East Anglia. When the Mercians drove them out, he and Foillan followed Fursey across the sea to France in 650; Ultan going to Fosses and Foillan to Peronne, on land given by St Gertrude. When St Gertrude asked Ultan for news of Foillan, he immediately had a vision of a dove with blood dripping from its wings – Foillan had died at the hands of robbers. Ultan took over the abbacy of Peronne as well as Fosses. Ultan was revered there as a saint as was his brother Foillan. Fosses remained an Irish monastery for many years.

REFLECTION

Visions seem to be rarer today, but they are a gift of the Holy Spirit. Has God ever told me something in this way? Am I open to guidance by a picture in the mind, though not always necessarily through symbols? Dreams too can be a way God can speak to us: am I open to that?

14 JUNE

St Melangell

D.590. FEAST DAY: *27 May*

Melangell was an Irish princess from Leinster, who escaped to Britain to avoid an arranged marriage. God led her to a place in Merionethshire in present-day Wales. She was praying in a copse when some hunters burst in on her; the hare they were hunting ran to take refuge under her cloak, or some say up her sleeve. The hunters' horses refused to go further. The chief huntsman – the local ruler, Prince Brochwel – was so impressed that he gave her a tract of land, promising that there would be no hunting there ever again. Melangell made it into a sanctuary of prayer and it is still a place of retreat and healing today, with a very tangible feeling of holiness about the church and the surroundings.

REFLECTION

Melangell went to a place of God's choosing and made it a place of retreat and healing. Have I ever been guided to a special place? Is there somewhere I can retreat to for peace and reflection or somewhere I can provide for others to have a sanctuary? Melangell was good with animals and offered protection to the hare. Can I improve my connection to animals?

15 JUNE

St Algise/Adalgisius

D. C.686. FEAST DAY: *2 June*

Algise was one of many Irish pioneers in France, who still holds a place in the folklore of the North and East of France. He and his brothers Gobain, Etto and Eloquius, were all St Fursey's disciples. They settled in the forest of Thiérache in Picardy, and evangelised the area around Arras and Laon. The town that grew up around their monastery became known as St Algise. His project has been quoted as an example of how the Irish gave financial support to their missionary work on the Continent. His three companions found him by following a dove with a twig in its mouth until they came to Algise's cell. He liberated several men from demons and banished all traces of idolatry from the Hannonia area, building a strong church there.

REFLECTION ~
Do I financially support missionary work abroad or another form of charity work? Even if not able to give much financial support, do I support the missionaries and people who give their time to charitable causes with my prayers?

16 JUNE
St Seadhna of East Ulster

D. SIXTH CENTURY. *FEAST DAY: 16 June*

Seadhna's father Tren was so cruel to his employees that St Patrick was obliged to remonstrate with him, and prophesy God's judgement on him. As a result, the horses pulling his chariot bolted into the lake now known as Lake Trena. His wife asked Patrick's blessing for the twin children in her womb: Jarlath and Seadhna. The twin boys were born safely and St Seachnall baptised them. Saint Jarlath succeeded Patrick and Benignus at Armagh as its third abbot and St Seadhna also became a bishop.

REFLECTION ~
Do I wait until a child is born before I pray for him or her? Can I say a prayer for a child before it is born just as St Patrick prayed for the twins? If St John the Baptist was filled with the Holy Spirit in his mother's womb, it can surely be no harm but a great good. Could I ask a priest or minister to bless my projects, my home, a shared meal, an expected child?

17 JUNE

St Moling

D.697. FEAST DAY: *18 January or 17 June*

Moling was an abandoned baby rescued by monks. Later he became healed of his extreme asceticism – which did not even permit him to listen to music – as the wax he had stuffed into his ears melted while the harpist played, his hardness melting as the wax melted. He then started seeing music and the arts as sources of good. He founded a monastery at St Mullins, Co. Carlow, and also its ferry service, which began with a homemade raft and continued until the 1900s. Moling built with his own hands a mile-long watercourse to power his mill – it took him seven years. *The Book of Mulling* is still extant and contains a plan of Moling's monastery. A number of poems attributed to him have survived. He became Bishop of Glendalough and then of Ferns after St Aedan's death.

REFLECTION
Moling is an example of perseverance, never giving up over the seven years it took to build his watercourse. Do I need to develop more perseverance? In what areas? Like Moling, can I enrich my life by listening to more music and appreciating the arts?

18 JUNE

St Brone

D.512. FEAST DAY: *8 June*

Brone founded a church on the Coolera peninsula near Strandhill, Co. Sligo, now called Killaspugbrone (Church of Bishop Brone). He is said to have been visited by St Patrick, who lost a tooth while with him. Patrick gave the tooth to Brone. Brone had it encased in silver and it is now in the National

Museum. While on his way to visit Patrick, Patrick had a vision that Brone and two others – Olcan and Marerca – were on their way but unable to cross the river. Patrick's prayers freed them from danger. Once at a Synod that Patrick and Brone were at together, a woman concocted a scandalous falsehood against Brone, but this was miraculously disproved. Brone assisted at the consecration of Cantellus, Bishop of Tamnach (a small piece of land rising over Cummeen Strand, now called *Doonan Patrick*).

REFLECTION
When I am faced with natural dangers like rivers in flood, does it occur to me to ask for divine or angelic protection? Or to claim the protection God promises in Psalm 121 – to keep us from all evil and keep our going out and coming in, and be our unslumbering shade at our right hand?

19 JUNE
St Moluag/Murlach/Lugadius

D.592. FEAST DAY: *2 June or 4 August in Scotland*

Moluag was educated at Bangor, and possibly also by St Brendan of Clonfert. He founded a hundred monasteries in Scotland, starting with Lismore in 562, and spreading throughout the Hebrides and mainland Scotland, including two on the shores of Loch Ness. He was known as the Apostle of the Picts. He arrived in Scotland a year before Columba, establishing his monastery and missionary base at Lismore, an island on Loch Linnhe off the west coast of Scotland. It was full of pagans at first, and Moluag worked hard to spread the Gospel. He and Columba are traditionally thought of as rivals. The Christian name Luke, common in Scotland, is said to be derived from St Moluag; Moluag being the affectionate form of Luaigh. He is credited with healing miracles and protection from insanity.

REFLECTION

To have converted a whole pagan island to Christianity and founded a hundred monasteries shows an amazing amount of tenacity and energy. Have I discovered yet that our energy comes from our belief in ourselves and our spiritual connection to the Divine?

20 JUNE

St Aifin/Aiféan

D. SEVENTH CENTURY. FEAST DAY: *3 June*

Aifin was the nephew of Glúnshalach, a reformed outlaw. He founded a church at Killafeen ('Church of Aifin') in the townland of Laragh, parish of Mullinacuff, near Shillelagh, Co. Wicklow. He was from Dalriada but associated with Glendalough. Saint Kevin often visited the church at Killafeen, which was part of the family of churches or *paruchia* of Glendalough.

REFLECTION

To have an uncle dramatically converted from a life of crime could actually have been an asset to Aifin. It might have provided a good example of how people can turn their lives around. It could also have highlighted the importance of compassion and not judging or dismissing others for their past mistakes. Have I judged someone unfairly because of their past mistakes? Could I see the good in such a person and believe that they can change or could I encourage them to release their true potential?

21 JUNE

St Cormac of Durrow

D. SIXTH CENTURY. FEAST DAY: *21 June*

Cormac was Abbot of Durrow, and is often referred to by his family name – Cormac ua Liatháin – to distinguish him from St Cormac of Cashel. Cormac had been a monk from an early age and became an ocean traveller. He was an energetic and courageous character. He travelled probably to convert pagans as well as to find the land of promise. Cormac had several unsuccessful voyages and also visited Iona. He is said to have sailed away in quest of a 'desert in the ocean'. He founded a church at Kintyre and on the Orkneys, but may not have left anyone in charge in the latter church. He reached intensely cold places and wanted to die abroad, but Columba sent him back to Durrow.

REFLECTION

Cormac's strong urge to travel was combined with doing good. Could I use my travels or holidays to attain something of value, either for a retreat or to learn something new at each place? Meeting strangers and blessing them inwardly can lead to some unexpectedly lovely encounters.

22 JUNE

St Concord/Cornelius/Conor

D.1176. FEAST DAY: *4 June*

Concord was born Conchobhar MacConchaille in Armagh, where he became an Augustinian Canon, later Abbot of Armagh and then Archbishop of Armagh in succession to Gelasius. He went on a pilgrimage to Rome to plead for support for the Irish cause at a time when his clergy were under severe pressure from the Norman bishops and the Ostmen (descendants of the Vikings). While returning from Rome Concord fell ill and died at Lemniec in Savoy. Miracles were witnessed in abundance at his tomb and he became the patron saint of the town. He used to climb a hill with a cross on top and prostrate himself there to pray. Local people built a chapel there in his memory.

REFLECTION

Concord found a special place for his private prayers. Have I managed to find one? Have I ever tried prostrating myself as a posture of prayer, as each different posture says different things to God? How about dancing to God as King David did – could I try that?

23 JUNE

St Mochae/Mochaoi/Mahee

D.496. FEAST DAY: 23 or 26 June

Mochae was the grandson of the pagan Miluic who had employed Patrick when he was a young slave aged sixteen. On Patrick's return as a bishop, Miluic locked himself up in his house and set fire to it rather than meet Patrick his ex-slave. While still a boy in around 433 Mochae met Patrick while herding pigs. Patrick taught and blessed Mochae. Legend claims that one day St Patrick was teaching when a crozier descended from heaven, its point at Mochae's breast and its handle at St Patrick's. He thus was consecrated bishop in spite of his protests of unworthiness. Mochae founded the monastery of Nendrum on an island in Strangford Lough (now called Mahee Island after him). While there he would join his monks in hewing wood to build the church. He went over to Scotland and ministered near Dumfries. Caylan was Mochae's successor at Nendrum, who in turn taught Finnian of Moville, who in turn taught St Columba.

REFLECTION

Would I be willing to work alongside my subordinates as Mochae did, as a way of good leadership?

24 JUNE
Rumold/Rombaut

D. C.775. FEAST DAYS: *24 June in Belgium and 3 July in Ireland*

Rumold was a prince born as a result of the prayers of the Archbishop of Dublin, Gualafer, who fostered him. He gave his wealth away to the poor and was one hundred per cent devoted to God. He refused an arranged marriage and was made Bishop of Dublin against his inclinations. Rumold laboured there until an angel appeared and told him to go abroad. He travelled to Malines in Belgium where he preached the Gospel. He had succeeded in winning most of the area of Malines and Mechlin to the Christian faith when he was murdered, and his body thrown into the river and covered with trees. Some fishermen found it because a great light was seen shining over the spot. It is now in a golden shrine at St Rumold's Cathedral in Malines.

REFLECTION
Although fostering is far less common, nurturing care comes in many forms and different people can provide parental care in a child's life. Am I a godparent, grandparent, uncle or aunt, or role model? A good one? How could I improve at that?

25 JUNE
Venerable Matt Talbot

D.1925. FEAST DAY: *19 June*

Matt was born in Dublin and was one of twelve children. He left school early in order to get a job to help provide for his family. He worked as a messenger boy for a firm of liquor merchants. He drank very heavily, which impacted his work. When he was twenty-eight he was out of work and his drinking cronies refused to buy him a drink and this set him thinking about his life. As a result, he took the pledge and kept it for the rest of his life. Matt started frequenting churches instead of pubs, he read spiritual books and lived an austere life. He attended Mass daily, and the altar boys reported that he seemed like a soul in ecstasy and was very fervent. He gave away a large portion of the small wages he earned, much of it to the Columban Fathers. He is often considered a patron for those struggling with alcoholism.

REFLECTION

Matt struggled with his addiction but eventually found ways to cope with it. He reformed his life and went on to help others. What most needs reforming in my life? Could I ask this question of myself on a regular basis? Could I support someone struggling to overcome an addiction?

26 JUNE

St Mothorian/Thorian

D. SIXTH CENTURY. FEAST DAY: *9 July*

Mothorian was the very first Abbot of the monastery St Columba founded at Drumcliffe, Co. Sligo. He probably was from Scotland, so Columba would have brought him over to Ireland with him when attending the Synod of Druimceatt. It is very reasonable to speculate that the reason Columba founded a monastery in Drumcliffe on the site where three thousand and one people had been killed in the Battle of Cooldrevny (sometimes called 'The Battle of the Books') was his expectation that the monks' prayers would make this blighted place holy. According to *The Book of Lismore*, Mothorian was left with a bell, a chalice and a crozier made by Columba himself. Mothorian is described in *The Martyrology of Donegal* as 'holy, radiant'.

REFLECTION

Columba clearly had a plan for Mothorian knowing that his guidance as an abbot would provide much needed spiritual healing to the area. Mothorian's holiness and radiance no doubt came from his giving room – by denying self – to the indwelling Christ and being filled with the Holy Spirit. Am I on a journey towards becoming more spiritual? What would help me here?

27 JUNE
St Colman of Cork/Colmus/Mocolmoc

D. SEVENTH CENTURY. FEAST DAY: *6 May*

Colman was a professor in St Finbarr's school in Cork. In 644 he composed a verse prayer for protection against the Yellow Plague that was devastating Ireland at the time, leaving only one in three people alive. So Colman took the schoolboys 'out beyond the ninth wave' to escape the plague and went to an island. His *Lorica* or protection-prayer has survived.

REFLECTION
Colman of Cork is a good example of a practical person who both prays to God for help and also does what humanly can be done (reminding us of the old saying: 'pray to God but keep your powder dry'). Do I leave it all to God when I pray for something or do I make an effort as well? There is no use asking God for a job if we don't also go out and look for one! It is well said that God does not always change our circumstances but can change our attitude to them. How would this apply to what I am praying about at present?

28 JUNE
St Bigseach

D. SIXTH CENTURY. FEAST DAY: *28 June or October 4*

Bigseach was the daughter of Bessal of the Hy Fiachra family. She became one of St Brigid's nuns at Kildare but later moved westwards to preach the Gospel in Co. Westmeath. A church founded by her near Ballynacargy is still a place of worship known by the anglicised version of her name, Kilbixy. Near here is the area known as Tristernagh where there was an Augustinian priory in 1200. There are also the remains of a mediaeval leper hospital in the grounds of the church. Bigseach was known to be very abstemious. Saint Bigseach's well is outside the walls of the Baronstown demesne and is said to cure arthritis.

REFLECTION

Possibly Bigseach herself had suffered from arthritis and was cured and so the well now cures it in others. Have I any stiffness of joints? Have I other kinds of stiffnesses, inflexibilities or irrational obstinacies? Could I bring them to God for healing? St Bigseach was reported to have been abstemious, which is the opposite of gluttonous. Where do I come on the scale between these two?

29 JUNE

St Cocca/Coca/Cocha/Coincha

D. FIFTH CENTURY. FEAST DAY: 29 *June*

Cocca became Abbess of Ros-Bennchir. She is claimed to be the sister of St Kevin of Glendalough and St Attracta. She used for prayer a rocky island in the sea off the west coast, in Co. Clare, in Moyarta townland, nineteen kilometres from Kilkee, and the island was named after her. She educated and looked after noble virgins. She is said to have been the nurse and guardian of St Ciarán of Saighir. Legend says that he would send oxen from Saighir (without a drover) every year to Ros-Bennchir to do the nuns' ploughing; and he would go and celebrate Christmas with them every year after he had celebrated at Saighir. There is a holy well called after her, *Tubbermohocca*, in the area. There may have been several saints with a similar name (one of them is Cocca the patron of Kilcock, whose feast day is 6 June).

REFLECTION

Cocca comes across as a motherly and caring person whose company St Ciarán sought and to whom he was loyal. She comes across also as an educated woman, her legend reports that she studied under a bishop, and educated her nuns herself. She also obviously organised the farming that the nuns did to be self-sufficient, so was a woman of great energy. Have I discovered that being a loving and caring person leads to having more energy as we are then highly motivated?

30 JUNE
St Dubhthach

D. FIFTH CENTURY. FEAST DAY: *7 October*

Dubhthach was a poet, the son of Lughar of Leinster. He was one of the only two people to arise from his seat when St Patrick entered Tara, to show him respect. The other was Dubhthach's pupil Fiacc, later Bishop of Sleatty. Saint Patrick blessed Dubhthach and his family which later included thirty saints. He is credited with being the first person at Tara to believe in the word of God and also it was claimed he was the first to build a wooden church and erect a stone cross. He is sometimes called Dubhthach the First to distinguish him from Dubhthach the Second, who was Archbishop of Armagh in 497.

REFLECTION

The poet Dubhthach's enthusiasm is exemplary, which suggests he was wholly given to God. 'Wholly' would mean one hundred per cent. What percentage of me is given to God? What areas of my life am I holding back? Which rooms of the house of my life are no-go areas for God at present? Could I think about them and then say a prayer inviting Him into those areas?

JULY

1 JULY
St Oliver Plunkett

D.1681. FEAST DAY: *1 July*

Oliver was from a landed family of Anglo-Irish Roman Catholics loyal to the crown. He was born in Loughcrew, Co. Meath. He studied for the priesthood in Rome and was ordained as Roman Catholic Archbishop of Armagh – in succession to a line of Archbishops of Armagh who had been killed, imprisoned or exiled. He was a courageous reformer of the priesthood, religious orders and the laity. He was arrested as a result of condemning the scandalous behaviour of some of his flock – on the testimony of nine witnesses, including quite a few priests he had suspended. He spent his time in prison in prayer. While in prison he became a Benedictine monk. He suffered martyrdom at Tyburn on 11 July 1681.

REFLECTION

How would I spend my time in solitude? Could it be a spiritual opportunity? Have I been guilty of condemning without any witnesses? What would be a better way to tackle or rectify the situation?

2 JULY
St Gibrian

D. C.515. FEAST DAY: *8 May*

Gibrian was an Irishman, possibly baptised by St Patrick, who went to preach abroad, with six of his brothers and three of his sisters. They probably spent time in Brittany first – many Breton place names honour his brothers. Eventually they were given places to live by Remigius Archbishop of Rheims. They worked in Rheims and each became solitaries at Chalons-sur-Marne, a little distance apart. A chapel was built over Gibrian's tomb and the village of St Gibrian on the River Marne grew up around it. His relics were later transferred to the Abbey of St Remigius and miracles were reported, especially restoration of sight.

REFLECTION

Gibrian and his brothers were living as both solitaries and hermits which was the early Irish Church pattern inherited from the Egyptian desert monks. They knew that no Christian need ever be lonely and walked in the awareness of God's presence knowing that God never withdraws Himself from them, but only that they withdraw from God at times. Do I need to learn this lesson too? What causes me to withdraw from God sometimes?

3 JULY

St Sunniva

D. C.950. FEAST DAY: 8 July

Sunniva was an Irish princess who went to Norway with several female companions to escape a forced marriage. They wanted to live lives consecrated to Christ in exile. They reached the Island of Selje off the west coast of Norway and lived there in caves. They were treated badly. An attempted attack by the local ruler Earl Haakon was prevented by a landslide of rock that buried her and her fellow nuns. Sunniva's uncorrupt body was found later thanks to a farmer on Selje finding a human head that was surrounded by phosphorescent light with an agreeable odour. Her remains were brought to Bergen in 1170. Her name means 'sun-gift' which is apt, as she brought the light of Jesus to the north.

REFLECTION

Sunniva had such a strong spiritual calling that she went against her family's wishes and set sail to a foreign land. Do I feel so strongly about something that I would take such a stance? What places of darkness could I bring the light of Christ to, as Sunniva did? Newspapers are full of reports of darkness; which particular darkness do I feel that God is calling me to pray about or even to help with?

4 JULY
St Indract

D.678. FEAST DAY: *8 May*

Indract is said to have abdicated his kingship to become a missionary. He and his sister Dominica were thought to have brought a stone altar with them in a boat from Ireland to Cornwall. He founded a community in Plymouth who were fed from fish in a miraculous pond, where as long as they never took more than they needed, the number of fishes remained constant. He and his companions moved on to the Somerset marshes, where they were attacked at Shapwick and all but one were killed. The bodies were never found; but the survivor reported their deaths and said that every year on the anniversary of their death a pillar of light rose from earth to heaven that lasted for three days. One woman was actually converted from paganism by this light.

REFLECTION
The miraculous fish pond is a good parable for today. Have I experienced that when I am greedy stores diminish and when moderate they seem to remain? It happens in personal lives and also on a planetary scale.

5 JULY
St Modwena of Polsworth

D. NINTH CENTURY. FEAST DAY: *5 July*

Modwena was an Irish woman whose monastery in Britain was destroyed in the Norse invasions. She travelled in Britain, along with her kinswoman St Arhea. She sought sanctuary from King Ethelwolfe, whose son was cured of an incurable disease by her. He granted her two abbeys and sent his own sister Edith to be a nun under her. Modwena later built many monasteries; her main headquarters being the first one at Polsworth in Warwickshire. For some years she lived as a solitary on an island, Andresey. This is where her body was interred, and where frequent miracles took place.

REFLECTION

These Irish saints were able to do amazing things because they had a strong faith and belief in themselves. They often had a strong support-network of like-minded people. Saint Arhea was St Modwena's kinswoman. Do I have someone similar in my life who supports me and who I can support and encourage?

6 JULY

St Moninna/Moninne/Darerca/Bline/Sarbile

D.518. FEAST DAY: *6 July*

Moninna, from north Co. Louth, was one of the early saints. Some accounts state that St Patrick baptised her when she was only a child; she is also believed to have received the veil from him. Her first community was at Faughart, but she found life too busy there because of continual visits from her extended family, so she then went with her community to Wexford where they lived with her uncle St Ibar on Beggary island. On his advice, she removed to Slieve Gullion in Armagh. A river in flood stopped their exit from Wexford, but Moninna had the gift of prophecy and declared that a stolen object was the cause. The object was discovered and the flood abated. She founded a nunnery at Killeavy. Moninna would visit the sick by night so as not to be seen. She was known for her healing powers, her great generosity, and kindness to strangers.

REFLECTION

Moninna's escape to Wexford shows her realisation of the need for quietness for contemplative prayer. Do I realise this need is in us all? What arrangements do I make to get such quiet?

7 JULY
St Maelruain/Mulroon

D.792. FEAST DAY: *7 July*

Maelruain founded the monastery at Tallaght on land named after a pestilence that had destroyed nine thousand people in a week. He was alarmed at the laxity of monks and imposed very strict discipline. With Aengus the Culdee he founded the *Céili Dé* movement, a reform of the rules of Irish monasteries, which restored prayer and soul-friendship to the centre of monastic life, and celibacy as a requirement. His monks had to be vegetarian and drink nothing but water and fast once a month. Maelruain produced a catalogue of Irish saints, *The Martyrology of Tallaght*, and directed the compiling of *The Stowe Missal*, the earliest surviving Irish liturgy. One of his sayings is: 'Labour with devotion is the most excellent work of all'.

REFLECTION

When I have hard work to do, could I lighten the load by doing it with devotion? St Paul told us to do all our work as for God, and Khalil Gibran said: 'Work is love made visible'. How could I apply this to the various different kinds of work in my week?

8 JULY

St Kilian of Würzburg/Cillian

D.689. FEAST DAY: *8 July*

Kilian was born in 640 in Mullagh, Co. Cavan. He had a taste for learning from infancy, especially the Bible. He depended on the Holy Spirit to help him to understand the difficult passages. He became a monk while very young and went to Europe and rebuilt the churches in Baden in Bavaria. Many German and Austrian cathedrals are dedicated to him. He was consecrated as a travelling bishop by Pope Conon. He sailed down the River Main to Würzburg with eleven companions. He was outspoken in his condemnation of breaches of faith and morals. He was murdered in Würzburg in 689, because of intervening in a marriage dispute by criticising Duke Gospert, one of their first converts, for marrying his brother's widow.

REFLECTION

Kilian had the courage to speak out against breaches of faith and morals. Have I the courage to speak out against abuses that are rife in the world today? Even if it would put me into danger? If I were to imagine my own sins being made public, which ones would I speak out against and put right?

9 JULY

St Wiro/Maelmuire

D. C.742. FEAST DAY: *8 May*

Wiro was born in Co. Clare. His models from earliest youth were St Patrick and St Columbanus. With his fellow priest Plechelm and the deacon Otger, he made a pilgrimage to Rome, where they were consecrated bishops and later they became known as 'the Apostles to the Guelderland'. After a short time back in Ireland they settled in the Netherlands on land given to them by the Emperor near Roermond, which they named St Peter's Hill. They built a church and monastery there, which remained their headquarters for long years of strenuous preaching, teaching and prayer. Wiro was ascetic, but generous to others and his calm demeanour drew people to him. The Emperor Pepin himself was said to go barefoot to receive absolution and penance from Wiro in Lent. At his funeral a miraculous fragrance was detected.

REFLECTION
Wiro's calm demeanour drawing people to him shows he was a person who had overcome the tendency to express anger in negative ways. How could I resolve issues with a calm and measured demeanour instead of flaring up with anger or negativity?

10 JULY
St Etto/Eton/Ze

D. C.670. FEAST DAY: *10 July*

Etto was an Irish missionary who went first with Fursey to East Anglia, and then on to Rome where he was consecrated a bishop. His work was in present-day Belgium with headquarters at the Abbey of Fescan in the village of Dompierre. He spent much time as a solitary, clearing the brambles and building himself a cell at Theirarche near Avesnes. After a claimant to the land gave it to him Etto built a church there. Many visitors came to seek his counsel. He was very humble and could not bear it if people thought highly of him. He once healed a cowherd whom he found asleep. He is deemed to be patron saint of cowherds and cattle drovers. He was greatly honoured locally and widely venerated outside Ireland.

REFLECTION
Etto and other Irish saints were not afraid of hard work! He succeeded because all he did was done in God. Could I clear some

brambles from my own patch, metaphorically speaking? What would they be? Would I benefit from facing up to them, and from learning to do all I do 'in God'?

11 JULY

St Drostan

D.606. FEAST DAY: *11 July (14 December in Scotland)*

Drostan was an Irishman who became one of St Columba's disciples. He was known as an apostle of Scotland. Drostan became Abbot of Deer Monastery in Buchan, which survived for a thousand years. After his abbacy, Drostan became a hermit at Glenesk in Angus, where he was known for his sanctity and his miracles. The account of his life in *The Book of Deer* is one of Scotland's oldest manuscripts. According to the legend, the name Deer came from the Gaelic *deora* meaning tears, as there were tears shed when Columba parted from Drostan never to meet again. There is a Killdrostan in Elphin Diocese, Co. Sligo.

REFLECTION

Deer Monastery probably continued for a thousand years because there was no dissension or conflict there. Could I try and live with minimum dissent or conflict? Can I apply this to my own life and that of my church family? Could we learn to live with having different opinions without conflict, and even to respect our difference and diversity?

12 JULY

St Menou

D. SEVENTH CENTURY. FEAST DAY: *12 July*

Menou was a native of South Leinster who went early with his family to Wales and later to France. He arrived at Brittany (known then as Armorica), and was ordained a priest shortly after his arrival by Bishop (St) Corentin who saw how well educated he was. He then became Bishop of Quimper, near Finistère in Brittany. A nobleman who had been unjustly imprisoned was released from prison merely by touching Menou's ring to his chains. Menou visited Rome where he carried out so many miracles that the Pope tried to detain him. There were more miracles at his tomb after his death.

REFLECTION

Menou obviously had discovered that fullness of the Holy Spirit is the prerequisite for a flow out to others, as miracles seemed to just flow from him. Jesus said once, 'from the abundance of the heart the mouth speaks', or more simply what is inside is what comes out, fullness precedes flow. Have I discovered this important principle yet?

13 JULY

Sts Espain, Maura and Britta

D.570. FEAST DAY: *13 July*

Espain was a son of King Aillil. When his sister Maura was baptised she declared that her mother was in heaven. When Britta was baptised she issued from the font surrounded with dazzling light. The two sisters accompanied their brother to the Continent. Espain probably worked in France before making the pilgrimage to Rome, as he is remembered in the town of St Épain. He healed and baptised Ursicin, the man they were lodging with, who accompanied them to Rome and the Holy Land. They then visited the shrine of St Martin of Tours. On their return journey, in the Diocese of Beauvais, the three siblings were set upon by pagans and killed. Ursicin escaped and told the tale of their martyrdom.

REFLECTION

It is inscribed on a memorial at Dromantine to priests who had been missionaries in Africa that 'they were missionaries from the bottom of their hearts'. This could be said in all probability of Espain, Maura and Britta. Could it be said of me that I am a Christian from the bottom of my heart?

14 JULY

St Cathal/Cataldo/Cathaldus

D.529. FEAST DAY: 10 May

Cathal was born near Thurles and educated at Lismore. As a young priest, he raised someone from the dead, but as a result he was thrown into prison by the local king for doing 'magic'. He was later rescued by angels. Cathal founded a school of manuscript illumination at Kildare. He taught at the monastic school in Lismore and became Bishop of Rachan in the Decies, Co. Waterford. He visited Jerusalem and wanted to remain in Palestine as a hermit but an angel directed him to Taranto in Italy. On the way Cathal met and healed a deaf and speechless girl. News of this miracle spread and many embraced Christianity because of it. He laboured hard there and became their bishop. He is very popular in Italy and many boys there are called Cataldo.

REFLECTION
What angels has God needed to send into my life to redirect me from what I want to do that is not His plan for me? How can I improve my listening skills to distinguish God's gentle voice from the voices of the world, my own desires and the tempter?

15 JULY
St Aenghus of Moyne

D. SEVENTH CENTURY. FEAST DAY: *4 March*

Aenghus' full name was Aenghus Láimhiodhan, meaning 'pure hand'. His mother was Fintan of Clonenagh's niece. He was a friend of St Moling. He looked after some of Moling's manuscripts after they had become water-damaged by their storage in the Dunmore cave. Aenghus founded three or four churches in Ossory Diocese. The main one was Moyne, the other ones were Killermogh, Kilderry and Sheepstown (Knocktopher).

REFLECTION

Keeping, preserving and possibly restoring damaged manuscripts would have required a lot of skill and patience. Could I offer my skills and patience to a friend in the same way? Taking on a lengthy and hard job is often called 'a labour of love'. What labour of love could I undertake to help others, whether it is knitting blankets for the homeless or collecting stamps for charity or raising money for good causes or simply helping a friend?

16 JULY
St Crone/Cróine Bheag

D. SEVENTH CENTURY. FEAST DAY: *7 July*

Crone was one of four St Crones, from Meath, Carlow, Westmeath and Donegal. She was from Templecrone in Boylagh, Co. Donegal. Her feast day on 7 July became a traditional day for digging up early potatoes.

REFLECTION

As a nun, a woman given wholly to God's service, Crone knew that possessions do not matter – it is what is inside a person that matters most. What about me? Do I get attached to possessions? Do I measure myself by my possessions? Have I yet realised that I cannot be measured by my job or my role or my house or my possessions? Have I got to the place where my treasure is interior? Have I discovered the truth of the saying: 'to be full of things is to be empty of God; to be empty of things is to be full of God'?

17 JULY

St Cathan

D. SIXTH CENTURY. FEAST DAY: *11 May (17 May in Scotland)*

Cathan was a friend of Comgall and Cainnech. Like his friends, he was an Irish Pict, from the Cruithni people. He studied at Bangor Monastery. Cathan went as a missionary to Alba, present-day Scotland, and worked in the area around Bute, where he became the bishop. Many churches in Scotland, usually called 'Cillchattan', are dedicated to him. He brought his sister Bertha with him. When she became pregnant by an an unknown man – some say King Aedan of the Scots – Cathan sent Bertha and her newborn son, Blane, adrift in an oarless boat. They landed on the coast of Ulster. Blane was educated at Bangor and later became an important saint in Scotland. Cathan is remembered in the Western Isles of Scotland, especially Bute and Colonsay.

REFLECTION

This story of Bertha was a sad story that worked out well in the end with God's help. Do I believe God is able to bring good out of a seemingly hopeless situation? Could I bring a situation to Him now that needs such transforming?

18 JULY
St Garbhan/Garvan/Germanus/German

D. SEVENTH CENTURY. FEAST DAY: *26 March or 14 May*

Garvan was a kinsman if not a brother of St Kevin of Glendalough, and a nephew of St Finnian of Clonard, being the son of St Finnian's saintly sister Ruignach. He had a hermit's cell at Clonshanbo, which later became famous for its association with him under his Latin name, Germanus or German. He also founded a church at Kilmacgarvogue near Rathvilly, Co. Carlow. Garvan's work was part of a monastic effort to preserve the knowledge and culture of Ireland during a time of uncertainty and battles. He is said to have put an end to his brother Kevin's wanderings as a pilgrim by remarking to him: 'It is not by flying that birds hatch their eggs'. He also gave his name to Athgarvan in Co. Kildare.

REFLECTION

Garvan did not take his own advice. It is invariably the case that the faults I upbraid others for are in fact my own. But also the qualities in others that we admire we often possess ourselves. Could I look at other people more positively in the light of this?

19 JULY
Corbán/Corbanus

D.732. FEAST DAY: *19 July*

Corbán founded the church at Kilcorban in Ballinakill parish, Co. Galway. Many things are named after St Corbán in Naas, Co. Kildare, including St Corbán's church at Kill near Naas, where many kings and heroes were buried according to the Irish Annals. Not much is known about his life except that he once brought a boy called Iobhar to Louth where St Mochta discovered the boy's talent for singing.

REFLECTION ←
Irish saints often visited each other, and in many cases, they were soul-friends or anamcharas. This could have been the case with Mochta and Corbán. Do I have a soul-friend? Many people today are desperate for someone to share their journey with who will understand and advise. The early Irish Church *anamchara* evolved into a confessor later, but the idea of two souls as equals sharing their path with each other is a lovely one. If I have not already found one, who would I pick? Could I pray for such a connection?

20 JULY

St Dymphna/Dimpna

D. SEVENTH CENTURY. FEAST DAY: *15 May*

Dymphna, born in Clogher in Co. Tyrone, was the daughter of a sixth-century pagan King of Oriel and his beautiful wife who died young. Dymphna was fostered by Christian women who taught her the faith. She was decorous and modest, aiming at God's approval not that of men. Her father tried to marry her, so she and her priest-confessor Gerebern fled to Gheel in Belgium, with two servants, so she could fulfil her desire to live in chastity for Christ. While there she was devoted to the poor and the suffering. Her father followed her and murdered her, Gerebern and the two servants. Miracles of healing were attributed to their veneration, especially for people with mental illness, and the town of Gheel has become a place of advanced study of mental health. She should not be confused with St Davnet although both names mean 'fawn'.

REFLECTION ←
Dymphna fled a traumatic event and helped others because of it. After witnessing her father's mental illness due to grief, she provided solace and healing to people suffering. Today there's a lot more awareness and support of mental illness. Have I looked after my own mental health? Can I support friends who struggle with their mental health?

21 JULY
St Arbogast

D. C.678. FEAST DAY: 21 *July*

Arbogast was an Irishman who arrived in Alsace as a missionary in 550. He spent some time in the forest of Haguenau as a hermit before founding a monastery at Strasbourg and was then made Bishop of Strasbourg. He raised to life the son of Dagobert III who had been killed by a boar while hunting. He was approved of by lay people and clerics alike. Arbogast was gentle and good, and people looked on him more as a father than a master. He was a peacemaker. If ever he had to reprove, he did it with such tenderness and consideration that he gained the hearts of all. He and his successor, Florentius, were described as the holiest of Strasbourg's holy patrons.

REFLECTION
Arbogast did not plunge straight into church work, he first spent time in prayer as a hermit. Has this an important message for me today? Could I develop a habit of prayerful preparation before actions? Do I reprove, when I have to do so, with Arbogast's gentleness and consideration?

22 JULY
St Gerebern/Gereburnus

D. SEVENTH CENTURY. FEAST DAY: 15 *May*

Gerebern was Princess Dymphna's chaplain. He helped her to escape to Belgium. He was murdered, along with Dymphna, by Dymphna's enraged father. At their tombs in Gheel, near Antwerp, miracles were reported – miracles of healing especially for epilepsy and mental illness. Gerebern is revered along with Dymphna in Belgium and also in America. His relics were stolen at one stage because they were so powerful for healing gout and jaundice. They are now at Sonsbeck in the Rhineland.

REFLECTION

Gerebern comes across to us as a Christ-like figure. It is written in Scripture that when a person is taught he becomes like his teacher. If Jesus Christ is my teacher I begin becoming like him. Is Jesus Christ my teacher? Do I read his words and listen to what he is saying to me personally? The more we listen to and the more we obey the words of Jesus the more Christ-like we all become. Do I revere older people for their wisdom and spirituality? Do I try to learn from them?

23 JULY

St Carantoc

D. SEVENTH CENTURY. FEAST DAY: 16 May

Carantoc left Ireland to be a missionary and established communities in Somerset and also in Brittany – he is known there as Caredec. His legend says that he cast his portable altar on the River Severn to try to find out where God wanted him to settle. He is said to have met King Arthur, who said he would tell Carantoc where the altar was if he tamed the dragon that was terrifying people in the area. Carantoc tamed the dragon: it bent its head in obeisance to the saint. He then led the dragon up the hill to the royal hall at Dunster, and no one was disturbed by it again.

REFLECTION

A community living in fear breeds more and more fear. How can I help save this from happening in my own community? Can I try to remain calm and positive while others are feeling fear and uncertainty. Seeing the dragon as interior, what is my dragon? Can I bring it out into the open and ask God to tame it for me?

24 JULY
St Declan

D. FIFTH CENTURY. FEAST DAY: 24 *July*

Declan was one of the four pre-Patrician Bishops in Ireland. A great globe of light was seen at his birth by seven men, who begged for him to be educated and become their bishop. After his education he went to Rome and was consecrated bishop by the Pope and sent back to Ireland. He founded the Christian community at Ardmore, Co. Waterford, described as a seminary. Multitudes flocked to him. Declan blessed and Christianised a large pillar stone with pagan origins. He raised to life a lot of people who had died of the plague and also put a stop to the plague. Legend credits him with restoring to life a dog he was being offered under the pretence that it was mutton. Dog's Pass in the Comeragh mountains marks this spot.

REFLECTION

Christianising a pagan stone seems a good missionary method. Could I bring good things and beliefs formerly pagan and subsume them into my beliefs, bringing them under Christ's influence? Do I listen well to what people already believe? Could I respect that as well as going further?

25 JULY
St Nessan of Mungret

D.552. FEAST DAY: 25 *July*

Nessan was a disciple of St Patrick's, known also as 'Nessan the Leper' or 'Nessan the Deacon'. He was reputed never to have told a lie. He was taught and trained by St Ailbhe. His monastery at Mungret had a great reputation, and there were said to be six churches and 1,500 monks there, whose learning was proverbial.

He was said to have gone to St Ailbhe for advice about whether to accept gifts. Ailbhe replied that one can receive what is offered but it does not make one greater than one's fellow men. It was said that of Nessan's one thousand five hundred monks at Mungret, five hundred of them were psalmists, five hundred of them were preachers and the remaining five hundred were given to spiritual exercises.

REFLECTION
Do I have the imagination to answer truthfully – yet not hurtfully – when I am asked to comment on something negative? Have I yet learned to see the good in each person and situation? Do I sit as lightly to possessions as Ailbhe advised, with no feeling of pride or superiority?

26 JULY

Sillao/Siollan/Sillaeus

D. C.1100. FEAST DAY: *21 May*

Sillao gave his patrimony to the poor so that he could live a religious life. The story goes that one night he wrote out the whole of the Gospel of St Matthew with his right hand while holding up his left hand to give light that emitted from his fingers. He was a monk in Clonfert and became abbot and was also consecrated bishop there, but had doubts about the validity of his consecration. He travelled to Rome to put this right. On his way home in 1100 he died at Lucca where his sister Mingar, on her journey back from her pilgrimage to Rome, had married a local nobleman. Miracles abounded at his tomb, which stopped when his brother-in-law demanded a share of the money from the monastery.

REFLECTION
Symbolically the flame issuing from the saint's hand is saying that the energy, light and power of the Holy Spirit was extra strong in

Sillao. Do I need a fresh infilling of the Holy Spirit to revivify my Christian life?

27 JULY
St Ronan Finn

D.637. FEAST DAY: 22 *May*

Ronan the Fair was from near Newry, Co. Down. He denounced Suibhne son of the King of Dalriada because Suibhne had dragged Ronan out of the church where he had been praising God and threw Ronan's psalter into a pool of water where it became submerged, and would not let Ronan return to the church. Ronan became a missionary to Scotland, possibly as a penance for denouncing Suibhne. A steep and rocky island called after him is North Ronan, ninety-six kilometres north of the Butt of Lewis, and the church on it is called *Teampall Ronan*.

REFLECTION
Ronan experienced real persecution and was not going to let the high social standing of the prince excuse him for his deed. Suibhne's actions can only be called bullying. Have I experienced persecution for my faith? Do I keep silent in the face of bullies or do I stand up to them and try to root out bullying from the work places and schools with which I am associated?

28 JULY
St Berthold

D.540. FEAST DAY: 16 *June*

Berthold was an Irishman who travelled to Rome and then to France in the sixth century, with a young companion, Amandus. They cleared a space from brambles, reptiles and demons to build hermitages. People were suspicious at first but later flocked to them. He was welcomed by Remigius Archbishop of Rheims. He became a solitary with a cell and oratory at Chaumont, and a community of monks gathered around him. After his death miracles were reported and a church was built on the site of his oratory. Several popes have honoured him. His friend Amandus also laboured nearby and they were buried together eventually and commemorated on the same day.

REFLECTION

Berthold must have acted like a magnet to those who gathered around him. He must have been communing with God which is easier to do in solitude and silence, and must have built people up and uplifted them. Do I allow myself any solitude and silence so that God can speak to my innermost heart? Do I bless people and build people up and uplift them?

29 JULY

St Diarmuid/Dermot

D.825. FEAST DAY: 21 June

Diarmuid was the grandson of the King of East Ulster. He became an anchorite or hermit. He was inclined to be very ascetic and belonged to the *Céili Dé* movement. He was a friend of St Maelruain of Tallaght. Then five years before his death he founded a monastery at present-day Castledermot, Co. Kildare. It became an important foundation and St Cormac, King of Munster and Bishop of Cashe, was educated there. Diarmuid wanted to go on a pilgrimage, but the sea rose up against him and prevented him. He was described as a 'teacher of religion for all Ireland'.

REFLECTION

Have I had any experiences of God using the weather to recall me to the path which is His will? We can also learn from the way Diarmuid and others first listened to God in solitude and silence, and then shared with others. Even if only preparing a talk or speech could I have a short time of silence and solitude first in which to hear God's voice and learn from Him before sharing?

30 JULY
St Gobain

D. C.670. FEAST DAY: *30 June*

Gobain was an Irishman from Galway. He accompanied St Fursey both to England and France. He was a solitary in the forest of Oise for some time and engaged in much missionary preaching in the area. He is said to have stilled a storm by saying Mass. His hermitage was built where a spring sprang up when his staff touched the ground. This spring had strong curative powers. Gobain was beheaded while at his prayers by vandals from the far north at a place now known as St Gobain, which was the scene of heavy fighting during the First World War. He is mentioned by the Venerable Bede in his *Ecclesiastical History of the English People*.

REFLECTION

Gobain seems to have been a man who was totally available to God, who values our availability above our ability. How available to God am I? Am I tempted to discount myself as fit for serving God for lack of ability? Have I learned that when God asks people to do something, He equips them for it, supplying the strength, the skill and the words to say?

31 JULY
St Assicus/Tassach/Assic/Assan

D. C.490. FEAST DAY: *27 April*

Assicus (pet name Tassach) was a close friend of St Patrick, appointed as the first Bishop of Elphin in 450. The Elphin church was built on land bought from a Druid with gold that miraculously appeared in a pigsty. The Druid later converted and returned the money. Assicus was a skilled metalworker. He founded the school of metalwork at Roscommon, which later produced the beautiful Ardagh Chalice and the Cross of Cong. Elphin became an ecclesiastical school. Assicus was possibly the earlier Bishop of Raholp in Co. Down, now Templemoyle. His prophecy that Patrick would receive the viaticum from him was fulfilled. He was known for austerity and penance, spending seven years doing penance as a hermit near Slieve League, because of a lie he told accidentally in innocence. He is buried at Raccoon near Assaroe.

REFLECTION ⁓

The gold in the pigsty shows that God can work in surprising ways. Am I open to God showing up less conventionally in my life?

AUGUST

1 AUGUST
St Nathy/Nathi

DATE UNKNOWN, POSSIBLY SIXTH CENTURY. FEAST DAY: 1 August

Nathy was the son of Seanach and his family was from the Glendalough area, Co. Wicklow. Nathy was also associated with Delgany, Co. Wicklow, of which he became the bishop. He was the bishop responsible for conferring orders on St Brigid's priests and nuns. He is remembered in Taney parish, Rathfarnham, Dublin, where a holy well called *Tobernea* still exists. The place name Taney is derived from *Tigh Nathi*, meaning Nathy's house.

REFLECTION

These early Irish saints were characterised by wholeheartedness. They had a wholehearted love for and commitment to God. God's love was the ground of their being. He was also their friend, their saviour, their teacher, their love, their inspiration. Could I give myself to God so wholeheartedly?

2 AUGUST
St Beatus of Honau

D. NINTH CENTURY. FEAST DAY: 9 May

Irishman Beatus was one of the Apostles of Switzerland. He had originally gone to the Continent with St Columbanus and St Gall. He chose to be a hermit in a cave thirty-five feet above Lake Thun on a high precipice above a waterfall, once he had cleared it of its previous inhabitant, a large snake. The place is now called after him – Beatenberg. He also became Abbot of the Irish Monastery of Honau, called the 'Monasterium Scottorum', on an island in the Rhine. He lived to the great age of ninety. Many pilgrims still visit the cave.

REFLECTION ✦

Would I have stayed and dealt with the snake or would I have run away? The pioneer Christian life can be exciting and dangerous. It required bravery and the strength given by God. What dangerous situation am I shying away from at present? How could God help me with it? Do I expect silence and solitude to just fall into my lap or am I willing to work for it as Beatus did?

3 AUGUST

St Dervilla/Dervla/Dairbhile

D. SIXTH CENTURY. FEAST DAY: *3 August but 1 August on Iniskea*

Dervilla was a woman of noble birth from the Erris area of Mayo, associated with the Island of Iniskea. She was a contemporary of St Columba. The site of her convent is marked by the ruins of a small primitive church with a Romanesque west door, an early cross-slab and a holy well with curative powers known as 'Dervla's Vat'.

REFLECTION ✦

Dervillla may have chosen an island for her hermitage for safety reasons, or she may have been attracted to its barrenness. Early Irish saints often sought a 'díseart.' away from other people and the Gaelic word for a hermitage is *díseart*. Have I heeded the promise of God that he will make a way in the wilderness and paths in the desert? What wildernesses and deserts have I in my life that God could be invited into to transform?

4 AUGUST
St Goar

D. C.575. FEAST DAY: *6 July*

Goar was an Irish hermit who is said to have acted as ferryman across the Rhine at a narrow place. As well as his hermitage, he also built a hostel for travellers and kept three cows to provide milk for them. The bishop sent two spies to find out why the hostel was so popular. The spies got lost in the forest on their way back, but found milk packed in their bags which saved them. Goar would use his bell to steer navigators away from dangerous rocks between St Goar and Goarshausen. Up to the nineteenth century boatmen would still ring a bell and say a prayer to St Goar when passing the Lorelei rock. Goar is the patron saint of ferrymen, Rhine boatmen and innkeepers.

REFLECTION

The warning bell may have saved many lives. Is there a warning that I need to give anyone about dangers they are in? Could I do so in as delicate, harmonious and lovely a way as Goar's bell?

5 AUGUST
St Abel

D. C.750. FEAST DAY: *5 August*

Abel was an Irishman who was a Benedictine monk in Lobbes, near Hainault in Belgium. He was highly honoured to be chosen as Archbishop of Rheims, the place where the kings of France were crowned. The appointment was confirmed by Pope Zachary, but his appointment was blocked because a usurper called Milo was occupying the see and refusing to relinquish it. So Abel became Abbot of Lobbes instead. He decided to curtail his missionary teaching and preaching rather than be the cause of bloodshed and scandal. At his death he was buried with full honours as Archbishop of Rheims. He is the patron saint of Liège and Hainault.

REFLECTION
Abel's standing down from his honoured position in order to avoid bloodshed was exemplary. In a similar way, is there any move I might need to make which would avoid metaphorical bloodshed, conflict of any sort, even if it meant being less honoured? Could I, for example, give some of my praise to those who have helped me rather than take it all for myself? Could I avoid saying things which would ignite a bonfire or fan a simmering blaze?

6 AUGUST

St Rioch

D. C.480. FEAST DAY: *1 August*

Rioch was the son of a Briton, said to be a nephew of St Patrick, though this is disputed. He was a disciple of Patrick's from an early age and served in Patrick's team in Ireland as librarian and secretary. He was very beautiful in appearance and legend has it that when an ugly chieftain was converted, he asked Patrick for a miracle to make him more good-looking like Rioch. Patrick consecrated Rioch a bishop, but Rioch was shy and reserved and doubted his own abilities. So Patrick encouraged Rioch to become a hermit on the island of Inisbofinde on Lough Ree instead. Rioch longed for silence and solitude, but people crowded to see him and join him.

REFLECTION
Can I relate to or understand Rioch's shyness and self-doubt? Could it encourage many other shy Christians and those who lack self-confidence? Do I realise that we all need some silence and solitude in our lives, and cannot be socialising all the time, or we would end up 'running on empty'?

7 AUGUST
St Eché/Echea/Eiche

D. FIFTH CENTURY. FEAST DAY: 5 *August*

Eché was said to have been St Mel's sister, and possibly St Patrick's niece, daughter of Darerca, Patrick's sister. She is described in a very interesting way as 'having fire in her chasuble'. The townland of Miltenagh near Ardagh is named after this harmless fire (*Maol Teine*). She was established by St Patrick in a nunnery at Drumkee, west of Slieve Gaulry, Co. Longford. This is said to be one of the oldest nunneries in Ireland. Eché is also associated with the ancient church of Kilglass, nearly five kilometres from Ardagh, where they had a pattern day in her honour every 8 September. She had a sister, Lalloc, who founded the church at Senlis.

REFLECTION
Could I be described as having fire anywhere about me? Where? Jesus said he came to cast fire on the earth: how can I make this 'living fire of love' – as St John of the Cross describes it – spread in the world?

8 AUGUST
St Feidlimidh/Felim/Phelim

D.560. FEAST DAY: *9 August*

Feidlimidh was from Breiffne, the great grandson of the first Druid to honour Patrick. His five brothers were monks and saints, as was his sister Femia. He was schooled for the church by St Columba, and by St Luthair at Slanore. He sought solitude and found it in Kilmore. His hermitage became the first church at Kilmore, called *Kill-mor* (large church) as it kept getting bigger. He was possibly the first Bishop of Kilmore. Owing to lack of solitude and silence, he retired to Trinity Island on Lough Oughter. The Church of Ireland cathedral at Kilmore is dedicated to him, and incorporates a thirteenth-century Romanesque doorway from Trinity Island Abbey. The Catholic church is also dedicated to him and St Patrick jointly.

REFLECTION ~

Feidlimidh must have been busy, but he avoided burnout by seeking silence and solitude. Can I pray in the midst of busyness? How can I seek solitude to be alone with God in the middle of a busy life? Do I realise God wants to spend time with me and commune with me?

9 AUGUST

St Crumnathy

D. C.610. FEAST DAY: *9 August*

Crumnathy – 'the Pious Presbyter' – was left in charge of a monastery Finnian of Clonard had founded at Achonry, Co. Sligo, on the instruction of an angel. It became a centre of prayer and study. Saint Fechin of Fore studied there. The cathedral there is known as the smallest cathedral in Europe. Crumnathy was an abbot and priest but not a bishop, hence his name Crum-nathy (Nathy the priest). Crumnathy is certainly not the same Nathi who opposed both Palladius and Patrick, being a century later, and unlikely to be the same as St Nathy of Taney, who was Bishop of Delgany. A story relates how once Columba, Comgall and Canice arrived at Achonry after supper time was over and he kept them hungry until morning, not wanting to break the monastery rules.

REFLECTION ~

'The Pious Presbyter' was a nickname applied to St Crumnathy, maybe to gently tease him for being such a stickler for the rules! Is there anything I am pedantic about? When no ethical issues are at stake, do I allow exceptions to help others?

10 AUGUST
St Liadain

D. FIFTH CENTURY. FEAST DAY: *unknown*

Liadain was from the area called Ross in West Cork. She was St Ciarán of Saighir's mother. She was one of the pre-Patrician saints. She founded a convent of nuns at Killyon (now Drumcullen parish) near Saighir. Both she and her son Ciarán were held in such respect that a virgin birth was attributed to her by popular belief: 'She lay down and a star fell in her mouth and the wondrous child Ciarán was born'. She is said to have later founded a nunnery at Clonmacnoise. She also acted as spiritual mother to several young women who later became saints themselves.

REFLECTION
Liadain's loving personality was like a flame that drew people to her and brought warmth into their lives and inspired them to higher aspirations spiritually. How could I become more like her? Am I a father in God or a mother in God to my godchildren? Do I take an interest in their spiritual progress and pray for them regularly?

11 AUGUST
Lelia/Liadahin

D. SIXTH CENTURY. FEAST DAY: *11 August*

Lelia was a sister of St Munchin the Wise of Limerick. She founded a nunnery at Kilteely, Co. Limerick, near her brother's monastery; the parish is partly in the liberties of Limerick and partly in Bunratty Barony. There is little known about her, it's possible that Lelia lived a life of very strict observance. Saints Lelia and Munchin are the patron saints of Limerick. Several churches are dedicated to her in Limerick, Killarney and Wexford. She also had a sister called St Rose of Kilrush, although even less is known about her.

REFLECTION ⁕

Do I see strict observance of a rule as something restricting? Or do I see it as a way of heightening my spiritual perception? Discipline certainly helps us to find time for God and spiritual reflection in each day, and to examine our conscience regularly. Do I have the wisdom and liberty not to impose similar rules and regulations and limits upon God, but to let His joy burst in upon me spontaneously? Could I learn to see discipline as a daily dying to self so that I can have a daily infilling of the spirit?

12 AUGUST

St Laserian of Devenish

D. C.563. FEAST DAY: *12 August or 12 September*

Laserian's pet name was Molaise. He was from Carbury, Co. Sligo, and educated by Finnian of Clonard. He founded a monastery on the island of Devenish in Lower Lough Erne in 530, where a round tower can still be seen. He brought back the soil of martyrs from the Colosseum at Rome to start the church there. The school there flourished until the arrival of the Anglo-Normans. Laserian was counted as one of the Twelve Apostles of Ireland. Once a fire broke out in the refectory and he told his monks not to flee but to pray; they did and all was well.

REFLECTION ⁕

Fleeing might have saved the monks' lives but would not have put out the fire! No doubt they did attempt this as well as praying. Panicking never solves anything. What things make me tend to panic? Is my first thought ever to turn to God in prayer? Could I establish that habit of first praying for all problems?

13 AUGUST
St Muredach/Murtagh

D. C.480. FEAST DAY: *12 or 13 August*

Muredach was reported to have been an old man in St Patrick's household. Patrick left him to be a bishop in the west of Sligo and Mayo. He was probably the first Bishop of Killala, and he blessed the port there. He became a recluse on the Island of Inishmurray towards the end of his life and the island is called after him. A round tower can still be seen in the small cathedral town of Killala, which is very close to the place regarded as the spot called 'The Wood of Foclut' in St Patrick's *Confessio*, where a vision of Victorinus was seen standing, calling Patrick back to Ireland. A cross-inscribed stone can still be seen in a field just outside the town, reckoned by historians to be the spot.

REFLECTION
Do I see old age as a barrier to achieving anything, or as an opportunity to do something new? Can I encourage elderly friends to follow a more creative, charitable or spiritual path, one that they didn't have time for when they were younger and busy with work or raising a family.

14 AUGUST
St Fachtna/Fachanan/Fachnanus

D.600. FEAST DAY: *14 August*

Fachtna was a pupil of Sts Ita and Finbar. He was struck blind in his youth, but his sight was miraculously restored by prayer. He was first Abbot of Molana on the River Blackwater and then founded another monastery, Rossaltair, in West Cork. He was the first Bishop of Ross. The school at Rossaltair was for lay people not just monks. It became known as the best in Ireland until it was destroyed by a Viking raid in 991. A charming legend claims that Fachtna left his office book behind on a grassy hillside where he used to pray. In the morning the book was found bone dry in spite of heavy rain overnight as the angels had built a little chapel over it.

REFLECTION

Have I ever found a corner of nature to be alone with God and listen to what He wants to say to me? Maybe my prayers are needed for nature itself, for the planet, because of the bad way humans have been treating it lately?

15 AUGUST

St Alto/Alton

D. C.760. FEAST DAY: *9 February or 5 September*

Alto was born of an ancient Irish family. He became a hermit missionary near Augsberg, having heard a voice from heaven instructing him to go to there. King Pepin, the father of Charlemagne, gave him a plot of land, a wooded site, for a monastery. Alto soon cleared the forest and founded his monastery. The monastery was along Benedictine lines. It was consecrated in 753 by St Boniface, who tried to persuade Alto not to let women into the area, but Alto argued against this successfully, allowing women to be there but not enter the monks' enclosure. When the monastery fell into ruins, Alto is said to have appeared in an apparition to the Duke of Bavaria to ask for its restoration. It is now called Altomünster and is a Brigittine convent.

REFLECTION

Alto stood firm for what he believed was right. Would I stand firm for my principles if others tried to persuade me into keeping their strict rules? Alto ensured that women were not excluded and the area was an inclusive place. What in my life now do I need to take a firm stand about? Can I become more inclusive in my outlook and actions?

16 AUGUST
St Faithlinn/Fallen

D. SEVENTH CENTURY. FEAST DAYS: *4 June and 5 September*

Faithlinn was a deacon, who was the son of a king in West Munster and suffered from some sort of skin disease. He lived in a hermitage on the island on Lough Leane, Killarney, now named after him *Inisfallen*. There are the remains of an ancient oratory to be seen there today. St Finan Lobhar – also a leper, or sufferer from skin disease – started the first monastery there later in the seventh century. An Augustinian priory, known as Inisfallen Abbey, was built on Inisfallen in the twelfth century, and monks from it wrote *The Annals of Inisfallen*, chronicling Ireland's history from 433 to 1450.

REFLECTION

Could I be satisfied with small beginnings no matter what my frailties and trust other people to continue the work? What would I like to start? Being a hermit was a way to simplify life and find more time for prayer and God. Is there some way I could simplify my life to be able to give God more time?

17 AUGUST
St Bee/Bega

D. SEVENTH CENTURY. FEAST DAY: *31 October*

Bee was an Irish princess from the Strangford Lough area, Co. Down. She fled to Cumbria to escape an arranged marriage with the King of Norway's son. She wanted to consecrate her life to God instead. She was a hermit in a wood beside the seashore in the Copeland area for a while. She became an expert on herbs. Seagulls and wolves fetched her food for her. Being frightened of pirates, she sought out Aidan of Lindisfarne, who received her vows and helped her set up a nunnery at Hartlepool. She also set up a convent at St Bee's in Cumbria. During the building, Bee prepared and served the builders their food herself, acting like a servant rather than a mistress, and teaching by example. She is also revered in Norway and elsewhere, famed for her charity to the poor, her austerity and her care for everyone with whom she came into contact.

REFLECTION

Does my care for people extend only to my friends and family, or – like Bee – to everyone I come into contact with? Do I show hospitality to everyone, regardless of status?

18 AUGUST

St Daig/Duig/Dega/Deganus

D.587. FEAST DAY: *18 August*

Daig was a nephew and foster son of St Molaise of Devenish. His mentor St Mochta lived in Co. Louth. One time, Mochta saw Daig's house encased in flames. People rushed to extinguish them but found Daig unharmed. Mochta said Daig would be inflamed by the Holy Spirit and be a great healer and metalworker. He studied metallurgy at Bangor. He travelled to Clonmacnoise and studied under St Ciarán. Ciarán told him to found his own monastery, which he did at Iniskeen in Co. Louth, near the Monaghan border, where he had a dual monastery for men and women, as at Kildare, with himself as the ruling abbot. But his colleague Oenu was scandalised and sent messengers to remind him of the impropriety of the practice. Although the messengers were placated by witnessing the nuns doing miracles, Daig did discontinue the practice.

REFLECTION

Daig was prophesied to be inflamed by the Holy Spirit. Isn't this what all Christians should be? Am I on the road to this in any way? How could I make more space and room for the Holy Spirit in me?

19 AUGUST
St Mochta/Mochuta/Mochetus

D.535. FEAST DAY: *19 August*

Mochta was a Briton and a disciple of St Patrick. He was brought to Ireland while an infant. Legend says he received his basic training from an angel. He then went to Rome and showed the Pope the heavenly alphabet on the slate! He received papal benediction, returned to Ireland and founded a church at Lughmade or Conaille, Co. Louth. He lit a fire there, and the local wizards came and tried to quench it with water, thinking that if it wasn't their own 'fire' it would be quenched. However, the more water they poured on, the bigger the fire became. People then flocked to Mochta, and old records show that there were eighty brethren, eight hundred priests and two hundred future bishops in his monastery, which was sited on a former Druidical sacred place. He converted many robbers to Christ and is believed by some to have raised people from the dead.

REFLECTION
If I was preaching the Gospel, would it occur to me to preach it to robbers or to witness to my faith in prisons? What 'fires' am I lighting today?

20 AUGUST
St Colman/Columbanus of Slanore

D.640. FEAST DAY: *9 September*

Colman founded a monastery at Slanore. Slanore's Irish name is *Snamh Luithir*, and it is near the townland of Kilmore, Co. Cavan. Saint Comaigh was Colman's sister. He had a second monastery at Myshall, Co. Carlow, and some of his siblings were also attached to both Slanore and Myshall. Colman was a contemporary of St Fechin of Fore, who often visited the monastery. Fechin healed Colman of blindness which had befallen him in his old age. Colman was Colmcille's charioteer at one time, on one of Colmcille's later visits to Ireland. The legend says that the chariot managed to cover long distances safely, despite having no retaining bolts on the wheels.

REFLECTION

The story of the chariot is very up to date: what Christian has not experienced miraculous help while on a journey or while driving vehicles that might not be one hundred per cent roadworthy? Can I recollect any incident like that in my own driving career? Do I pray for protection before starting my car or starting out on a journey?

21 AUGUST

St Senach

D. SIXTH CENTURY. FEAST DAY: *3 or 21 August*

Senach became Abbot of Clonard in succession to Finnian. As a young boy he was abandoned by a gang of bandits and left at the door of a church, probably in Aghowle, Co. Carlow. Finnian found him there the following morning. He took him in, looked after him and educated him. Senach later studied at Clonard after Finnian had gone there. He became known as 'Senach the Eloquent'. Finnian trusted him and later prophesied that Senach would be his successor.

REFLECTION

To have started life as a member of a gang of bandits was hardly an auspicious start for an abbot. Through Finnian's kindness and care, Senach flourished. Have I ever judged anyone harshly because of their upbringing or where they are from? Can I show a similar kindness and care to encourage a young person to flourish?

22 AUGUST
St Andrew of Fiesole/Andrew of San Martino

D.877. FEAST DAY: 22 *August*

Andrew and his sister St Brigid of Opacum, when they walked together to school as children, would pause at the church door to pray. They were especially compassionate to unhappy people and would comfort them. Donatus befriended Andrew and took him to his school at Iniscaltra on Lough Derg. When Donatus went to Italy, Andrew went as his companion, to Brigid's grief. After the death of Donatus – by then Bishop of Fiesole – Andrew became archdeacon of the diocese. He helped restore a little ruined church at San Martino, and used it for a society of priests living a common life that he had founded. When he was dying, his sister Brigid appeared and a great light filled the place that no one could bear and the house was filled with a fragrant odour, and there were miracles at his tomb.

REFLECTION
How good am I at seeking out and comforting unhappy people? Do I spread a fragrant odour of caring love and kindness wherever I go, and do I allow my life to be a bright shining light for Christ?

23 AUGUST
St Eugene/Eoghan

D.618. FEAST DAY: 23 *August*

As a boy, Eugene was taken captive by pirates who walked into the classroom while he was reading the Gospel manuscript, which he hid in his tunic. They brought him, Tigernach and Corpre to Britain. He baptised and hid a hundred people who had also been kidnapped, by passing unseen through the pirate camp. Saint Ninian liberated and educated them. Following a second capture, in Brittany, they were put to work at a millwheel. They longed to have time to read, so an angel came and turned the mill wheel. The King heard of this and liberated them. Eugene met a leper by the River Bann and gave him his two chariot horses. When he left to become Bishop of Ardstraw, his Wicklow monks, bereft, asked who would be abbot. Eugene replied: 'You can all be abbot and prior and ministers, and I will be with you in spirit'.

REFLECTION

Do I regard Holy Scripture with the same importance as St Eugene did? Is my Bible precious, and marked at passages which have spoken to me? Do I regard all people as equal in God's sight?

24 AUGUST

St Gunifort/Bonifort

D.303. FEAST DAY: 22 or 26 August

Gunifort was a third-century saint, who left Ireland with his brother Gunibald and two sisters to go to Germany to preach to the Teutons, and also to escape from persecution in their own country. They lived a century before St Patrick, when not many people were Christians, and were very much pioneers. All four of them were martyred. The two sisters were killed by Teutons, who left the brothers alive as they could see they were good men. Gunibald was martyred in Como in Italy, and Gunifort at Pavia to which he had escaped. There he died of his wounds after being prayed for during three days by a pious matron. It is said that when he died all the bells of Pavia rang out of their own accord.

REFLECTION

How willing am I to be a pioneer, forging new paths? Would willingness to give my life be part of the dream? If I cannot do it personally, do I support and encourage and pray for those who are doing these pioneer works?

25 AUGUST
St Osmana/Osmanna

D. C.650. FEAST DAY: *9 September*

Osmana was born Agariana, but took Osmana as her baptismal name. Her pagan Irish parents were opposed to her becoming a Christian and tried to marry her to a pagan prince. She escaped to a place near St Brieuc in Brittany, retreating into the forest to practise contemplative prayer. A boar once sought shelter in her hut from the hunters who later found the boar lying quietly at Osmana's feet. She wore a dress woven of grass and rushes, and her bed was made of thorns. She healed a blind man just by touching him, and the man was baptised. After the baptism the Bishop paid a man to make a garden and lawn around Osmana's hermitage and build her a proper oratory. She healed blind, deaf and speechless people. She became the patron saint of Fericy-en-Brie.

REFLECTION

Is there any way I could make my life more simple? An oratory or prayer space was essential for Osmana. But even if I only have a small hut to live in, is there prayer space or a prayer corner there?

26 AUGUST
St Silvester

D.500. FEAST DAY: *10 March*

Silvester was a Roman Christian who came to Ireland in 430 with St Palladius as part of the mission Pope Celestine had sent to Ireland. After Palladius' departure, Silvester decided to stay on as a missionary to Wicklow. He founded a church at Donard, Co. Wicklow, and became a bishop. After his death he was interred at Donard and venerated there. His remains were moved later for safety to St Baithen's monastery at Innisboyne.

REFLECTION

Silvester was obviously resolute, resilient and tenacious. Do I have any of these attributes? What project inspires me so strongly that I would keep on with it even when others had given up? Silvester was loyal to his original commission. Do we appreciate the value of loyalty enough today?

27 AUGUST

St Auxilius/Usaille

D.454. FEAST DAY: *27 August*

Auxilius was possibly a nephew of St Patrick and acted as one of St Patrick's assistants – along with Benen, Seachnall and Iserninus – in the early days of his ministry. He was made a bishop in 439. He is commemorated in the area of Killashee near Naas, Co. Kildare (also known as Killossy), and also Aghade. Gaining converts wasn't easy as one of St Patrick's stipulations was that a new convert had to fast for forty days before they received baptism. Auxilius had the particular task in St Patrick's team of being an exorcist. An old account says that at first Auxilius was unwilling to go to Ireland when Bishop Germanus told him to, but he was forced to go there by the wind! This story is also told of Iserninus, as they were together.

REFLECTION

Auxilius' name implies that he was a helper; can that be said of me? What help could I be giving that I am withholding now?

28 AUGUST

St Tegan/Tacan/Tecan/Tagán/Tecce

D. FIFTH CENTURY. FEAST DAY: *9 September*

St Tegan was a contemporary of St Patrick. He was said to be one of the seven disciples who St Patrick left with St Fiacc of Sleatty. Having evangelised South Carlow and the area around Rathvilly, Tegan built a church over a kilometre from the present village of Kiltegan. In the old cemetery there used to be St Tegan's holy well. He was an active missionary whose work took him to Stradbally and other areas of South Leinster, including Inistioge. Saint Moling wrote a poem in his honour which suggests that he is buried near the Rock of Dunamase, Co. Laois. Tegan is mainly associated with Curraclone near Stradbally, Co. Waterford and Kiltegan, Co. Wicklow.

REFLECTION

The Gospel the Irish saints preached was not a soft Gospel but robust, calling sins by their names. What sort of Gospel do I preach if any? When presenting repentance to people would I put the stress on the culpability and guilt of the sinner or on the depth of God's mercy and forgiveness?

29 AUGUST

St Winoc/Uinoc/Vinnoc

D. FIFTH CENTURY. FEAST DAY: *29 August*

Winoc was a confidential friend to Patrick. Once they were both sitting at a religious conference and were speaking of charity and willingness to part with their garments to clothe persons in need. That moment a cloak descended and fell between them. They took this as divine approval of their sentiments, each ascribing the miracle to the other's merits. Patrick said it was for Winoc, who had renounced earthly possessions for the sake of Christ. Winoc said it was for Patrick, who had clothed many poor people. Meanwhile, the cloak went back up to heaven and two cloaks descended instead. St Winoc became Bishop of Tynan and Rathaspic and was a person of true wisdom and profound humility.

REFLECTION
This charming story shows that both Winoc and Patrick were equally humble and self-denying. Could this be because they had overcome all desire for worldly success and knew their worth came from their being children of God not from what the world thought of them? Could I say the same of myself?

30 AUGUST

St Fiacre/Fiachra

D.670. FEAST DAY: *30 August*

Fiacre rejected the offer of a throne and became Abbot of Ullard near Kilkenny instead, with a hermitage on the River Nore. So many people flocked to his hermitage that his peace was destroyed. So he went to France in 636 and built his small hermitage in the forest of Breuil in Brie province, later enlarging it to be the first hostel to accommodate Irish pilgrims on the Continent. He received all men kindly. He is the patron saint of gardeners and was renowned for his vegetables and herbs. He had great compassion, healing people of syphilis and haemorrhoids – and fistula, in particular, which became known as 'St Fiacre's malady'. Thirty towns in Brittany and thirty French churches bear his name. The Hotel St Fiacre was the terminus for horse-drawn cabs, thus called fiacres.

REFLECTION
Do I use my abilities such as green fingers to help others, as St Fiacre did at his hostel? How well do I tend God's garden, our

planet, at this time of climate change? St Vincent de Paul was inspired by Fiacre's work. The charity St Vincent de Paul provides practical support for people in need. How can I support people in need?

31 AUGUST
St Aidan of Lindisfarne

D.651. FEAST DAY: *31 August*

Aidan, often known as the Apostle of Northumberland, was an Irish monk on Iona. Aidan was sent in 631 to be Bishop of Lindisfarne. His work there was a great success. When he was given money gifts, he used them to help the poor or buy slaves their freedom. Aidan was gentle and humble, travelling everywhere on foot, trying to reach the outlying villages and hilly regions with a gospel of love and forgiveness rather than the harsh hellfire and judgement his predecessor had been preaching. He also organised for pastoral care for those he was reaching so successfully.

REFLECTION

Aidan obviously lived what he preached, and his love, care and gentleness were evident to all. How loving and gentle has been my own witness to Christ, in my life and in my words? Aedh of Kildare, who died in 588, was the Bishop of Iona while Aidan was there. Aedh advised fasting on Wednesdays and Fridays, and thus influenced the Irish language words for those days of the week, meaning first fast and main fast (*Ceadaon* and *dia hAoine*). Fasting provides room for a stronger spiritual connection. Could I fast occasionally to build my connection to God?

SEPTEMBER

1 SEPTEMBER
St Mansuy/Mansuetus/Fethgo

D.350. FEAST DAY: *3 September*

Mansuy was an Irishman who went to Rome where he was ordained as a missionary to the Rhone valley. Initially there was much opposition to his work. So he built a cabin in the woods and lived a life of prayer and meditation. Gradually people came to him seeking instruction, including the governor's wife. Many people were converted after they heard that Mansuy had restored the governor's son back to life after he had drowned. He then ordained priests, built monasteries and churches and rooted out paganism in the area. He became the first Bishop of Toul in Lorraine, France around the year 338.

REFLECTION

Mansuy learnt in a way that you cannot sow seeds until you have ploughed the land, and people are not ready to listen to your preaching yet until they have seen your life and been influenced by your prayers. Am I getting better at learning from my mistakes as Mansuy did? Could a regular evening examen help here, or a journal where I record what I am learning?

2 SEPTEMBER
St Lupait/Liemnania

D. FIFTH CENTURY. FEAST DAY: *27 September*

Lupait was St Patrick's sister. It is recorded that once she was tending sheep with him after being taken into captivity by pirates, when she fell and fractured her skull against a stone. Patrick healed her, and the white scar remained to testify. She married Restitutus the Lombard and had seven sons, the youngest of which was Patrick's pilot. For a while Lupait lived with her nephew St Mel in order to benefit from his teaching. This caused a local scandal. St Patrick advised separate houses to avoid further scandal after their innocence had been proved by a miracle. She founded a convent for women in Armagh, where they wove and embroidered vestments and linens for the church.

REFLECTION

St Paul advises to avoid every appearance of evil, and to avoid actions that would 'offend the weaker brethren'. Even though I know I am innocent, do I avoid being in situations which would cause scandal? Do I, like Lupait with her nephew, recognise wisdom in the younger generation, and benefit by it?

3 SEPTEMBER

St Macnessa/Macanisius/Oengus Macnissi

D.514. FEAST DAY: *3 September*

Macnessa was the first Bishop of Connor and abbot of a large community. Once he found local lawyers had decreed that a small boy, Colman, should be put to a cruel death by being tossed into the air and falling onto the spears of the assembled warriors. They wanted to carry out this act to punish his father, for killing his own father, Colman's grandfather. Macnessa begged the High King to commute the sentence, but to no avail. He then prayed and fasted. On the day a whirlwind arose that blew the boy high over the spears of the warriors to land in Bishop Macnessa's arms. Macnessa brought Colman up as a Christian and he became Bishop of Dromore. Macnessa was said to have respected the Holy Scriptures so much that he refused to tie the gospel books with cords when he was travelling, so held them on his hunched back or else went on all fours.

REFLECTION

Are there any glaring injustices in my country today pricking my conscience in which I can try to intervene or at least pray about?

4 SEPTEMBER
St Ultan of Ardbraccan

D.657. FEAST DAY: *4 September*

Ultan was one of the first Bishops of Ardbraccan, Co. Meath. He was known to have powerful hands. A legend tells that he repelled a Viking raid with his left hand while feeding porridge to sick children with his right. He was very generous to the poor, and they said of him that he 'fed every child in Erin who had no support', between fifty and a hundred and fifty children, particularly those whose mothers had died of the plague. He also had literary and antiquarian interests, and was the teacher of St Patrick's biographer, Tírechán. He wrote a poem in honour of St Brigid, to whom he was related through her mother. Ultan founded a school for illuminating manuscripts.

REFLECTION

The legends depict a man who could multitask and was not afraid of hard work. How could I translate my compassion for those who are suffering now into action? How could I help others by doing a little multitasking? Which group of people inspire my compassion most?

5 SEPTEMBER
St Bricin

D. SEVENTH CENTURY. FEAST DAY: *5 September*

Bricin was known as 'Bricin the Wise'. He was attached to the lay University of Tomregan (*Túaim Drecain*) which taught Irish law and literature and Latin learning, and is now part of Kildallan parish, on the Cavan-Fermanagh border. Bricin was a skilful and well-known surgeon, even performing a brain operation successfully on the university's most illustrious pupil

Cenn Faelad, who turned from the sword to the pen in his three-year convalescence. He was also famous as a missionary and went abroad to preach the Gospel. He was listed as in the second order of saints as he was a priest but not a bishop. Slievebricin Hill is named after him.

REFLECTION
Being a surgeon and attached to the university and also preaching the Gospel must have been a busy life. Do I use my busyness as an excuse not to do anything outside my daily routine? Do I see a role for people working part-time to serve God in useful ways?

6 SEPTEMBER

St Magnus/Magnobaldus

D.655. FEAST DAY: *6 September*

Magnus was St Gall's brother. They were both fellow disciples of their uncle St Columbanus. They went to Europe with Columbanus when Magnus was only nine. A story about the brothers is that Columbanus sent them to the desert with only a loaf of bread. They made the bread last for three days and thereafter they foraged. When Columbanus went on to Bobbio in Italy, Magnus stayed in Switzerland to help Gall, and he was ordained deacon at this point. At first he had refused an offer to be ordained saying he was unworthy, but Bishop Wictherpe insisted as he had seen a great crown of glory emanating from Magnus' head. Magnus went to Bobbio to try to make peace between Gall and Columbanus, who had fallen out over Columbanus disbelieving in Gall's sickness. He was successful. He had a gift for expelling dragons and demons; in art he is depicted transfixing a dragon.

REFLECTION
In these days of instant wisdom do I miss out on savouring a 'loaf' of wisdom, a teaching or a lesson I have learnt, until it becomes part of me?

7 SEPTEMBER
St Tida/Taoide/Thady/Toit

DATE UNKNOWN. FEAST DAY: 7 September

Tida is associated with Church Island on Lough Beg in Ballyscullion, Co. Derry. The Island's Irish name is *Inis Taoide*. A holy stone on the island contained curative water, and a well nearby called Thady's Well had the power to cure jaundice.

REFLECTION

This sounds as if Tida was a hermit on the island. He must have felt the need to be alone. We need to remember that aloneness is not the same as loneliness. Once a person has given their life to God and welcomed Jesus as a living reality in their life they can never really be lonely. Have I made this wonderful discovery for myself? Times of being alone can also have the effect of purifying a person's character and helping them to find their true identity. Our need for simplicity on the inside has to be matched by simplicity on the outside. Have I discovered yet that a cluttered environment does not help in cultivating silent prayer and communion with God?

8 SEPTEMBER
Blessed John Sullivan

D.1933. FEAST DAY: 8 May

John Sullivan was born in Dublin, brought up as an Anglican, but at age thirty-five he was received into the Roman Catholic Church. He lived a very simple life. He joined the Jesuits and was eventually ordained priest. John gave his life to teaching and influencing for good the pupils at Clongowes Wood College. He gained a reputation for holiness and being a man of prayer, and always being available to the sick, the poor and anyone in need. His was the first beatification in Ireland.

REFLECTION

What a wonderful reputation to have! The availability to those in need is especially to be admired and emulated. How available am I to God for his purposes of love towards those in need – of healing, of guidance, of practical help, or simply in need of a friend?

9 SEPTEMBER

St Ciarán of Clonmacnoise

D.545. FEAST DAY: 9 September

Ciarán was the son of Beoadh, a carpenter and chariot-builder who moved to Co. Roscommon where the taxes were less heavy. He studied under Finnian of Clonard, where his favourite cow followed him and where he generously lent his Gospel book to Ninnidh who had none. He also was a monk under Enda of Aran, and later Senan of Scattery Island, Co. Clare. Enda was depressed when Ciarán left as the guardian angels seemed to be leaving with him. Ciarán founded the monastery of Clonmacnoise. He died of the plague seven years later aged thirty-three. The monastery lasted another thousand years, producing many manuscripts, including: *The Book of the Dun Cow, The Annals of Clonmacnoise, The Annals of Tigernach,* and *The Chronicle of the Irish.* Ciarán was said to have the gift for turning peoples' attraction from himself to attraction to God.

REFLECTION

The gift of turning someone's attraction from oneself towards God instead would be wonderful to have if there was some way of doing it without seeming prudish or over-pious. Could I develop this?

10 SEPTEMBER
St Finnian of Moville

D.576. FEAST DAY: *10 September*

Finnian was fostered and educated by St Colman of Dromore, then Abbot Caolan of Nendrum. Once Caolan was about to cane Finnian when his arm became rigid and the boy asked why. Caolan answered: 'the Holy Spirit is preventing me from punishing you, holy boy'. Caolan sent him to Whithorn to continue his education, feeling himself unworthy to teach a young man with such a bright future. Finnian stayed on to teach there and travelled round Scotland for twenty years returning to Strangford Lough to found the monastery of *Magh Bile*/Moville there. Saint Columba was one of his students, as were St Canice, St Comgall and St Crumnathy. He also founded Dromin, Co. Louth, which is where St Columba without his permission copied his precious psalter. When he was elderly and Comgall was Abbot in Bangor he urged Comgall to go easier on the monks. He is possibly the author of *The Penitential of Vinnian*.

REFLECTION

Do I respect the advice of elders? Am I keen to learn their wisdom, and draw on their experience? Who?

11 SEPTEMBER
St Lugaidh/Lugadius/Luach

DATE UNKNOWN. FEAST DAY: *24 March*

Lugaidh was one of many of that name, several of them saints. The name is pronounced 'Lewy'. He was from the Inishowen peninsula, and the church at Clonleigh near Raphoe was under his patronage. His two brothers were also saints, Dochonna of Assylin near Boyle, Co. Roscommon, and Cormac, a Bishop of Moville on Inishowen.

REFLECTION

These early Irish saints lived in a God-filled world, seeing Him in every part of His creation, all of it indwelt by Him. This is not to say that they were pantheists, they also believed in the transcendence and infinity of God – the early Irish Church was completely orthodox in its doctrines. The dimension of immanence was lost or downplayed for many centuries and is now being rediscovered. These saints lived and moved and had their being in God, which gave them the ability to pray continuously. Have I come to realise the indwelling of God in all of creation? Do I find this helps me to pray at all times? Am I making efforts in that direction?

12 SEPTEMBER

St Ailbhe/Alibeus/Ailbeus/Alby

D. C.530. FEAST DAY: 12 September

Ailbhe, one of the four bishops who were in Ireland before Patrick, was the son of a slave girl, and was left on a Tipperary hillside to die. Legend claims he was brought up by a wolf alongside her cubs until rescued by a hunter. He later saved that wolf from hunters, feeding her daily. A priest found him praying outside and asking to know the creator of all things. The priest taught him all he could and baptised him. Ailbhe went to Rome, studied with St Hilary and was made a bishop. He returned to Ireland with fifty followers in an unseaworthy boat. They landed safely (Ailbhe had blessed the sea) in Dalriada, converted the King, raising his three sons to life, with many other miracles. He travelled round Ireland preaching, settling in Emly, Co. Tipperary. Once St Sinchell came asking for a place to live, Ailbhe gave him his own house and all that was in it.

REFLECTION

Creation was a pointer to the Creator for Ailbhe: how much is it also for me?

13 SEPTEMBER
St Dagan/Daganus

D.639. FEAST DAY: *29 May or 13 September*

Dagan was said to be mild-tempered and suave. One day he was minding the calves when raiders came and decapitated him and brought his body to a monastery where St Canice was staying. Saint Canice united the head and the body and healed Dagan, who lived for long time after that, with only a circular scar on his neck to remind him of the episode. After his schooling he went east to Ennereilly, Co. Wicklow, six kilometres from present-day Arklow and started a monastery there under the rule of St Molua. He went to Rome to get papal authority for the Rule. Nicknamed 'The Traveller', he also attended a conference on the date of Easter in Britain. This mild man was so vehemently in favour of the Irish dating method that he refused to sleep under the same roof as British bishops!

REFLECTION
About what do I feel vehemently enough that it would cause me to make a protest?

14 SEPTEMBER
St Cormac

D.908. FEAST DAY: *14 September*

Cormac was both King of Munster and Bishop of Cashel. He compiled the *Psalter of Cashel*. He was very austere, sleeping in a hair shirt, which he also wore to Matins, and singing the psalms while immersed in cold water. He became bishop before he inherited the throne, which happened in 903, in a period of comparative peace, the Danes having settled or gone home. He wrote psalms telling of Ireland's history. A portion of this *Psalter of Cashel* is in the Bodleian Library in Oxford. An Irish glossary or dictionary of etymologies, *Sanas Chormaic*, is also ascribed to him. There were a few battles in the last years of his life and he died in battle after appointing his friend Lorcan King of Thomond as his successor.

REFLECTION

Have I ever tried writing psalms myself as Cormac did? They don't need to rhyme, they are a pouring out of one's soul to God. What is stopping me trying? It can be surprising what emerges once pen and paper are handy!

15 SEPTEMBER

St Mirren/Mirinus/Mirin

D. SIXTH CENTURY. *FEAST DAY: 15 September*

Mirren was an Irish monk who trained under Comgall at Bangor from an early age and was a contemporary of St Columba. He went to Alba (Scotland) and became Abbot of Paisley. He was said to be gentle and greatly loved by the monks, who saw him surrounded by light as he sat in his cell. He had a powerful influence on the Strathclyde area and is honoured by both Catholics and Protestants. He is the patron of a football club, St Mirren's of Paisley. The ruins of a chapel dedicated to him can be seen on the largest island on Loch Lomond.

REFLECTION

Scripture teaches that we are to receive the light of Christ; we are to walk in the light; we are to be lights to the world; and others. Mirren put all these into practice, which was why the rather fey early Irish monks were able to literally see the light surrounding him. How conscious am I of having the light of Christ within me? Of letting my light shine? Of being a light to the world?

16 SEPTEMBER
St Maculin

D. C.497. FEAST DAY: *16 September*

Maculin founded a monastery at Lusk in north Co. Dublin. His lovely story goes that he was so humble that he wanted to serve under someone else even in his own monastery and chose Eolang. Eolang replied that they both should serve only Jesus Christ. Then Jesus appeared to them with a choir of angels and took Maculin by the right hand and raised him to be abbot. A wonderful effulgence spread around the hand Jesus had held so it could not be seen for brightness, so in humility Maculin always wore a glove on that hand. He visited Scotland twice and was held in repute there. Popular tradition has it that angels were heard singing when he died.

REFLECTION
Do I realise that the service I do is for God? Do I see my 'bosses' as equals in status though above me in function? Am I modest about any elevation I am given by others? Do I realise modesty and confidence can both have room in my life?

17 SEPTEMBER
St Grellan/Greallain/Grellanus

D. FIFTH OR EARLY SIXTH CENTURY. FEAST DAY: *17 September*

Grellan was a disciple of St Patrick, who prophesied about Grellan's birth which was three months premature during a very loud thunderstorm. He is the best known of a number of St Grellans. He settled at Kilclooney in the Diocese of Clonfert and built a monastery there. Once he was caught between two opposing armies, and as both leaders respected him, he was able to bring about a truce. Later he had to pray hard for peace as the locals were killing their hostages. He is patron of Hy Many and the Kelly tribe, and revered in Galway and Roscommon.

REFLECTION
Have I ever found myself caught between two people opposed to each other or even fighting? The story of Grellan shows how important it is to keep on friendly terms with both sides if we are to become peacemakers. How have I been managing to do this? In the family? At work? Politically? Among my friends? My neighbours? Would praying more for the people I live amongst help here?

18 SEPTEMBER

St Disibode

D. C.700. FEAST DAY: *18 September or 8 July*

Disibode was apparently a bishop in Ireland before he resigned his see and left with Giswold, Salust and Clement to preach in Germany. He founded a missionary centre near Bingen, on a hill later called Mount St Disibode or Disenberg. All four became hermits. His life was written by Hildegard of Bingen who began her religious training at Disenberg, and who claimed that the life of the saint had been revealed to her. He was devoted to the sick and the poor, and received unfailing answers to prayer. People flocked to him because of the aura of his holiness and his many miracles. When he died a delightful odour of myrrh and frankincense filled his cell and continued at his grave.

REFLECTION
Disibode was probably a man with one hundred per cent devotion to God. What percentage of me is surrendered to God? How could I increase that? What part do I play in reaching all nations with the Christian Gospel? By giving? By prayer? Supporting a missionary or missionary society?

19 SEPTEMBER
St Maeldoid

D. EIGHTH CENTURY. FEAST DAY: 13 May

Maeldoid was from the Omeath area of Co. Louth. He founded a church at Muckno, Co. Monaghan. A legend about the founding of Muckno – which appears to mean 'the swimming place of the pig' – recounts that the spot chosen was indicated to Maeldoid by a pig who swam across a neighbouring lake. Scholars have dismissed this as based on inaccurate etymology; however, no other explanation has been offered. Another legend claims he had a miraculous escape from burning when St Patrick and a local chieftain agreed on a conflagration as a test of the truth of the Christian faith. Chronology would disprove this one.

REFLECTION

The spiritual meaning of Maeldoid's escape from burning could be that he escaped burning for his sins by reforming his life. To have become a saint he would have had to be a hundred per cent honest before God. God can work with the real me, not a false front or mask. Am I honest in this way before God when I do my evening examen or make my confession?

20 SEPTEMBER
St Manchán of Lemanaghan/Manchianus

D.665. FEAST DAY: 29 September

Manchán founded a monastery in Lemanaghan which is in Garrycastle barony in Co. Offaly. Kilmanaghan takes its name from him. He is said to have written a number of pious poems and to have been regarded as an authoritative commentator on Holy Scripture. He is thought to have been a peacemaker or go-between between St Mochuda (Carthage) who lived in the next parish and other local people, at risk to himself and at his own expense. His twelfth century shrine is very impressive. He died in the great plague of 665. His mother Mealla's cell is near to St Manchán's holy well.

REFLECTION

When there is trouble locally, do I steer clear of it and try not to get involved, or do I offer to be a go-between at my own expense and risk? Peacemaking is not easy, but Jesus said in the Beatitudes that peacemakers were blessed, implying that Christians should try to be peacemakers. What situation could I help with in this way?

21 SEPTEMBER

St Blathe/Flora

D.523. FEAST DAY: *29 January*

Blathe was the lay sister in charge of St Brigid's kitchen at Kildare. She therefore would have shared something of Brigid's generosity. She had the job of ensuring there was enough food for all the monks and nuns and also the beggars – who were never turned away. Her job must have been extra hard at the times when the feasts prepared for visiting clergy were given away by Brigid to the beggars clamouring at the gate. As a result, Blathe would have had to conjure up new food for the guests! She was renowned for her holiness and her loyalty to Brigid in good times and bad.

REFLECTION

Given St Brigid's extreme generosity, Blathe's job would have been difficult. She must have been a woman of much faith and also ingenuity. Do I feel God will provide and thus do I go ahead and offer hospitality or do I hold back from fear of scarcity? When I give do I do so with love, knowing the spirit in which even a small gift is given makes all the difference?

22 SEPTEMBER
St Pappan/Pappin/Papán/Papanus

DATE UNKNOWN. FEAST DAY: *31 July*

Pappan was the patron saint of Poppintree in Finglas, North Dublin. There is also a St Pappin's well near the church in nearby Santry. According to O'Riain, his sacred tree was recalled annually in his pattern on 31 July.

REFLECTION

We know very little of the life of this saint and can only speculate on what his sacred tree was. But we can say with certainty of all these Irish saints that they lived joyful Christian lives. Their discipline of regular confession meant that they rejoiced in being regularly forgiven and cleansed, receiving God's forgiveness, healing and love. When a priest says a prayer of absolution, do I actually receive into myself this forgiveness God is offering me? As well as receiving His forgiveness do I receive his cleansing and healing power, and his liberation from the bondage to sin? Do I rejoice in regular receiving of forgiveness, at an evening examen maybe, in addition to Sundays?

23 SEPTEMBER
St Adamnan/Eunan of Iona

D.704. FEAST DAY: *23 September and 7 September in Raphoe*

Adamnan was born at Raphoe, Co. Donegal. He is also associated with Drumhome, and Kilmacrennan, Co. Donegal and Skreen, Co. Sligo (its full name is *Scrín Adhamhnáin*). He became a monk at Iona under Ségène and ninth abbot in 679. He wrote the definitive biography of St Columba and *De Locis Sanctis*, about the places of the Holy Land. His friend Bishop Asculf was said to have seen the chalice used at the Last Supper and described it to Adamnan as very similar to the Ardagh Chalice. He achieved the passing of the *Law of the Innocents* or *Cain Adamnain* at the Synod of Birr in 697, protecting non-combatants and excusing monks and women from fighting in battles, and imposing sterner penalties for assaulting women. He had never forgotten seeing as a youth one woman dragging another from the field of battle with a reaping sickle through her chest.

REFLECTION
Are there any situations of injustice that I would have a chance of fighting against, even later in life?

24 SEPTEMBER
St Grimonia/Germana

D. FOURTH CENTURY. FEAST DAY: *24 September*

Grimonia was an Irishwoman who became a Christian at the young age of twelve. She was imprisoned by her pagan father for refusing to agree to an arranged marriage. She escaped and with her companion Proba landed in France and became a hermit in the forest of Thiérache in Picardy. Her father sent his henchmen to find her and they beheaded her. Her grave became famous for miracles. A church was built on the site and the town of La Chapelle developed around this. Her relics and those of Proba, who died beside her, were moved in the thirteenth century to Lesquilles and in the sixteenth century to Henin-Lietard near Douai. Her companion Proba is known as Sainte Preuve in France.

REFLECTION
A grave of a little-known saint being famous for miracles of healing shows that people often are looking not for religion but for healing for their ills, and peace of mind. Have I realised how important, then, it is to make clear to the people I pray for that the power to heal and bring peace of mind comes from God and not myself?

25 SEPTEMBER

St Finbarr/Barre/Barry/Barra/Find-Barr

D.610. FEAST DAY: *25 September*

Finbarr was the son of a Cork blacksmith. After training at Bangor he became a hermit at Gougane Barra. King Fachtna presented the land to Finbarr as a gift to thank him for healing his children (his son was blind and his daughter unable to speak) and raising his wife back to life. He established a school there famous for sanctity and learning and people flocked to him. Some students turned up and told him it was their place of resurrection and he humbly turned the whole place over to them. He set out wandering, eventually building a hermitage on a spot indicated by an angel, where Saint Fin Barre's Cathedral, Cork now stands. He became Bishop of Cork. He was a lovable man, performing many healing miracles. His monks went on a mission to the Hebrides and called the island of Barra after him.

REFLECTION

Can I see unpleasant events as hints or pointers in the right direction? Can I accept a period of waiting, of transition, knowing that God's timing is different from and better than mine?

26 SEPTEMBER

St Colman Elo/Colman Moccu Sailnu/Colmanell/Colman Eile

D. SEVENTH CENTURY. FEAST DAY: *26 September*

Colman was possibly a nephew of St Columba. He spent some time in Iona, returning to Ireland in 597 when Columba died. Columba said, when Colman was having difficulty on the crossing to Ireland because of a whirlpool, that God had designed this to help him pray more strongly. He was the probable author of *The Alphabet of Devotion*. He settled in Meath where he founded the famous monastery of Lann Elo – Lynally – near Tullamore.

Colman Elo and his monastery took their names from the swans that the monks befriended as they were building a causeway. These swans sang to them to help them work more efficiently. Saint Mochua cured Colman of a sudden loss of memory brought on by pride. He was said to have second sight and to have heard the bells tolling in Rome for Pope Gregory's funeral.

REFLECTION
What beautiful songs could help me do my work more efficiently? Could some 'whirlpools' in my life have been promptings to pray more strongly? Have I increased in spiritual strength because of them?

27 SEPTEMBER

St Moengal/Marcellus

D. C.887. FEAST DAY: *27 September*

Moengal was one of a party of pilgrims returning from Rome, when they put up for the night at the Abbey of St Gall. Moengal and his uncle Bishop Marcus decided to stay on, giving their horses and packs to the returning travellers to see them home to Ireland. However, they kept their books and vestments and these enriched the St Gall Abbey Library. Moengal was given charge of the cathedral school and trained Notker, Ratopert and Tutilo there. He trained the choir and it became a famous music school. The Abbey supplied Germany with manuscripts of Gregorian chant, often embellished with artistic illuminations. The Abbey flourished in his day.

REFLECTION
Moengal was able to make a life-changing decision when he decided to stay on at St Gall, and his contribution to the abbey was very worthwhile. How ready am I to make complete changes like this? Do I pray about big decisions I have to make? Do I listen to God's voice guiding me?

28 SEPTEMBER
St Sinach MacDara

D. SIXTH CENTURY. FEAST DAY: *16 July*

Sinach was a hermit who lived on what is now called MacDara's island in Connemara off the coast near Roundwood. Traditionally fishermen would dip their sails or make the sign of the cross when passing the island. An annual Mass used to be held on the island on his feast day, 16 July.

REFLECTION

Saints like Sinach were enthusiastic about their Rule of Life, their discipline and their asceticism. Have I made out a Rule of Life for myself? How enthusiastic am I about it? They knew that contemplative prayer, or what nowadays is more often called meditation due to Eastern influence, was a way of becoming aware of the presence of God and our inseparability from Him; and was an essential need for ministry, spilling over to it and to all the everyday activities. Do I give priority to prayer during my day? Have I learnt like the Irish saints that perpetual surrender is the first prerequisite for transformation to begin?

29 SEPTEMBER
St Eigneach/Agney/Egnaghus

DATE UNKNOWN. FEAST DAY: *24 April*

Eigneach is a patron of the Diocese of Derry. He was from present-day Desertegney in Inishowen West, Co. Donegal. Desertegney means 'Agney's hermitage', so clearly the saint left his mark, though not much else is known about him. He is said to have meditated by the well in the Gap of Mamore.

REFLECTION

Many early Irish saints found inspiration and enlightenment from meditating in nature. One wonders what Eigneach's thoughts might have been as he looked at the well? Possibly along the lines of flow, fullness, dryness, emptiness. Could he have come to the realisation that if his love was to flow out to other people it must flow from a fullness, because if the well was dry there would be little to offer other people? Do I appreciate this truth? Have I ever tried to 'run on dry' or 'run on empty'? What was the result? How could I link fullness with flow better in my own life, my own Christian walk and ministry to others? Or could Eigneach also have thought about Jesus Christ being an inexhaustible wellspring of life from which to draw?

30 SEPTEMBER

St Brigid of Kilbready

D. SIXTH CENTURY. FEAST DAY: *30 September*

Brigid was a recluse on the banks of the River Shannon and her holy well, St Bride's Well, is near Rathdowney, Co. Laois. An amazing story about her recounts that once she prepared a cope or chasuble for St Senan, but did not know how to get it to him, so she wrapped it in hay and put it into a basket with some letters asking that St Senan would send her the Holy Sacrament and launched it onto the river. By a miracle it landed on the shore near Senan's church and he was given knowledge of it. He placed a pyx and two portions of salt along with the host into the basket and relaunched it onto the river. The second portion of salt was for St Diarmaid of Inis Clothrann – another recluse – who also was given divine knowledge that it was coming.

REFLECTION

Would I be open, after praying, to receiving unconventional solutions to problems of mine that seem insuperable? Am I listening to God?

OCTOBER

1 OCTOBER
St Becan/Beacon/Peacon

D. SIXTH CENTURY. FEAST DAY: *26 May*

Becan was of Muskerry and Stagonil, Co. Wicklow (present-day Powerscourt). When the High King killed his son by mistake, he consulted St Columba who told him to go to St Becan at Kilpeacon. He found the saint in his old work clothes digging a ditch around a graveyard. As the king approached, Becan called out: 'Oh murderer! Down on your knees!' So the king prostrated himself before the saint. When Becan saw the king's genuine grief, he prayed to heaven fervently three times and the king's son, Breasal, was restored to life. He was a very holy recluse given to frequent fasting and constant prayer. He is said to have erected a stone cross outside the monastery in the open air and would recite the whole Psalter beside it.

REFLECTION
Becan did not let status get in the way of speaking the truth to people and didn't excuse the king from repenting. Do I similarly discount status, or do I let it blind me to realities?

2 OCTOBER
St Donard

D.506. FEAST DAY: *24 March*

Donard's mother was converted by St Patrick while expecting him, and Patrick blessed the child in her womb. He set up a hermitage and oratory on the Mountains of Mourne, above today's town of Newcastle. His principal church was at Maghera, Co. Down. Slieve Donard is named after him, and still has prehistoric cairns, suggesting that he used sites previously sacred for the Druids to establish his Christian settlements. The hermitage was much used in penal times. There are still regular pilgrimages to the summit of Slieve Donard. The locals believe Donard still celebrates Mass there every Sunday.

REFLECTION

Do I bless the child in the womb of my pregnant friends or family members? St Patrick's doing so had good results; my blessing could have good results too. The Irish saints were great blessers; would I be in favour of restoring this wonderful habit? What is to stop me beginning to do so more each day? Could I include a blessing for someone when I include them in my prayers?

3 OCTOBER

St Dallan

D. SIXTH CENTURY. FEAST DAY: *14 December*

Dallan was a saint who came from Glendallan, the old name for the western end of Glencar Lake. This western half of Glencar Lake is in Co. Sligo, while the eastern half is in Co. Leitrim. The fact that Dallan was the father of St Loman of Lough Gill is all that is known about him. However, his son was known to have attended the Synod of Druimceatt, which would place the father as a generation older than the other Saint Dallan, Dallan Forgaill, who also attended that Synod and whose church was further north at Kildallan.

REFLECTION

Dallan obviously passed on to his son Loman something very precious, a living flame of love in his heart and a vision of giving his life to serving God. This bears out the saying that Christianity is caught rather than taught. Who passed on to me the flame and vision that inspired me in my life? Am I trying to inspire the young people with in my life with my own love for Christ and desire to serve him?

4 OCTOBER
St Munis/Mun

D. SIXTH CENTURY. FEAST DAY: *6 February*

Munis was St Patrick's nephew and St Loman of Trim's brother. He is also said to be a brother of St Mel and of Rioch of Inishboffin, but scholars cast doubt on this. Brother could be meant in the Christian sense. He possibly was a hermit for some while on an island on Lough Ree. His monastery was in Forgney, Co. Longford. Saint Patrick established Munis as Bishop of Forgney after he had returned from Rome where he had been on a mission for St Patrick.

REFLECTION

Munis was obviously a person St Patrick depended on for his reliability and trustworthiness. Am I someone people can depend on to be in charge of important messages? What qualities in a person send messages to others about the person's trustworthiness? Do I have these qualities, or should I be trying to cultivate them with God's help?

5 OCTOBER
St Sedna

D.570. FEAST DAY: *10 March*

Sedna was a speechless cowherd, who was healed by St Fintan of Clonenagh and St Colm of Terryglass. When his speech recovered it was found he had the gift of prophecy. Sedna also wrote poetry and went on to become Bishop of Ossory and Abbot of Seir-Kieran. He was said to be the brother of St Multose or Eltin. Saint Sedna's well near Clonbeg church in the Glen of Aherlow has healing waters, especially for eye diseases. Every year on 18 July there is an ecumenical service at his holy well.

REFLECTION

We all have need for healing of our eyesight in a spiritual sense. With full spiritual vision we would see that God is all around us, in people and creatures, plants and minerals and the sky, and also see that God is within us as well as around us and beyond us. Saint Paul spoke of: 'Christ in you, the hope of glory' and that we 'live and move and have our being in Him'. Have I opened my eyes to these inspiring truths yet?

6 OCTOBER

St Lugdach

Date unknown. An early saint. Feast day: 6 October

Lugdach was Bishop of Coolbanagher, Co. Offaly. He was known as 'Lugdach the Gentle', in *The Feilire of Aengus*. Aengus the Culdee was also associated with Coolbanagher and is reputed to have composed the Feilire there.

REFLECTION

Gentleness is not a quality that excites admiration in people nowadays. But it is not weak to be gentle as some suppose, it is a quality that is possessed by people who are strong and know their own strength and have confidence. It is the quality of a lion rather than a mouse. A gentle person is moderate, fair, forbearing and considerate. Gentleness is the quality of a patient teacher. Could I be said to be gentle? Can I claim this quality without apology? St Paul exhorts the Philippians: 'Let your gentleness be evident to all' and he applied the word to himself.

7 OCTOBER
St Landelin

D.640. FEAST DAY: *7 October*

Landelin was an Irish prince who went to Alsace to preach the Gospel. He was known for healing the sick, the blind and the lame. His hermit's cell in the area even had an effect on the local animals and the hounds refused to chase deer in the vicinity of his cell but became meek and docile. A huntsman killed Landelin, and a spring of water gushed out from where his body lay and formed a healing pool. Ettnheimmunster is still a place of pilgrimage. (Not to be confused with the French St Landelin Abbot of Lobes.)

REFLECTION

How one treats animals can be a good indicator of a person's spirituality. Animals are very sensitive to a person's unseen emanations. Could my treatment of animals be described as respectful and kind? Do I encourage my family and friends to treat all creatures with love and respect? The way in which North American Indians used to treat the animals they killed for food – with a prayer and respect – is a good example to us all.

8 OCTOBER
St Triduana/Trullen/Tredwell

D.532. FEAST DAY: *8 October*

Triduana travelled to Scotland with Riadhail/Regulus from Lough Derg, Tipperary. She, with two other young women, was looking for a desert place to be a solitary. They settled in Forfarshire, until a tyrant pursued Triduana and she was forced to flee from him. He sent his ministers after her and she inquired of them: 'What does the great prince require of me, a virgin dedicated to God?' They replied: 'He desires the most lustrous beauty of thine eyes, which if he obtain not he most assuredly shall die'. So she plucked out her eyes saying: 'Take what your prince loved'. The prince admired her constancy and left her alone thereafter. She lived a life of prayer and the place where she lived was known for cures for blindness.

REFLECTION

Have I a similar assurance that I am on the right path? Could Triduana's confidence have come from having dealt with her dark side and being totally honest with God? Have I any unresolved conflicts that could be brought to God in prayer?

9 OCTOBER

St John Henry Newman

1801–1890. FEAST DAY: 9 October

John Henry Newman's canonisation in 2019 was welcomed by many Christian denominations, because his influence was so wide. He was an Anglican priest before later converting to Roman Catholicism, and he was catholic in the widest sense. He brought stability to the newly emancipated Roman Catholic Church in England. He was seen as an honorary Irishman after founding the Catholic University in Dublin during his time in Ireland, which University College Dublin regards as its forerunner. Newman's books *The Idea of a University* and *Apologia Pro Vita Sua* (A Defence of One's Own Life) have been widely acclaimed. His poem *The Dream of Gerontius* was put to music by Elgar. It is a sublime piece of music and worth a listen, especially in times of reflection.

REFLECTION

Newman was not afraid of change, including converting to Catholicism. One of his sayings is: 'To live is to change and to be perfect is to have changed often'. An impressive theologian, he is held in great esteem by many Christian denominations. He was creative as well as spiritual. He wrote books, hymns and poems. Can I make more time to listen to music, read poetry or pursue a creative activity I enjoy?

10 OCTOBER
St Loman/Lomman of Lough Gill

D. SIXTH CENTURY. FEAST DAY: 11 *October or 4 February*

Loman was St Dallan of Glendallan's son. He became a hermit on an island in Lough Gill, Co. Sligo, now known as Church Island. Later a nunnery was founded on the island, and then a renowned monastery known for having the best library in the west – which sadly burnt down in the fifteenth century. *The Book of Armagh* calls St Loman an exorcist. He is credited with being a contemporary of St Columba. He is believed to have assisted at the Synod of Druimceatt, welcoming Columba to it, and trying to read a eulogy about him that Columba forbade him to read during his lifetime.

REFLECTION
Loman certainly had a sense of beauty in choosing Lough Gill for his hermitage. Do I let the beauty of God's creation speak to me of Him and spark me to joy, worship and praise? Loman seemed to have had a gift with words, which maybe came from his sense of awe and wonder at God's beauty and majesty, a quality there is not enough of today. Do I encourage my children to wonder at creation?

11 OCTOBER
St Canice/Canicus/Kenneth

D.600. FEAST DAY: 11 *October*

Canice was born in Keenaght, Co. Derry. His father was a celebrated but impoverished bard. He started life as a cowherd before embarking on his spiritual education. He studied under Cadoc in Wales, under Finnian of Clonard, where he made friends with Columba, then again with Columba under St Mobhí of Glasnevin. Canice founded several monasteries in Scotland and Ireland, including Aghaboe, Co. Laois. He had a close communion with nature and wild animals, using a stag's antlers as a bookrest while saying the psalms. The animal stood still in respect for the saint. He accompanied Columba to the fortress of Brude King of the Picts, his Cruithnian language being close to Pictish. He once calmed a storm off Iona by his prayers, sensing Columba's urgent plea while in the refectory. He ran to the chapel to pray with only one shoe on.

REFLECTION
Columba said of Canice that God had granted him a calm even in the midst of storm. Have I learnt to claim this calm and peace which passes understanding? Do I pray for my friends in danger and on their travels?

12 OCTOBER

St Mobhí/Berchan/Clairinech

D.545. FEAST DAY: 12 October

Mobhí was one of the Twleve Apostles of Ireland. After studying with St Finnian of Clonard, where he was one of the earliest pupils, he founded a monastery at Glasnevin on the banks of the river Tolka. The monastery became a famed school and was attended by Saints Columba and Canice, and possibly also Comgall and Ciarán. He lost his eyesight, but was said to be wonderfully gifted with prophetic light. He was considered an outstanding abbot and a man of great sanctity as well as learning. Mobhí's school was badly hit and closed down by the Yellow Plague that he had predicted and during which he himself died. Although his monastery lasted only a few years before the plague, his memory is still revered today. He was buried between Rush and Skerries.

REFLECTION
Losing his eyesight Mobhí became strong in inner seeing, or prophecy. What have I lost that God has compensated me for in a different way? Can I see the hidden benefit in every seeming loss?

13 OCTOBER
St Colman of Austria

D.1012. FEAST DAY: *13 October*

Colman, a son of Malachy King of Ireland and grandson of Brian Boru, wanted to preach in France and Germany but first made a pilgrimage to Rome and the Holy Land. On his return he was passing through Austria at a time of war when he was seized. He was mistaken for a spy because he was unable to speak the language. He was tortured and hanged in a public place with a robber on each side. Wild animals ate the other corpses, but none touched Colman. His body remained incorrupt and unmolested for a year and a half; even the scaffolding took root and bore branches. Colman's remains are now in the Abbey of Melk, where he is venerated as St Koloman. All sorts of miracles happened at his tomb, which had a beautiful fragrant odour around it. He is the most universally known of the three hundred Saint Colmans in the Irish martyrologies.

REFLECTION
Do I spread a fragrance wherever I go, meaning do I spread happiness and cheerfulness? We make more impression on other people than we realise!

14 OCTOBER

St Fiacc/Fiach/Fiace/Fiech

D. FIFTH CENTURY. FEAST DAY: *12 October*

Fiacc the Fair, with remarkable powers of intellect, was educated by his uncle Dubtach, the chief poet of Ireland. He too was a bard and was the only one to answer to Patrick's description of who he wanted to ordain – someone of good family without liability, with one wife (Fiacc was then a widower) and one child, neither too poor nor too rich. So St Patrick gave him the tonsure, cut off his beard and left him with a bell, a reliquary, a staff and a writing tablet, and seven monks, including St Tegan. Later Patrick consecrated Fiacc as Bishop of Sletty, and a school or ecclesiastical seminary was founded later at Sletty. He was the first native of Leinster to become a bishop. The monastery was on the eastern side of the River Barrow, but after sixty monks fell ill, an angel guided St Fiacc to move the monastery to the western bank of the river.

REFLECTION
Could it have been the saints' greater awareness of angels that led to their having guidance from them?

15 OCTOBER

St Cuan of Ahascragh

D.788. FEAST DAY: *15 October*

Cuan was Abbot of Clonmore, Co. Carlow, probably as successor to St Finan Lobhar. He went with St Moling on a mission to obtain freedom for the Dalriadans from 'The Boromean Tribute' – a very heavy tax of livestock going back hundreds of years. There was a manuscript called *The Book of Cuan* that was said to have contributed very largely to the compilation of *The Annals of Ulster*. Cuan is venerated both at Clonmore and Ahascragh, Co. Galway.

REFLECTION ~

Helping the Dalriadans to gain freedom from their crippling tax was an excellent way of putting Cuan's Christian values into practice. What could I do to make someone's life more bearable? Have I noticed any injustice that could do with support to put right? Maybe in the newspapers? Do I read the papers or listen to the news in a spirit of prayerfulness rather than just complaining? What might God be asking me to help with now?

16 OCTOBER
St Gall

D.630. FEAST DAY: *16 October*

Gall was an Irish monk and poet from Leinster. He was taught by St Columbanus at Bangor and later became one of Columbanus' companions on his mission to Europe. Gall fell ill in Switzerland and stayed on in present day St Gallen. This caused a quarrel as Columbanus did not believe the illness was genuine; but before Gall died Columbanus sent Gall his belt and crozier as a sign of forgiveness. His enthusiasm and impetuosity almost spoiled the work in Switzerland as he burned the pagan shrines, incurring the wrath of the inhabitants. Gall escaped to Bregenz and became a hermit, taming a bear which fetched his firewood and healing an epileptic girl. Known for his sanctity, Gall refused honours and bishoprics preferring to live as a hermit.

REFLECTION ~

Do I also crave the silence and solitude that will return me to my true self in God and deepen my faith? Do I avoid solitude or do I seek it? How could I get more of it than at present?

17 OCTOBER

St Eliph

D. C.362. FEAST DAY: *16 October*

Eliph was an Irish prince who chose to serve Christ in poverty in the city of Toul in France. He was imprisoned there at one stage but released miraculously. His preaching led to the conversion of four hundred people before his beheading by Pope Julian the Apostate. He was beheaded for rebuking Jews and pagans for worshipping a devil, although the devil they worshipped actually appeared and sank below the earth. Eliph's brother Eucharius and his two sisters shared his martyrdom. Mount Eliph is the place where it happened, between Neufchâteau and the Vair River. His relics are now in St Martin's church, Cologne.

REFLECTION

This was one of several cases of a mass conversion due to the ability of a saint to open peoples' eyes to let them see the demon they were worshipping in their idol worship. Such a gift would be very worthwhile having. Am I able yet to open peoples' eyes to what they have been regarding as most important in life – their unexamined values? Should I pray for this ability?

18 OCTOBER

St Dichu

D. FIFTH CENTURY. FEAST DAY: *29 April*

Dichu was St Patrick's first convert. Dichu first saw Patrick when his boat arrived at Strangford Lough. Their coming was alerted to him by the swine. Dichu was an enormously tall man. As he thought Patrick and his followers were pirates, he tried to draw his sword against them, but his arm became miraculously paralysed. Dichu became humble and mild. He was converted

October 227

when he saw Patrick's face and he then realised that Patrick was a good man. He became Patrick's most devoted follower and gave Patrick a barn for his first church. The barn was called *Sabhall Padraig*, and it gave its name to present-day Saul.

REFLECTION

Am I able to see the goodness in someone's face? Am I able to see things which can aid me in helping them? Dichu gave Patrick very good help along the way. Do I remember and respect those who have helped me in my spiritual journey? Could I list them and thank God for them now?

19 OCTOBER
St Ethbin

D. C.600. FEAST DAY: *19 October*

Ethbin was fostered and taught by St Samson of Dol in Brittany. He was deeply impressed with Our Lord's words about renouncing all worldly goods so he became a monk at Tauriac. He fled to Ireland when a war destroyed Tauriac. Ethbin became a hermit in Nectan's Wood, Co. Kildare, founding a community there. Once the mother of a paralytic brought her son to Ethbin for healing saying a voice had told her to go to Nectan's Wood and Ethbin would heal him. Ethbin prayed for a long time and the boy was healed. Ethbin only ate on Thursdays, surviving on only bread and water. He drank no wine except for the wine of Holy Communion. Ethbin became very ill near the end and announced his death to his disciples. Miracles occurred at his tomb.

REFLECTION

St Ethbin continued to pray for healing for a long time. Could our expectation of everything being instant today be hindering God's work of healing? What things do I need to persevere with and not give up on?

20 OCTOBER

St Maeldubh

D. SEVENTH CENTURY. FEAST DAY: *18 December and 20 October*

Maeldubh was associated with Cloncurry (*Cluain Conaire*), Co. Kildare and also Ummeas. Saint Fechin of Fore was fostered with Maeldubh, and Fechin said of him on his death: 'Maeldubh the foe of the great black demons… A crooked midge would not be weary for the evil or error that he wrought; a midge would carry in its claw what of evil Maeldubh wrought'. His only belongings were his shirt and his quilt.

REFLECTION

His foster brother's words about Maeldubh are very moving: 'a midge could not carry in its claw what of evil Maeldubh wrought'. It was a wonderful compliment. It is a great pity that people wait until the recipient of the compliment has died to pay them compliments. Paying sincere compliments – though not too fulsome – or even just declaring what we appreciate about a person, can be such an encouragement during our lives, especially when going through difficult times.

21 OCTOBER

St Wendel/Wendelin/Vindolinus/Waldolen

D.617. FEAST DAY: *21 October*

Wendel was the son of an Irish king, who went on a pilgrimage to Rome and on the way back stayed to preach in Germany. He settled in a solitary place near Trier. Gradually a community grew up around his cell that later became the Benedictine Abbey of Tholey. When Wendel died he was buried at Tholey, and when so many wonders and visions took place at his grave they built a church on the spot. He was widely venerated, including by the

Emperor. The town of St Wendel was built there in the fourteenth century. Many Americans have this Christian name, as emigrants from Trier named their villages after the saint. There are seventeen St Wendel villages in the United States. A mission society in his name is also active there.

REFLECTION

Sustained prayer, continuous abiding and doing their work in partnership with God was normal for these Irish saints. Could their dedication inspire and encourage me? How could I apply this principle to my own life?

22 OCTOBER
St Donagh/Donat/Donatus

D. C.876. FEAST DAY: 22 *October*

Donagh was an Irishman who, when returning from a pilgrimage to Rome in 829, stopped at Fiesole where a crowd had gathered to elect a bishop. It was miraculously indicated that he should be their bishop. Donagh held the office for forty-seven years, building up local schools and leading a military expedition against the Saracens. He was a man of letters and wrote two lives of St Brigid, in prose and in verse, and he built the church of St Brigid at Piacenza. The devotion of Irish missionaries on the Continent to St Brigid would explain why there are so many St Brigid's churches there. Emperor Charles the Bald trusted Donagh so much that he gave him the right to levy his own taxes and hold his own court.

REFLECTION

St Donagh obviously was the man of God's choice for the job. When I am faced with choosing someone, do I pray and let God indicate who it is to be? Or when facing a mid-career move? Or any important decision?

23 OCTOBER

St Maglorious

D.575. FEAST DAY: 24 October

Maglorious was an Irishman who trained at Illtyd's monastery in Wales. Samson took him with him to Brittany. He preferred to be a hermit on the coast, but crowds sought him out for counsel and healing. After healing the ruler of the island of Sark of a skin disease, Maglorious was given land there where he established a monastery. He nobly served the poor there during times of plague and famine and organised their defence against raiders. He may have also founded a monastery on Jersey, where he tamed a wild beast. During his last days he refused to budge from the church, interpreting literally the words of Psalm 27:4: 'I desire to live in the Lord's house to the end of my days'.

REFLECTION

We smile at Maglorious spending his last days in the church because of a literal interpretation of a psalm verse, but do I take much of the Bible literally? Could I ask God the Holy Spirit to teach me how to discover the spiritual meaning in the Bible stories and parables?

24 OCTOBER

Blessed Thaddeus MacCarthy/Tadgh

1455–1492. FEAST DAY: 24 October

Thaddeus was born in Cork and educated by the Franciscans. Thaddeus happened to be in Rome when he heard news of the Bishop of Ross' death. Pope Sixtus IV was impressed with Thaddeus, and immediately consecrated him Bishop of Ross aged twenty-seven. But when he returned to Ireland, he found the post already filled by Odo, in favour of whom the last bishop had resigned. Therefore, both men were legitimately bishop of Ross.

Pope Sixtus had died, so Thaddeus appealed to the new pope, Innocent. He was then appointed Bishop of Cork and Cloyne, which he was said to highly deserve because of his honesty, prudence and other virtues. Thaddeus died while lodging in a hostel at Aosta en route for Rome. His papal document of appointment was in his wallet and he was buried with full honours. Numerous cures occurred at his tomb.

REFLECTION

Thaddeus impressed the Pope with his honesty. What attributes about me would impress people? Jesus said the outside is unimportant and what is inside will come bubbling out. How would I like to be regarded?

25 OCTOBER

St Mearnóg of Kilmarnock/Marnock/Ernene

D.625. FEAST DAY: *25 October*

Mearnóg is thought to have been from South Armagh. O'Riain links him to Kilnasaggart in the parish of Forkhill. He went to Scotland to be a monk at Iona and left to be a missionary on the mainland. King Aidan of Dalriada asked his help resisting the Angles and Saxons. Mearnóg inspired Aidan's army by getting them to make the sign of the cross on their foreheads and charge into battle shouting the name of Jesus Christ. He had a cell on the bank of the River Deveron near the church he founded at Aberchirder. Mearnóg gave his name to Kilmarnock in Scotland as well as several other places. He is also celebrated in Scotland on 25 October. He died at Aberchirder.

REFLECTION

The ability to inspire a whole crowd of people is rare. Perhaps a similar method might work for individuals, encouraging them to increase their spiritual connection? People do need encouragers. Could I be one?

26 OCTOBER

Blessed Margaret Ball and Blessed Francis Taylor

D.1584 AND 1621. FEAST DAY (JOINT): *30 January*

Margaret Ball was thrown into prison for teaching the faith, harbouring priests in her house and having the sacrament celebrated in her home. She died in prison in Dublin Castle from the harsh conditions there. She was beatified in 1992. Francis Taylor, born in Swords, was Mayor of Dublin (1595–1596). He also was thrown into prison for practising his faith, and died of the hardships he endured there. (His wife was Margaret Ball's granddaughter.)

REFLECTION

How would I have fared during the repressive regimes in Dublin in the sixteenth and early seventeenth centuries? Would I have been a target because of my strong faith? What can I do now for those in prison for their faith or political beliefs in many countries around the world?

27 OCTOBER

St Torannan

D.921. FEAST DAY: *12 June*

St Torannan was the saintly tenth-century abbot of the monastery founded by St Columba in Drumcliffe, Co. Sligo. He was considered the monastery's patron saint for many years. He is described in *The Martyrology of Donegal* as 'lasting, deedful, over a wide shipful sea'. He was different from St Torannan or Ternan who was the apostle to the Orkneys. He was also associated with Bangor and with Kilternan.

October 233

REFLECTION

The Columban monastery in Drumcliffe lasted from the sixth to the sixteenth century – one of the few early Irish monasteries not to be taken over by a continental order of monks. Thus St Torannan's rule there was in the middle of the time span. His dates coincide with the probable date of some of the High Crosses and possibly the start of building the Round Tower, so that would explain the epithet 'deedful' being applied to him. 'Lasting' could refer to his reputation for holiness. What epithets would suitably apply to me? What would I consider my reputation to be? Could I answer these questions prayerfully and honestly?

28 OCTOBER
St Luran/Lurach/Luireach

D. SEVENTH CENTURY. FEAST DAY: *17 February; 29 October in Derryloran*

Luran was from Maghera, Co. Derry. He was the Bishop of Derryloran, Co. Tyrone. He was the bishop chosen to come from afar to baptise Cainnech, later St Canice of Aghaboe, who was at that time a native of Dungiven, Co. Derry. Luran's brother Bega obtained the kingship of Oirghialla and died in the Battle of Dun Bolg at the side of his overlord Aedh son of Ainmire, a relative and friend of Columba's. Luran's other brother and a sister also entered religious life. His church was associated with the production of a book of poems.

REFLECTION

To be a poet one has to be observant, happy with one's own company and above all silent. Can I be happily alone or do I need company all the time? Silence is the first essential to self-knowledge and to God-knowledge. The deepest kind of prayer is contemplation or silent prayer, connecting with God deep within ourselves, sometimes called meditation, in the Eastern sense. Have I tried this yet?

29 OCTOBER

St Colman of Kilmacduagh

D.632. FEAST DAY: *29 October*

Colman son of Duach was renowned for fasting and mortification, living on only vegetables and water. He was a hermit first in a beehive hut on the Aran Islands and then in the Burren near Kinvara. Legend claims that after a total Lenten fast, angels picked up King Guaire's meal and whisked it off to Colman's cell, the King following! The King and the saint together founded the Diocese of Kilmacduagh ('church of the son of Duac') with Colman as its first bishop. He had an affinity with animals: a cockerel woke him, a mouse stopped him from going to sleep again, and a fly kept his place in his service book. The leaning tower of Kilmacduagh is almost twice as old as the leaning tower of Pisa.

REFLECTION

Would I have set a mousetrap and swatted the fly? Could I see respect and love for all of God's creation as part of my Christian path of being unconditionally loving, using deterrents such as lavender or electronic devices, rather than killing, to keep unwanted creatures out?

30 OCTOBER

St Ergnat/Herenat/Erenai/Ercnacta

D. FIFTH CENTURY. FEAST DAY: *8 January or 30 October*

Ergnat was associated mainly with Tamlacht, also Duneen, Co. Antrim, Dalriada. She was a noble lady who received the veil from St Patrick. She loved music and admired St Benignus' singing. Ergnat used to repair and wash the vestments. She did penance for her love of music. She did many signs and miracles. This early Christian saint is buried at Tamlacht.

REFLECTION

It is sad that St Ergnat felt she should do penance for loving music. If one enjoys things God made in company with Him and in gratitude to Him for them, they are good and need not be repented of. Art can lead us to God and inspire us. Ergnat's work of repairing and washing vestments must have given her an opportunity for glorifying God in the way she did her everyday tasks and finding His beauty in the ordinary things. Have I found this yet in my life?

31 OCTOBER
St Foillan/Faolan

D.655. FEAST DAY: *31 October*

Foillan was the brother of St Fursey, a holy man with a strong missionary spirit. After considerable and successful missionary work in Ireland, Foillan went with Fursey first to England, succeeding his brother as abbot in East Anglia as Fursey wished to be a hermit in the Fens. Mercians drove them out and took the fleeing monks prisoner. Foillan begged for money until he had enough to ransom his monks. He salvaged the monastery's books and brought them to France. He became the first Abbot of Peronne where Fursey was interred. Foillan was given land at Fosses by Abbess Itta of Nivelles. Later his brother Ultan became Abbot of Fosses. While visiting Nivelles, Foillan and his two companions were set upon and killed in the forest by a band of robbers. In Belgium he is known as St Pholien and in France as St Feuillen. He was a friend of St Gertrude and taught her nuns psalmody.

REFLECTION

Foillan had unshakeable faith and courage in dark times. He may have learnt that difficulties are for our spiritual growth. Have I learnt this yet?

NOVEMBER

1 NOVEMBER
St Caoimhe

Date unknown. Feast day: 2 November

Caoimhe's name is pronounced 'kwee-va' and means 'beautiful'. She was specially celebrated at Killeavy, Co. Down. Caoimhe died at the age of seventeen. Very little is known about her except her young age at death and the wonderful fact that she read the Bible to people in the streets who could not read. This alone should guarantee her a place among the saints of Ireland.

REFLECTION

Her name described her well. Reading the Bible to people in the streets who could not read when you are barely seventeen is a beautiful thing to do. Do I ever shy away from doing something beautiful for God – as St Teresa of Calcutta's and St Caoimhe's work was justly described? Could I think of a modern equivalent to Caoimhe's work that would benefit others? Perhaps if you listen to God carefully He will give you guidance about this.

2 NOVEMBER
St Erc

D.513. Feast day: 2 November

Erc was one of St Patrick's first converts, a young man in the retinue of King Laoghaire who greeted Patrick courteously and became a Christian. He lived an eremitical style of life and was known for austerities. Erc was said to have lived alone among his geese, who loved him because his heart was pure and his voice gentle. He first tried to be a hermit because the noise of his charges was getting too much for him; but when he awoke the next day he found the geese had followed him into solitude! His church at Tralee became a school for saints, including St Brendan of Clonfert. He became Bishop of Slane and was St Patrick's judge. Patrick said: 'Bishop Erc: everything he adjudged was just'. He is also remembered in Killerig (Church of Erc), Co. Carlow.

REFLECTION ~

One understanding of austerity is as a pruning of one's life. Have I sought to prune my life, or is the Holy Spirit having to do it for me in a more painful way?

3 NOVEMBER

St Malachy

D.1148. FEAST DAY: 3 or 4 November

Malachy O'Morgair was a famous Archbishop of Armagh. He undertook the complete reform of the Irish Church, re-establishing discipline, regularising worship and re-introducing monastic life. He is known to have raised King David of Scotland's son back to life. A pope – Eugenius III – was advised by the Cistercians to model his life on that of Malachy of Armagh. Malachy is well known for his prophecies about the popes and the end of the world. He was a friend of St Bernard of Clairvaux, and died at Clairvaux. Saint Bernard said of him: 'one thought he was born only for his country; and if you saw him alone, living on his own, you would have thought he lived only in God and for Him'.

REFLECTION ~

If someone was advised to model their life on mine, what would that be? What would have to change in my life for me to be described as living only in and for God?

4 NOVEMBER
St Baithen/Baithen Mór/Comin/Cominus

D.599. FEAST DAY: *9 June*

Baithen was St Columba's cousin and was chosen by him as one of the band of twelve to go on the mission to Scotland. Baithen became Abbot of Tiree, an island monastery near Iona founded by St Comgall. He later became the successor of St Columba as Abbot of Iona in 597. Baithen was held in high esteem as a wise counsellor. Columba once was so angry with him for starting divine service without him, that he sent Baithen to Ireland for confession and penance. During the last years of Columba's life, Baithen was very much Columba's right-hand man. He is called Baithen Mór (the great) to distinguish him from the other eight St Baithens. He was said to have been communing with God all day, including in between mouthfuls of his food, and that even when reaping a grain harvest he worked with one hand and held the other up to God.

REFLECTION
How possible is it for me to commune with God while doing my daily work? Are there in-between times as there were for Baithen?

5 NOVEMBER
St Lassar

D. SIXTH CENTURY. FEAST DAY: *2 March*

Lassar was a sister of St Davnet, both of them daughters of St Ronan. Her name – which means 'flame'– was given to her by St Molaise of Devenish in memory of her preservation from the flames that surrounded her cell at Devenish when it was set on fire by a band of marauders. Lassar is revered in the parish of Aughavea, near Brookeborough. The church of Killesher was founded by her. She settled at Lough Meelagh, Co. Roscommon, with her father, who became a hermit on the lake's island and died there. She founded a church called Kilronan whose ruins can still be seen near Keadue. She used to recite the psalms sitting on a high rock above Kilronan, and she wrought many miracles. Her holy well at Lough Meelagh is a place of pilgrimage.

REFLECTION

Lassar must have been preserved from the flames for a purpose. Do I see wonderful or 'lucky' escapes as God's hand in my life? Do I ever try praying or worshipping out of doors in a place that is special to me?

6 NOVEMBER

St Senell/Sinilis/Sinell

D. SIXTH CENTURY. FEAST DAY: 12 November

Senell was one of the Twelve Apostles of Ireland, tutored by St Finnian of Clonard. He founded his monastery at Cleenish (*Cluain Inis*), an island on Lough Erne, Co. Fermanagh. His regime there was very severe, not allowing any winnowing of wheat, so straw and grain were all mixed up together, ground, water added and then baked on hot stones. This was named as severe even for those days! The monastery became famous for scholarly pursuits. Columbanus studied with Senell, learning Latin grammar, rhetoric, geometry and scripture.

REFLECTION

Early Irish saints saw the harsh disciplines as a means of submitting themselves to the searching, chastening and cleansing work of the Holy Spirit. Have I experienced any of these? Perhaps at Lent we all experience some chastening; and we experience the searching of the Spirit when we examine ourselves before confession of sin. The cleansing power of the spirit is available to everyone whenever the absolution is pronounced; it is important to actually receive this cleansing absolution into oneself – imagination can help here.

7 NOVEMBER
St Begnet

D. SEVENTH CENTURY. FEAST DAY: *12 November*

Begnet, daughter of Colman son of Aedh, probably from a ruling family in Leinster, is credited with the founding of two churches. One of the churches is in Dalkey, Co. Dublin, next to Dalkey Castle. The other is on Dalkey Island, which also contains St Begnet's Holy Well and many medicinal herbs. Little is known about her, she could have been an anchorite or an abbess. Some accounts say she first started a women's convent on an island off the west coast of England but she has often been confused with St Bee/Bega. Both of Begnet's churches were under the protection of Glendalough. An icon of her written by Colette Leahy is in the modern St Begnet's church, Dalkey.

REFLECTION

Begnet would not have wandered far from God at any time but kept close. How often do I wander? How could I keep closer? These saints were able to resist temptation because they were saturated with the words of Scripture. Do I memorise scripture verses so the Spirit can bring them to my mind when in need of comfort, strength or guidance?

8 NOVEMBER
St Gerardine

D.934. FEAST DAY: *8 November*

Gerardine was one of the Cruithni or Irish Picts, who fled to Moray in Scotland in order to escape Danish invaders. He first landed at Holyman's Head near Lossiemouth, where St Gerardine's cave can still be seen. Lossiemouth has him on their coat of arms. He used to patrol the beach to offer assistance to any ships in danger of shipwreck. A legend about him says that when he came to build his little cell at Kinnedor, a flood miraculously helped him by floating the exact amount of timber needed to the spot where he planned to build.

REFLECTION

Could I expect good to come out of some situation that formerly I saw as bad, like Gerardine's timber? Patrolling the coast would have had many quiet and unoccupied moments conducive to prayer. Have I such quieter moments in my daily life? Saints were people who knew how to use silence to good effect. Am I comfortable with silence? Can I regard it as a chance to be in God's company and bask in His love?

9 NOVEMBER

St Benen/Benignus/Beannan/Mionnan

D.468. FEAST DAY: *9 November*

Benen was one of St Patrick's assistants. When Benen was very young, St Patrick came to his father Sesgne's house and converted all there. Still a child, Benen followed Patrick with great dedication, although criticised by others for his extreme devotion, continually bringing him flowers and refusing to be parted from the saint. So Sesgne gave his son to Patrick to foster. Benen became Patrick's psalm singer. He later founded two churches: one at Kilbennan in Galway, where Jarlath of Tuam later became a pupil; the other on Inis Mór in the Aran Islands. Along with St Patrick, Benen healed and baptised nine lepers, and confronted Druids successfully. He also was in Drumlease, Co. Leitrim, for seventeen years; a place where scholars believe St Patrick once thought of making his headquarters. Benen later founded an ecclesiastical school at Armagh and became the second Bishop of Armagh.

REFLECTION
Who do I feel strongly drawn to, like Benen to Patrick? Have I benefitted from their company spiritually? Patrick was a spiritual mentor to Benen, could I be a mentor or a good role model to others?

10 NOVEMBER
Venerable Catherine McAuley

D.1841. FEAST DAY: *10 November*

Catherine was the foundress of the order of Irish Sisters of Mercy. Her two great passions were education in the faith and helping the poor. She felt that only a lay organisation would be able to reach out to the street urchins of Dublin's back lanes and alleys and to people in penitentiaries. Two other women – Anna Maria Doyle and Elizabeth Harley – joined her in the effort to run a school, and the community was born. She did her novitiate in Nano Nagle's Dublin Presentation Convent. Her own community lived austerely and wore a simple uniform. By the time she died she had founded ten houses in Ireland and one in England. Some of the sisters helped Florence Nightingale with nursing in the Crimean War. Catherine was a woman of great faith and sanctity.

REFLECTION
Have I ever noticed a need or a gap needing filling and tried to do something about it as Catherine did? Are there things lay people can do that ordained cannot? Can I think of some now?

11 NOVEMBER

St Bithe

D. FIFTH CENTURY. FEAST DAY: 29 *July*

Bithe was a nephew and fellow metalworker of Assicus/Tassach who was with him, along with his mother Cipia, at Elphin. When Assicus went to be Bishop of Raholp, Bithe became the priest at Raccoon Hill in the Donegal parish of Drumhome. Assicus died and was buried in Drumhome. Legend claims that Bithe had a miraculous birth; this was due to St Mochua, who was chastised and beaten by Comgall. The legend claims that Mochua's tears while he was being chastised 'entered a barren woman's womb', and Bithe was the result. (The chronology of this would not really work, as Comgall was a century or more later; but maybe the legend refers to another St Bithe as there were quite a few St Bithes, both male and female.)

REFLECTION
St Mochua's tears healing a barren womb seems fanciful but is probably symbolic; possibly he prayed for her when in his sadness and those prayers worked. Have I found that when we are suffering it enables us to be more compassionate to others' suffering? Could I offer my tears of sadness to God to be used in a creative way to help someone in need?

12 NOVEMBER

St Cummian the Tall/Cummian Fota

D.665. FEAST DAY: 12 *November*

Cummian was an abandoned child found in a basket outside St Ita's convent at Killeady. He was named Cummian after the basket he was found in. He wrote a famous letter trying to get the Iona monks to accept the 'Roman' date for Easter in order to be in line with the rest of Christendom. Cummian had wide learning and wrote a *Lorica* for protection against the Yellow Plague. He was also the author of a very severe penitential, used by the *Céili Dé* movement and influenced by John Cassian. He was a monk at Clonfert and then became Abbot of Durrow. He may also have been the fourth successor to Brendan as Abbot of Clonfert. Not to be confused with his nephew Cumine. Cummian was regarded as Ireland's most distinguished seventh-century scholar.

REFLECTION
A *Lorica* is a protection prayer. *St Patrick's Breastplate* is one example. When I need protection, do I turn to God and His angels? Do I realise they only need an invitation, wanting to both help us but also to respect our freedom of will?

13 NOVEMBER
St Caillin

D. SIXTH CENTURY. *FEAST DAY:* 13 *November*

Caillin is associated with St Aedan of Ferns. It is possible that he was his tutor. He was descended from the Druid Dubhtach. An old story claims that when Caillin was building his monastic foundation at Fiodhnach (Fenagh), the King of Breiffne sent some Druids against him. Caillin responded by turning the Druids into stone. The old records mention a sea of signs and miracles, and that he was a burning fire against the persecution of God and his church. Another story is of the famous bell of St Caillin or Bell of Fenagh – *Clog-na-Righ* – which was used to hold the water for the baptism of nineteen Irish kings. One of Caillin's poems is in *The Book of Fenagh*. He was brother to the chief bard of Ireland, Seanchan. He was instrumental in bringing about the recovery of the then lost epic poem *Táin Bó Cúailnge*.

REFLECTION
Caillin was on fire about persecution. Am I on fire for anything?

What? Do I need to pray about this? Ireland will always be grateful for Caillin saving the valuable archive of the Tain. Do I realise the value historic things have for the light they throw on history, which is after all something we all should be learning from?

14 NOVEMBER
St Lawrence O'Toole/Lorcan Ua Tuathail

D.1180. FEAST DAY: *14 November*

Lawrence O'Toole was a man of self-effacing and self-denying ministry. He became Abbot of Glendalough at the age of twenty-five, then in 1161 was chosen unanimously by the clergy and laity of Dublin to be their first archbishop. His icon shows him with loaves of bread because he attempted to feed the poor of Dublin. He rebuilt wooden Christchurch Cathedral in stone. He was made a papal legate, and was asked to mediate between Dermot MacMurrough and Henry II, but Henry went to France. Lawrence followed him but died at Eu in Normandy before he could see Henry. Miracles occurred at his tomb and he was declared a saint forty-five years after his death. His heart hangs in a heart-shaped shrine in Christchurch Cathedral, Dublin – once stolen, but now restored.

REFLECTION

Trying to feed the poor of Dublin must have been like trying to fill a swimming pool with a thimble! Do I ever refuse to help because I feel that my help would be such a 'drop in the ocean'? Who might I begin to help in a small way now?

15 NOVEMBER
St Fintan of Rheinau

D.878. FEAST DAY: *15 November*

Fintan was an Irishman from Leinster who was abducted by Viking raiders. He prayed to God for help vowing that if he escaped he would make a pilgrimage to Rome. He plunged into the sea at the Orkneys and swam to shore. A kindly bishop took him in. Fintan accomplished his pilgrimage to Rome two years later on foot, and then settled as a hermit on the island of Rheinau on the River Rhine near Schaffhausen. He was the founder of the monastery in Rheinau. He was given to visions and hearing the voice of angels (in the Gaelic tongue). Fintan's calendar and missal are preserved at Zurich and St Gall, and his feasts are still kept at Rheinau.

REFLECTION

Fintan was courageous to leap from the ship. God answered his prayer even more than he had asked for, by providing for him and his education. Has God answered my prayers in a similar way? Do I need to pray for something I haven't wanted to 'bother God about'?

16 NOVEMBER
St Cillian/Killian/Chillen of Artois

D.681. FEAST DAY: *13 November*

Cillian was a prince of Dalriada, who was tempted by military victory, but eventually opted for heavenly victory. He was very humble and refused an abbacy at first then reluctantly agreed, and later became a bishop. He was very successful but desired solitude and prayer. He prayed to God to lead him to a place of spiritual toil where his princely rank would not be known. While returning from a pilgrimage to Rome, at age fifty, Cillian visited his kinsman Fiacre in France, and stayed on as a missionary. Based at Aubigny near Arras, he preached the Gospel throughout Artois until his death, keeping up his austerities. Cillian was offered the papacy but refused – the only Irishman to have been offered this.

REFLECTION

Would I be capable of starting a new career in a foreign land at the age of fifty? And would I be as dismissive of status as Cillian was? Have I yet discovered that victory over my own weaknesses and temptations is far more worthwhile than military victory or other kinds of worldly victories?

17 NOVEMBER

St Doulaigh/Doolagh/Dúileach

D. EARLY EIGHTH CENTURY. FEAST DAY: *1 August, 17 November in Christchurch Cathedral*

Doulaigh was from the West of Ireland, Co. Clare, near Loop Head. Doulaigh's uncle, one of several Baodáns, was patron of a Leinster church. Christchurch's first grange was called *Kildulyc* (Church of Doulaigh) and was situated at present-day Grangegorman. Doulaigh is revered in North Dublin churches. His 'bed' at St Doulaigh's Church, a Church of Ireland church near Malahide, was held in high repute by women fearful of dying in childbirth. In 697 he was one of the guarantors of Adamnan's *Law of the Innocents*, exempting women, children and monks from fighting in battles.

REFLECTION

Despite being from the West of Ireland, Doulaigh must have been willing to go where God guided him, open to the wind of the Spirit. He knew that when we belong to God we are moving gradually from a self-centred life to a God-centred life. Could I say the same of myself? Am I ready for wherever the Spirit may lead?

18 NOVEMBER
St Deicuil/Desle

D. C.625. FEAST DAY: *18 January*

Deicuil was a monk at Bangor who accompanied St Columbanus on his journeys as far as Luxeuil in France. He succumbed to fatigue at that point and was blessed by Columbanus and then left behind. Deicuil knelt to pray for help, dying of thirst and a little spring of water gushed out from under his staff. He built a cell there, and used to pray in a small chapel nearby, whose priest complained of this man for whom doors opened without keys. This called attention to him and disciples flocked to him attracted by his learning and his miracles. A monastery grew up there and became the Abbey of Lure, where he is still revered as St Desle. The spring had the reputation of healing childhood illnesses.

REFLECTION

This is a good example of acceptance and making the best of a less than perfect situation. Do I accept the weaker areas of my life? Do I make the best of them, and pray that good may come out of a potentially bad situation? (Nothing is impossible for God!)

19 NOVEMBER
St Cathbad/Chathbad/Cathbhadhe/Cobthach

D.555. FEAST DAY: *6 April*

Cathbad was a follower of St Patrick and had been left by him to look after a church now called Kilmakevit (*Cill-mo-Chathbad*) in Co. Antrim, in the townland of Markstown. An incorrect rumour grew up locally that this church was founded by a Druid as St Cathbad had the same name as Cathbad the Magician who features in stories in *The Ulster Cycle*. According to *The Annals of Inisfallen*, Cathbad became the Bishop of Lieth Cuind.

REFLECTION

All sorts of incorrect rumours can spring up. If we know of them we can correct them; if we don't we have no need to worry about them. Have I managed to become resilient and not be upset by false rumours, especially if I cannot trace their origin? Can I react and deal with them in a calm manner? Can I help dispel any rumours about other people I know to be false? If I am in a position to do God's work, I should acknowledge and accept that I will be somewhat visible in public, which might make some people speculate. If I have been hurt by this, could I pray and ask for God's healing?

20 NOVEMBER

St Vougay/Vie/Vio/Vauk

D.585. FEAST DAY: 15 June

Vougay was possibly a bishop in Ireland before going to Brittany as a missionary where he became an archbishop. Legend says he went abroad because he was made a canon in Armagh and he hated the honour. He lived first as a hermit before large crowds came to him to be healed. Vougay founded a church between present-day St Pol-de-Leon and Saint-Thégonnec, today known as Saint Vougay. Vougay is credited with being a saint of such spiritual resources that he was able when needed to appease the raging of the sea in that part of the Finisterre coast.

REFLECTION

Do I seek honours or can I do without them? Do I realise that Vougay's spiritual resources that even quelled storms are available to me as well? It was not his own power but God's spirit working through him. Do I believe that with God nothing is impossible? What seems impossible in my life today? Or in the world? Could I ask God's help to transform either the situation, or my attitude to it?

21 NOVEMBER

Venerable Nano Nagle

D.1784. FEAST DAY: *26 April*

Honora Nagle, known as Nano, was a spirited girl from a well-to-do background in north Co. Cork, born in penal times. She was educated in France due to the penal laws. On her return, she brought her mother home a present of some silk. When she discovered that her mother had sold it to give alms to the poor, this started Nano's vocation, especially as her mother died soon afterwards. Nano became determined to devote herself to helping the poor. After a short time as a nun in Paris, she returned to Ireland and started schools in mud cabins helping and educating the sick and the poor. Soon other girls joined her and she started the Presentation Order, which is now worldwide. Nano founded seven schools.

REFLECTION
Nano knew the value and importance of education for everyone. When have I seen an event of my life as a 'wake-up call'? Am I supporting the kind of charities which educate and teach skills to people in order to help them to help themselves?

22 NOVEMBER

St Enan

D. EARLY SIXTH CENTURY. FEAST DAY: *25 March*

Enan was a monk at St Comgall's monastery at Bangor. One day he saw Comgall making a coffin with his own hands. He admired it and said he would like to be buried in it! He died soon afterwards and was put in the coffin; but Comgall raised him to life again. Enan lived a long time after that and often spoke of his death experience. Apparently two angels carried him to heaven, but on the way they met two blessed spirits who said that Enan had to be re-united with his body.

REFLECTION

Enan's wish to be buried in the coffin his abbot had made became a self-fulfilling prophecy! Have I experienced my own words coming true in this way? Do I fully realise the power of words? Could saying negative things about a person bind them closer to that sin rather than releasing them? Could I ask Jesus' help to try and always say positive things about people?

23 NOVEMBER

St Columbanus/Columban

D.615. Feast day: 23 November

Columbanus trained under Finnian at Moville and then at Bangor under Comgall, where he stayed on to teach. He desired to go on a *peregrinatio pro Christi*, a pilgrimage for Christ, so as to shine the light of Christ into dark places on the Continent. At the age of fifty-four he set off for Europe with twelve companions, founding three monasteries in present-day France: at Annegray, Luxeuil and Fontaines. He continued on to Italy where he founded a fourth monastery in Bobbio, which lasted until 1802. His penitential shows he had a particularly harsh Rule. Columbanus wrote to the Pope on several occasions, once about the date of Easter. He stubbornly kept to the early Irish rather than Roman ways but submitted to the authority of the Pope. Today twenty-three Italian churches are dedicated to him.

REFLECTION

Does age ever hold me back? If I feel something is wrong could I be productive about it and write to the Pope, an archbishop, a bishop, a member of parliament or even the editor of a newspaper about it?

24 NOVEMBER
St Colman of Cloyne

D.606. FEAST DAY: 24 November

Colman was a native of Muskerry who succeeded his father as poet laureate at the court of the King of Cashel. He was one of the first Irish poets to use Latin rhymes. While there, he was so impressed by St Brendan of Birr's miraculous finding of St Ailbhe's stolen relics, which Brendan rescued from a lake, that he became a Christian. Brendan of Clonfert baptised him. Colman studied under St Brendan and St Jarlath of Tuam. He went on to become the first Bishop of Cloyne. He is one of the most famous of the ninety-six recorded St Colmans. He had six saintly sisters. He wrote a poem in praise of St Brendan and a life of St Senan of Scattery Island.

REFLECTION

What miracle inspires me to rejoice in the Christian faith? How about the miracle of rebirth in nature every year? And the sheer beauty of creation? Have I enough awe and wonder at such beauty and grandeur? Does the poet in me need nurturing?

25 NOVEMBER
St Finchu

D.664. FEAST DAY: 25 November

Finchu became a bishop at Brigown, the monastery founded by St Abban near present-day Mitchelstown, Co. Cork. He was a man of remarkable asceticism. He is said to have surrendered his place in heaven to a king of the Decies. He commenced to win a new place for himself by mortifying his flesh with 'seven sickles made by seven smiths'. He died of the Yellow Plague. The remains of a round tower can still be seen at Brigown.

REFLECTION ∽

Giving up his place in heaven for someone else was surely the ultimate sacrifice; however, trying to win a new place in heaven seems to lessen its splendour somewhat! Do I ever make huge promises that I am unable to keep? Certainly the King of the Decies would have been a key figure locally and his conversion would likely have led to many more in his kingdom embracing Christianity. Could I pray for world leaders to respond and rule with more kindness?

26 NOVEMBER
St Connoc/Thégonnec/Tegoneg (in Breton)/Goennec

D. SIXTH CENTURY. FEAST DAY: *unknown*

Connoc was an Irish bishop who arrived in Brittany in 530 with Paulus Aurelius from Wales. Paulus became St Pol-de-Leon, and Connoc became known as St Thégonnec in French. Both saints have towns named after them in Finisterre. Possibly Connoc's full Irish name might have been Tigernach; there was a Bishop of Quimper called Goennec who might be him. The only legend we have about him claims that a wolf devoured Connoc's horse. Not wanting to kill the wolf, Connoc imposed a penance on it instead. The wolf was harnessed to a cart and pulled the logs used to build the monastery.

REFLECTION ∽

Connoc made the punishment fit the crime and it was better to use the wolf rather than kill him. Have I ever been able to similarly save the life of an animal? Could I harness the animals' energies as people did long ago? Could I conceive of the fact that dogs, cats, horses, pigs and poultry are not the only animals capable of being domesticated? Could I pray about our use of animals today?

27 NOVEMBER
St Fergal/Virgil/Virgilius

D. C.784. FEAST DAY: 27 November

Fergal was the Abbot of Aghaboe who left the monastery and set out for the Continent. He preached the Gospel faithfully there alongside many other Irish missionaries in Bavaria and Carinthia, founding monasteries, churches and schools. After St Boniface attempted to denounce Fergal because of his cosmological theories, Fergal became Bishop of Salzburg. He was a humble bishop, joining in with his monks in their preaching journeys to the boundaries of Bavaria, often as far as the Hungarian border. Fergal was also well known as an astronomer and theologian.

REFLECTION
St Fergal's boundless energy no doubt came from his being filled with the Spirit. Do I regard spirit-filledness as something special, or could I see it as a normal part of the Christian day-to-day life? Fergal was a keen missionary; deserving of the epitaph in the garden of Dromantine to the African Mission Fathers: 'They were missionaries from the bottom of their hearts'. What am I doing or what could I be doing from the bottom of my heart?

28 NOVEMBER
St Seachnall/Secundinus

D.448. FEAST DAY: 27 November

Seachnall, in 453, founded the original church where St Seachnall's Church of Ireland Church stands today in Dunshaughlin, Co. Meath. He is described as a man of great wisdom and sanctity. An old story tells that Seachnall had a disagreement with Patrick due to a chance remark someone twisted that spread. Patrick called to him to explain. Then an angel appeared and addressed them both with words of love and wisdom and they were reconciled. He was not shy of reproving Patrick. A hymn to St Patrick in *The Antiphonary of Bangor* is attributed to him. Seachnall was fourteen years older than Patrick, which makes him less likely to have been Patrick's nephew as some have suggested.

REFLECTION

Am I careful about chance remarks that could be twisted or misinterpreted? If shy of saying anything negative to my superiors, could I make the comment in a gracious and gentle way without giving offence? Have I heard the old saying that 'one can say anything to anybody if one says it in the right way'?

29 NOVEMBER

St Brendan of Birr

D.573. FEAST DAY: *29 November*

Brendan was one of the Twelve Apostles of Ireland and known as the 'chief of the prophets of Ireland'. He was the Abbot of Birr monastery which produced *The MacRegol Gospels*. He was a loyal friend of St Columba and defended him in a synod at Teltown where he was being threatened with excommunication after the Battle of Cooldrevny. Brendan was the only one to stand and greet him and said: 'I dare not slight the man chosen by God to lead nations into life.' Columba had a vision of angels receiving St Brendan's soul at his death and said a Requiem Mass for him before his death had been confirmed.

REFLECTION

Brendan would have known about Columba's future great mission in Scotland, by his ability to hear God's voice. God speaks to us all if only we would listen. Do I listen to God enough? Have I learned to discern His gentle voice from the loud voices of the world, my own ego, and the subtle voice of the enemy?

30 NOVEMBER
St Odhrán

D. FIFTH CENTURY. FEAST DAY: *19 February*

Odhrán drove the cart or chariot in which St Patrick travelled. Sensing that there would be an attack on the saint's life, he pretended to be tired in order to change places with the saint, sending him to lead the horses, and sitting in the cart himself. Odhrán was killed, thus saving Patrick's life. Patrick was about to curse the murderer but the dying Odhrán begged him to place the curse instead on a large tree on a nearby hill. The murderer, a pagan chief whose idol Patrick had destroyed, was called Failge Berraide, and he became deaf.

REFLECTION

Odhrán was completely selfless. His dying request was to ask Patrick not to curse the pagan chief to death. Odhrán was also pragmatic for he realised that if the chieftain did convert he would have the influence to bring many others with him. Have I any opportunities to bear witness to my faith to someone with influence over others?

DECEMBER

1 DECEMBER
St Comghan

D. EIGHTH CENTURY. FEAST DAY: *13 October*

Comghan was a trained warrior. He succeeded his father Cellach Cualan as Prince of Leinster in 715. However, an arrow pierced his foot and he was left with a limp. In 717 he sailed to Scotland – forced to seek asylum because of the hostility of neighbouring tribes. He went as a servant of Christ, taking with him his widowed sister Kentigerna and her sons, including his nephew Fillan. They probably landed near Whithorn, near the village of Kirkcowan. They settled in Lochalsh, on the mainland opposite the island of Skye. He became abbot of a Culdee settlement at Turriff. Both Comghan and his nephew Fillan are buried on Iona.

REFLECTION

The arrow that pierced Comghan's foot led to a happy change of career. Can I think of times in my life when an accident forced me to change course, or when things turned out differently – but better – than expected? Could I see these as examples of God bringing good out of bad situations?

2 DECEMBER
St Ronan of Kilronan

D. SEVENTH CENTURY. FEAST DAY: *23 June*

Ronan was eighth in descent from Niall of the Nine Hostages, probably from a part of Co. Monaghan near Lough Erne. He is the patron of Aughalurcher near Lisnaskea. Saints Davnet and Lassar were his daughters. Saint Lassar was educated by St Molaise of Devenish. Ronan and his daughter Lassar had their headquarters on the shores of Lough Meelagh, in present-day

Kilronan parish which they founded. Kilronan is on the borders of Leitrim and Roscommon. There they used to pray daily on the island of Inishmore on Lough Meelagh, later named the Island of the Saints. He took himself off permanently to the solitude of that island when he felt his end was near.

REFLECTION

Regular contemplative prayer breaks down our masks and makes us more real and allows God to do His work of transformation in us. How available am I to God for this to happen in my life? Would it be best not to wait until our end is near to start this process?

3 DECEMBER

St Colm McCrimthann

D.549. FEAST DAY: *24 March*

Colm was a hermit on the island of Iniscaltra on Lough Derg. A friend asked him why the birds did not fly away from him the way they did from other people. His answer is very revealing of the man: 'Why should birds fly from a bird? For just as a bird flies, my soul never ceases to fly up to heaven'.

REFLECTION

We could add that the birds would have felt at home and completely unthreatened by Colm, as with Sts Kevin and Francis of Assisi. Animals, birds and even plants can sense a person's love towards them. Have I yet discovered this secret of how to get on with the Kingdom of Nature? What am I doing to help protect our animals, plants, minerals and the planet we all share? A desire to fly is deep within us all; have I discovered that ecstasy of spiritually flying to God, the lightness of the joy of knowing Him? How could I get to that as my 'default mode'?

4 DECEMBER
St Brochan/Berchan/Broghan

D. SEVENTH CENTURY. FEAST DAY: *4 December*

Brochan was known as 'Berchan of the Prophecy'. There is a holy well at Clonsast, the church he founded, called St Brochan's well. Many cures have been attributed to it. Clonsast is eight kilometres from Portarlington, Co. Laois. *The Book of Clonsast* is one of the lost books of Erin but part of it, including a beautiful hymn or prayer to the Virgin Mary, is contained in the *Leabhar Breac* (the Speckled Book) which is in the Royal Irish Academy in Dublin. Saint Canice visited the monastery of Clonsast at a time when a blind, deaf and speechless boy, Ermine, had just died. They had all been very fond of Ermine; the community was grieving and fasting around the bier. Canice prayed over Ermine's corpse and returned him to life with his sight, hearing and speech. Ermine became a great and holy man.

REFLECTION

Ermine was obviously taken into the monastery and became part of the family there. Do I treat disabled people with a similar welcome and give them a chance to become part of my family or community so that people may become fond of them?

5 DECEMBER
St Beircheart/Beretchert/Benjamin/Beireachtuine

D.839. FEAST DAY: *6 December*

Beircheart was from Tullylease, in Duhallow parish, Co. Cork. There is a cross-slab there inviting prayer for him. There are several townlands named Kilberrihert after him, and also holy wells. Otherwise not much is known about him, except that possibly he could have been a great, great nephew of St Gerald of

Mayo, as his name is an Irish edition of an Anglo-Saxon name – Beorhtwine.

REFLECTION

One can only speculate that if he was an Anglo-Saxon who felt called by God to come to Ireland, Beircheart was a brave man to come to an unknown land with no certainty about where he would settle, or if he would be welcomed and no guarantees of success in his mission. This prompts me to ask myself, do I only set out to serve God when I am guaranteed success, or do I take a leap in the dark? How comfortable am I with uncertainty? Can I learn to put my whole trust in God for my future as obviously Beircheart did?

6 DECEMBER

St Gobban/Gobhan

D.567. FEAST DAY: *6 December*

Gobban was a holy man who started a monastery at (Old) Leighlin in present-day Co. Carlow. There were said to be as many as fifteen hundred monks under his charge there. He prophesied the coming of St Laserian to Leighlin, when he saw a vision of a crowd of angels hovering over the place. Gobban said a saintly stranger would come and gather as many servants of God there as there were angels in the heavenly host. He resigned his abbacy to Laserian, and then founded Seagoe, Co. Armagh, and finally retired to Killamery, where he is said to have ruled over a thousand monks. There is a fine, carved ninth-century high cross on a hill above the village of Killamery. Gobban is buried at Clonenagh.

REFLECTION

It takes humility to publicly praise one's successor as better than oneself. Could I do the same? Could I resign my place to another in a similar way to Gobban, and move on? How do I decide when to move on? Do I pray about it?

7 DECEMBER
St Buite/Boiote/Byuithin/Buin/Boecius

D.521. FEAST DAY: *7 December*

Buite was one of the most illustrious disciples of St Teilo in Llandaff, Wales, who also founded some churches in Scotland. His missionary work among the Picts included baptising King Nechtan and restoring the King's son to life. He then returned to his native Co. Louth *circa* 500 and became the founder-Abbot of Monasterboice (which is named after him). This was built on a previously pagan site. Today one of the finest high crosses – St Muredach's Cross – can be seen there. When Buite lay dying, on the day of St Columba's birth, he predicted 'a child illustrious before God and Men'.

REFLECTION

Am I as quick to praise others as Buite was? Can I inspire and have faith in the next generation? How easy would it be for me to cultivate the habit of always seeing the best in people, their potential rather than their faults? Likewise with my country, could I see it as becoming part of the God's Kingdom of Love?

8 DECEMBER
St Aifric/Afraic/Affrica

D. NINTH CENTURY. FEAST DAY: *unknown*

Aifric was the daughter of Cumlachtach. She was from Clonfad, in Upperwoods, Co. Laois. She was one of the only two abbesses of St Brigid's monastery in Kildare not to have had an Irish name. She had links with the church of Imleach Tuaiscirt. Aifric has become a fairly common Christian name for girls.

REFLECTION

Although not much is known about Aifric, no news could be good news: because she was in a position of public responsibility, if there was anything amiss it would have been known about. She was probably a person who quietly got on with the work and avoided anything spectacular. Also, to be counted a saint, she must have been a person who abided in Christ – thinking the same thoughts as Him and loving with the same love as Him and guided by the same Spirit. Have I made any progress towards a more continuous abiding in the vine that is Jesus Christ? What more is needed?

9 DECEMBER

St Charles of St Andrew

D.1893. FEAST DAY: 5 January

Charles was a Passionist priest who spent all of his ministry in Dublin. He was born John Andrew Houben in the Netherlands but came to Ireland in 1857. His ministry in the confessional was renowned, and the poor of Dublin found him a great support. He was canonised in 2007.

REFLECTION

As a confessor Charles was exercising a wonderful ministry. There are many ways of exercising ministries, and St Paul lists a number of them. How could some of the work I do become a ministry to others? Could I visualise this happening and pray about it?

10 DECEMBER
St Emer

D. FIFTH CENTURY. FEAST DAY: *11 December*

Emer was one of the two daughters – both called Emer – of Miluic for whom St Patrick had worked as a slave. Miluic immolated himself rather than meet his former slave, but his family followed Patrick. Patrick gave the veil to the two sisters, who were possibly the first nuns in Ireland. They were in all likelihood the founders of the convent of Clonbroney that St Fuinnech and then St Samthann became abbesses of later. Their nephews, Colman Muilinn and Mochae, both became saints.

REFLECTION

Miluic's daughters had no such problems as their father had with meeting Patrick, his former slave now returned as a bishop. Do I regard class as a barrier or do I totally disregard such a thing? What would Jesus have done? Would I agree that there is no room for snobbery in the Christian church? Can I honestly say I have lived up to that ideal?

11 DECEMBER
St Multose/Eltin/Maeltog

D. SIXTH CENTURY. FEAST DAY: *11 December*

Multose – who was possibly the son of Cobhtach – founded a monastery on the site of the present-day St Multose's Church in Kinsale, Co. Cork. Little is known about him, but there is a legend that as he was building the church and lifting stones to do so, he called for help. As no one local helped him, Multose put a curse on the place saying that it would be peopled with foreigners. He is also the patron of several other Munster churches in Co. Kerry and Co. Waterford.

REFLECTION

The people of Kinsale today – especially in the tourist trade – might well see the prophecy of the town being peopled with foreigners as a blessing rather than a curse! It is a pretty seaside town and has been a desirable place to move to. Today the town is quite cosmopolitan. Is there anything in my life which started out as a curse but turned out to be a blessing? Have I confidence that God can bring good out of a bad situation?

12 DECEMBER

St Finnian of Clonard

D.549. FEAST DAY: *12 December or 23 February*

Finnian was tutored by Bishop Fortchern and Gildas the Wise. His first monastery was at Aghowle ('Apple Tree Field'), Co. Carlow. He was called 'the Tutor of the Saints of Ireland', as many well-known saints of Ireland were tutored by him, including Colmcille, Comgall, Canice, Brendan and Ciarán. He was an excellent role model for them all. He lived very ascetically using earth as a bed and a stone for a pillow; eating only barley bread and water, with fish on Sundays and holy days. Legend claims St Brigid at Kildare gave him a gold ring that he tried to refuse; on his way home he met a man who needed an ounce of gold to pay his ransom to the King and the ring came in handy. His large monastic university at Clonard, Co. Meath, founded *circa* 520, also welcomed many scholars from abroad. Finnian died of yellow fever having put himself at risk to save others' lives.

REFLECTION

God had a plan for that gold ring. Do I realise that unusual things that happen, taking me outside my comfort zone, are often God's will? God works in mysterious ways. Can I apply that to my life now?

13 DECEMBER

St Colm/Colum/Colman of Terryglass

D.549. FEAST DAY: *13 December*

Colm was one of the Twelve Saints of Ireland tutored by St Finnian of Clonard. Saint Finnian's successor at Clonard, St Senach, was asked once by Finnian to report on what all the students were doing. Of Colm he said he was praying, with his arms outstretched towards heaven oblivious to all, with the birds alighting on his shoulders. Finnian said that he would be the one to give him the last rites. Saint Colm became the Abbot of Terryglass, Co. Tipperary, on the River Shannon. He also founded the monastery of Iniscaltra, on Lough Derg, and also the monastery of Clonenagh, where his disciple St Fintan stayed on to become a famous abbot. Terryglass was where he used to retreat for private prayer.

REFLECTION

One does not need to be an abbot to have a need to retire for private prayer! Have I established a place where I can go quietly for prayer or meditation? Maybe even a corner of a room, or a hut in the garden?

14 DECEMBER

St Palladius

D.432. FEAST DAY: *31 July*

Palladius had been archdeacon to Pope Celestine at Rome who sent him to Ireland in 431, a year before Patrick's arrival, to combat the Pelagian heresy into which the church in Ireland had fallen. Not much is known of his ministry in Ireland, except that the people were not willing to accept his doctrine. Some of his deeds may well have been attributed to Patrick and he may even have been known also as Patricius, a patrician, as *The Book of Armagh* claims, as being a patrician gave the authority to travel in those early days. However, Palladius is said to have baptised and taught the holy saint Ailbhe. A year before his death, Pope Celestine sent him to Scotland and he died there at the church of Fordun near Aberdeen which he had founded.

REFLECTION

Palladius' doctrine being unacceptable could have been because it was not offered with love or presented as joyful good news. Although Palladius gets very little credit for good things he may have done, baptising Ailbhe made up for it all!

15 DECEMBER

St Cadán/Gedanus

D. FIFTH CENTURY. FEAST DAY: *12 December*

Cadán was Bishop of Tamlaghtard, near Magilligan, Co. Derry. The son of Madán, his tomb is under the gable end of the ancient church at Tamlaght. The local surname of McIllhatton – an anglicisation of Mac Giolla Chatáin – reflects devotion to him. He is listed as a servant in the lists of orders under Patrick.

REFLECTION

In Christian life there should be no hierarchy, all are equal in the eyes of God. Choosing bishops was more of a community affair then and Cadán/Gedanus must have been the best man for the job, God's choice for the Christian family in that place. Rather than having great plans for God, these early Irish saints allowed God's plans for them to be accomplished. Have I erred in this regard? It is all too easy to plan God's work rather than wait for his plans to be accomplished in and through us. The prayer of Jesus was always 'Your will be done'. Could it be mine?

16 DECEMBER
St Maighnenn/Maghnend

D. SEVENTH CENTURY. FEAST DAY: *18 December*

Maighnenn was one of the four sons of Aodh, a king of Oirthir, who had died in Clonmacnoise where he had gone as a pilgrim. He founded the church of Kilmainham in Dublin, which in the thirteenth century was the headquarters of the Knights Hospitaller. Maighnenn also gave his name to Kilmainham Beg and Kilmainham Wood, Co. Meath. He visited many other saints in Ireland. Maighnenn and St Fursey 'exchanged troubles' – Fursey giving Maighnenn a headache, piles and other troubles, including a ravenous reptile!

REFLECTION

Maighnenn seems to have been friendly and compassionate, more than just a good listener, as taking other peoples' troubles on himself seems a Christ-like thing to do. Maybe it meant he had a ministry of intercession. Even though I cannot take my friends' troubles on myself, could I have a ministry of intercession for them? Even to think of a sufferer with compassion is a kind of prayer. How compassionate am I for those suffering? How patient am I at listening to their woes, small as well as big?

17 DECEMBER
Michan/Michean/Michanus

DATE UNKNOWN. FEAST DAY: *25 August*

Michan has a large church dedicated to him in Dublin close to the Liffey, but little is known of him. It is thought he was from Danish stock. As he is mentioned in a list of martyrs, Michan may have been martyred himself. A rather fantastic life was written about him saying he was the son of a Canaanite king who travelled to Dublin from the Holy Land. Scholars are undecided about whether or not he was Irish. He obviously founded several churches and was also included in a list of the chief saints in Ireland, by his biographer, Henry Fitzsimon.

REFLECTION

Whether or not Michan was martyred for his faith, he was a martyr in the sense of witnessing to the faith. How do I witness to my faith? Do I share what Christ means to me and how he came to be a reality in my life today? Maybe I do it by my life? We live in a wordy society and Masses and church services are very wordy, so we often forget that meeting God is done in silence.

18 DECEMBER

St Flannan

D.640. FEAST DAY: *18 December*

Flannan was a monk and disciple of St Molua. He spent a lot of time travelling on missionary pilgrimages, and possibly reached Scotland where he is remembered – the Flannan Isles in the Hebrides are named after him. He is said to have made a pilgrimage to Rome 'on a floating stone' (his portable altar) where he was consecrated bishop by Pope John IV. When Flannan returned his fellow pilgrims gave him a gift of Friar's Island on the River Shannon. He is said to have been disappointed by his listeners' lack of interest. He succeeded Molua as Bishop of Killaloe taking on the abbot's duties during Molua's lifetime. Saint Flannan's oratory can still be seen beside the cathedral.

REFLECTION

What object would be best to pack when travelling to help make my journey and my stay into a pilgrimage rather than just a vacation? Flannan might have been failing to inspire his listeners; how could he have caught their attention? How can I help inspire the people I meet every day?

19 DECEMBER
St Samthann/Safan

D.739. FEAST DAY: *19 December*

Samthann became a nun after being widowed. She was in Urney, Co. Cavan, as a stewardess when called to be Abbess of Clonbroney. She was a poet, and a strong influence upon the *Céili Dé* movement. Her convent at Clonbroney was small at first, with only six cows, but was later reckoned to be one of the three most important convents of Ireland. Many miracles have been attributed to her and she interceded with kings on behalf of prisoners and hostages. When asked about the best posture for prayer she said, 'Each and all of them'. She advised a monk who wanted to give up study for prayer only, that he needed to study to develop his concentration to help keep his mind on his prayers. One of her sayings is: 'The distance to heaven is the same from every part of the earth'.

REFLECTION

Might several postures for prayer, in each of which one can say different sorts of things to God, be as yet untried by me? Samthann's view of every part of the earth being equal is inspirational. Do I share the same view or do I judge certain countries, places or people unfairly? How can I amend my view to be more like Samthann?

20 DECEMBER
St Fraoch/Fraochan/Frign/Cruimther Fraoch/Criffer Ree

D. C.570. FEAST DAY: *20 December*

Fraoch was the founder of the monastery at Cloone, near Mohill in Ardagh Diocese. Columba is reputed to have visited this holy man to say farewell before setting out for Scotland. Saint Fraoch gave Columba an upbraiding for the Battle of Cooldrevny.

Columba tried to put the blame on King Dairmuid and Fraoch is said to have told him it would have been more godly to have submitted to the unfair judgement. 'It is better to stifle wrath lest it make matter for regret,' Fraoch advised Columba. They parted friends. He was a good friend of St Caillin (his foster father) and succeeded him as Abbot at Fenagh.

REFLECTION
Fraoch was unafraid to speak the truth to Columba, but did so in a fatherly way. Can I learn from this? The way we say a thing makes a big difference. Have I some way to go yet in learning how to master in myself a tendency to impulsive anger? Or is there some friend or family member I could help to achieve such mastery?

21 DECEMBER

St Ursin/Ursinus/Ursanne/Ursicinus

D. C.625. FEAST DAY: *20 December*

Ursin was one of Columbanus' band of Irish disciples. While accompanying Columbanus on his journey from Luxeuil, they came to a wilderness inhabited by bears, in present-day Switzerland. Ursin is said to have stayed there and trained the bears to do his bidding – the word 'ursine' means of or relating to bears. When other disciples joined him, he moved to the valley and started a hospice for the poor and needy. Ursin would keep special oxen for transporting the sick to the hospice. He was known for his holiness and his miracles. He was known as St Ursanne in Switzerland, and his monastery grew into the town of St Ursanne.

REFLECTION
Ursin certainly had a way with animals, and humans have often been able to tame bears for domestic use. However, metaphorically there is a lesson here: do I push down into my subconscious the wild animals of my lower self or do I tame them? Do I realise that their energy and their good qualities, if tamed, could help me in

my life? Could I think about the possibilities of this under the guidance of the Holy Spirit?

22 DECEMBER
St Nessan of Lambay

D. SIXTH CENTURY. FEAST DAY: *15 March*

Nessan had a hermitage on Lambay Island off the coast of Co. Dublin, the ruins of which can still be seen. He had seven sons who all entered the church, among them Dichull Dearg of Ireland's Eye, Nesas and Neslugha. The copy of the Gospels known as *The Garland of Howth*, now in Trinity College Dublin, probably came from the Lambay monastery. Nessan shares his feast day with his sons.

REFLECTION
Nessan's life shows that family life is not a bar to sanctity! Do I ever use the excuse of family life to avoid taking steps to increase my spiritual connection and grow in spiritual maturity to become holy and Christ-like? Do I realise that family life is a steep learning curve and you need to take the rough with the smooth (sometimes painfully)? Have I experienced this abrasion as something positive? Could I change my attitude to it if not? Have I benefited from the practice family life gives me in forgiving, especially difficult people, and in accepting and even celebrating differences in others?

23 DECEMBER
St Mochorogh

D. C.700. FEAST DAY: *23 December*

Mochorogh was the son of a British king and a Saxon queen, who came over with his brother Canoc in search of St

Kevin. He founded churches at Delgany and Enniskerry, Co. Wicklow. He retired as a hermit to present-day Kilmacurragh near Rathdrum, whose church was built later by King Ronan of Leinster, named for his daughter Cred. The abbey there lasted until the sixteenth century. Saint Mochorogh helped Kevin establish Glendalough as a centre of learning and it was he who administered the last rites to St Kevin as he lay dying.

REFLECTION

Mochorogh was a good friend to Kevin, helping him in his work, but allowing the credit to go to his friend. Have I any friends who could do with such selfless help? People rarely ask for help, but if an offer is made it is usually accepted gladly. Could I start offering help a little more often, when I have the time and the opportunity? Christianity is very much about friendship. Would I call myself a good friend?

24 DECEMBER

St Mochua

D.657. FEAST DAY: *24 December*

Mochua had been a famous warrior and was a late entrant to monasticism. His main foundation was Timahoe (*Tech Mochua*), Co. Laois. He is also remembered at Derenish in Co. Cavan, which he founded and where he is buried. He is the best known of the fifty-nine Saint Mochuas in the Irish martyrologies. He was distinguished as a healer and healed two abbots who were afflicted with physical ailments because of spiritual shortcomings – Colman Ello of a sudden loss of memory and Fintan Munnu of leprosy. The way he healed Colman was interesting. A little bird was singing beside them and Mochua asked Colman what it was saying in its song. Colman did not know, and Mochua told him it was that Colman had lost all his wisdom. Colman then admitted this to his friend and confessed his sin of pride and was healed.

REFLECTION ~
If called upon to heal someone, do I use my imagination as Mochua did? Imagination can be used in healing, in prayer and in meditation. As Jesus demonstrated, imagination is a powerful aid in understanding spiritual matters.

25 DECEMBER
St Forannan

D. C.982. FEAST DAY: *30 April*

Forannan was from the Decies and was Bishop of Donaghmore, Co. Tipperary, for a short while before leaving Ireland. He left Ireland because of a dream he had of an angel telling him to leave his native land and find the 'beautiful valley'. This led him to the Abbey of Waulsort on the River Meuse, which was an Irish monastery in Belgium. He was elected abbot in the year of his arrival. (The constitution stated that an Irish monk should rule the Abbey as long as there was an Irish monk in the community.) It flourished so well under Forannan that they had to annexe the neighbouring abbey to provide space. His work renewed the spirit of Benedictinism. Forannan was said to have been of a happy disposition and always ready to forgive and forget.

REFLECTION ~
Forannan's happy disposition may have been a large contributory cause of his monastery being full to overflowing. Do I realise how much my habitual or frequent disposition affects those around me? Should I try to improve in this respect? Learning to forgive and forget is not easy; could I pray about it?

26 DECEMBER

St Tathan/Tatheus/Dathai

D. SIXTH CENTURY. FEAST DAY: *26 December*

Tathan was the son of an Irish prince who was educated and ordained in Ireland. Tathan set out with six companions in a little coracle without sail or oar. They were carried to the River Severn and landed at Gwent, Glamorganshire in Wales. The King, Caradoc, invited Tathan and his monks to settle there permanently so they founded the church now called Llandathan (Tathan's church). The school at Llandathan attracted many scholars, including the famous St Cadoc. Caradoc's son Ynyr built them a monastery at present-day Caerwent, and appointed Tathan as the first abbot. His fame as a teacher spread far and wide. He was remembered as a miracle worker and a wise, hospitable man who never gave way to anger.

REFLECTION

Do I give way to anger? Have I learned how to express my anger in non-violent ways when alone? How could the energy of my anger be used in a positive way?

27 DECEMBER

St Aedh Dubh/Hugh/Aedh/Aidus

D.638. FEAST DAY: *10 May or 4 January*

Aedh was of the royal blood of Leinster but gave up his patrimony to be ordained. He became Abbot and Bishop of Kildare. He is described by some annalists as having actually been King of Leinster before becoming bishop but possibly he was just in line for the provincial kingship, in the *Derbhfine*, as was St Columba. He was called Aedh Dubh because of his black hair and also to distinguish him from another St Aedh of Kildare, who died a century earlier in 588.

REFLECTION

Giving things up is not popular today, though those who offer to serve often have to give up something – to do anything new the old has to go. What old things are going now in my life to make room for the new? What do I consider worth giving up for the sake of serving Jesus Christ? Maybe some small sacrifices could be achieved to help others in need in the penitential seasons of Lent and Advent?

28 DECEMBER

St Maughold/Machalus

D.498. FEAST DAY: *27 April or 28 December*

Maughold (originally Machalus; Maughold is his Manx name) was a robber chief who tried to deceive St Patrick by pretending one of the band was dead. Patrick knew the truth by the Holy Spirit and prayed, and the 'dead' man became truly dead. They fell at Patrick's feet, confessed and were baptised. Patrick restored the dead man to life and told them to make proper restitution. Maughold asked for a life of penitence so Patrick put him in a curragh without oars, telling him to serve Christ wherever he landed up, which was Eubonia (the Isle of Man). A holy man, Romulus, and the bishop, Concudrius, welcomed Maughold warmly. They taught and trained him, and he became bishop after Concudrius' death by general consent, as his preaching and his holy life had won all hearts. Maughold is honoured as an Apostle of the Isle of Man.

REFLECTION

Conversion is instant, an act of will; transformation is a slow process. Am I willing to work and pray and wait for a gradual transformation?

29 DECEMBER

St Mudhnat/Muadhnata/Monat

D. SIXTH CENTURY. FEAST DAY: *6 January*

Mudhnat was from the area of Glencar Lake which spans Co. Sligo and Co. Leitrim. She was one of Naitfrech's three daughters. Her two sisters were St Tullala and St Osnata, and her brother was St Laserian of Devenish. She founded a convent of nuns, probably at Keelty, a name derived from *caille*, a nun. This was further west than Glencar, nearer to the Drumcliffe Monastery. Possibly her nuns did the laundry and needlework for the monks at Drumcliffe. The convent later came under the protection of the Augustinian convent near Tuam, Co. Mayo. The ruined church there now is called St Mudhnat's. The Keelty Slab – an unfinished high cross that was discovered in the area – is in the basement of the National Museum.

REFLECTION

Mudhnat's life was obviously one of service, caring for others – her parents, her fellow nuns and the monastery nearby. People who live that sort of life are rarely celebrated or famous, they work away quietly and devotedly. It is easy to overlook such devoted service. Do I notice people who serve me quietly without a fuss?

30 DECEMBER

St Tullala

D. SIXTH CENTURY. FEAST DAY: *6 January*

Tullala was the third sister of St Laserian/Molaise of Devenish, along with St Mudhnat and St Osnata. She went on to become a nun at Kildare and eventually became abbess there. Her father was Naitfrech, and mother was Monua, living in Glendallan near Glencar, on the Sligo–Leitrim border.

REFLECTION
Tullala felt called to move away from her home in God's service; her two sisters were staying locally so she knew her parents would be well cared for. That she rose to such a high position in Kildare is a tribute to her parents' upbringing of their family. She would have gained confidence and a strong faith. Has my career been aided by my upbringing or have I been one of the ones who have succeeded in spite of an inauspicious start? People who do not have the family support Tullala had are still specially supported by the angels and the Communion of Saints – am I aware of that support? People whose parents gave them a poor self-image can gain confidence from knowing that they are children of God, made in His image. Have I that confidence?

31 DECEMBER
St Osnata/Osnat

D. SIXTH CENTURY. FEAST DAY: *6 January*

Osnata, from Glendallan, was one of Naitfrech and Monua's three daughters. Her brother was St Laserian/Molaise of Devenish, and her sisters were St Mudhnat and St Tullala. Osnata continued to live quietly in the Glencar area. She went on to found a church down past the Leitrim end of Glencar Lake, which is now called Killasnet. She is known to have visited St Farran at Drumcliffe. Possibly Osnata's visits to St Farran were to obtain soul-friendship and advice.

REFLECTION
Osnata is said to have founded the church at Killasnet rather than founding a convent like her sister Mudhnat or joining one like her sister Tullala. Local community and spreading the Gospel of Jesus Christ locally must have meant a lot to her. How important to me are community and family? If I have none or very little, do I realise that the church is a family and part of a larger worldwide family? How could I make my local church more of a family to me and others?

BIBLIOGRAPHY

Bede, *A History of the English Church and People* tr. Leo Sherley-Price, Harmondsworth: Penguin, 1955.

Bunson, Matthew and Margaret, *Our Sunday Visitor's Encyclopedia of Saints*, Huntingdon, Indiana: Our Sunday Visitor Publishing Division, 2014.

Carrigan, William, *History and Antiquities of the Diocese of Ossory*, Facsimile edition ed. John Bradley, Kilkenny: Wellbrook Press, 1981.

Carthage, Father O.C.S.O., *The Story of Saint Carthage: Otherwise Saint Mochuda*, Dublin: Browne and Nolan, 1937.

Cerebelaud-Salagnac, G. and B., *Ireland Land of Saints*, Dublin and London: Clonmore and Reynolds and Burns & Oates, 1966.

Comerford, Revd M., *Collections relating to the Dioceses of Kildare and Leighlin, Vols I and II*, Dublin: James Duffy and Sons, 1883.

Curtayne, Alice, *More Tales of Irish Saints*, Dublin: Talbot Press, 1967.

D'Arcy, Mary Ryan, *The Saints of Ireland: A Chronological Account of the Lives and Works of Ireland's Saints and Missionaries at Home and Abroad*, St. Paul, Minnesota: The Irish-American Cultural Institute, 1974.

De Paor, Liam, *Saint Patrick's World*, Dublin: Four Courts Press, 1996.

Duckett, Eleanor, *The Wandering Saints*, London: The Catholic Book Club, 1960.

Flanagan, Laurence, *A Chronicle of Irish Saints*, Belfast: The Blackstaff Press, 1990.

Gleeson, John, *Cashel of the Kings: A History of the Ancient Capital of Munster from the Date of its foundation until the present day*, Dublin: James Duffy 1927.

Hull, Eleanor, *Early Christian Ireland*, London and Dublin: Nutt and Gill, 1905.

James MacNamee: *History of the Diocese of Ardagh*, Dublin: Browne and Nolan, 1954.

Maguire, The Revd Canon: *A History of the Diocese of Raphoe*, Dublin: Browne and Nolan, 1920.

Montague, H. Patrick, *The Saints and Martyrs of Ireland*, Gerrards' Cross: Colin Smythe, 1981.

Neeson, Eoin, *The Book of Irish Saints*, Cork: Mercier Press, 1967.

Ní Mheara, Roísín, *Early Irish Saints in Europe: Their Sites and Their Stories*, Armagh: Cumann Seanchais Ard Macha, 2001.

O'Connell, Philip, *The Diocese of Kilmore: Its History and Antiquities*, Dublin: Browne and Nolan, 1937.

O'Hanlon, John, *Lives of the Irish Saints in 10 vols.*, London and Dublin: Duffy and Burns Oates, 1873.

Pochin Mould, Daphne: *The Irish Saints*, Dublin and London: Clonmore and Reynolds, 1964.

Power, Patrick, *Waterford and Lismore: A Compendious History of the United Dioceses*, Cork and London: Cork University Press, Longmans Green and Co. Ltd., 1937.

Roche, Aloysius, *A Bedside Book of Irish Saints*, Dublin: Browne and Nolan, 1941.

Stokes, George T., *Ireland and the Celtic Church*, London: Hodder and Stoughton, 1886.

Toulson, Shirley, *The Celtic Year*, Shaftesbury: Element, 1993.

Waddell, Helen, *The Wandering Scholars*, Harmondsworth: Pelican, 1954.

Woods, Richard J., *The Spirituality of the Celtic Saints*, Maryknoll, New York: Orbis Books, 2000.

INDEX OF SAINTS

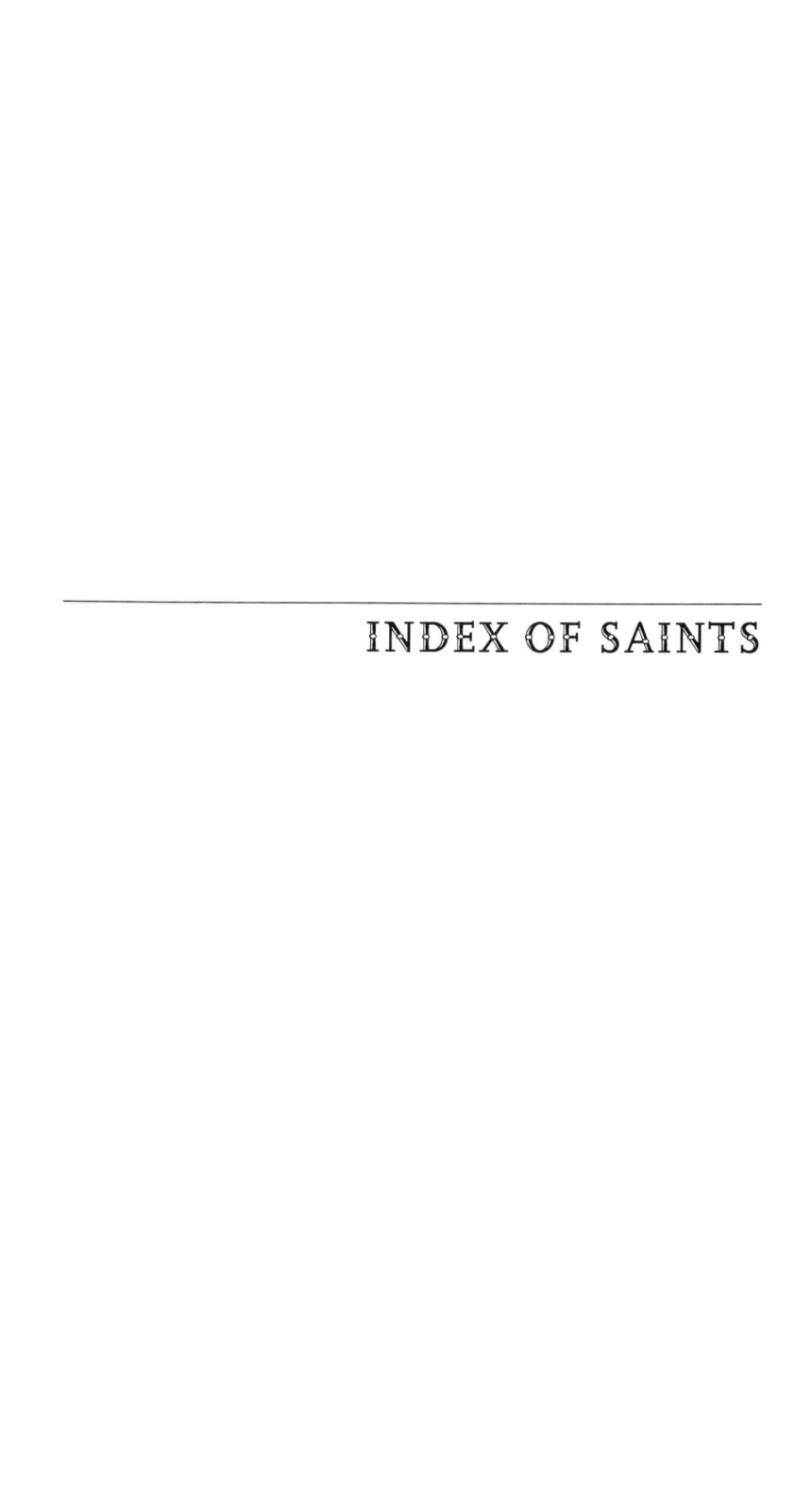

Abban, 13 May
Abbanus, see Abban
Abel, 5 August
Adalgisius, see Algise
Adamnan of Coldingham,
    20 March
Adamnan of Iona, 23 September
Aedamair, 18 January
Aedan of Ferns, 31 January
Aedh Dubh, 27 December
Aedh Mac Bruic, 28 February
Aenghus of Burt, 27 April
Aengus the Culdee, 11 March
Aenghus Macnisse, see
    Macanisius
Aenghus of Moyne, 15 July
Aifric, 8 December
Affrica, see Aifric
Aglenn, 6 March
Aidan, 31 August
Aidus, see Aedh Dubh
Aiféan, see Aifin
Aifin, 20 June
Aiglend, see Aglenn
Ailbeus, see Ailbhe
Ailbhe, 12 September
Albert, 8 January
Alby, see Ailbhe
Algise, 15 June
Alibeus, see Ailbhe
Alto, 15 August
Alton, see Alto
Anatolius, 3 February
Andrew of Fiesole, 22 August
Anmchadh, 14 March
Arbogast, 21 July
Assan, see Assicus
Assic, see Assicus

Assicus, 31 July
Attracta, 27 January
Auxilius, 27 August

Baithen, 4 November
Baoithin, see Baithen
Barrind, 21 May
Barry, see Finbarr
Beagán of Emlagh, 5 April
Beatus of Ardcarne, see Beoadh
Beatus of Honau, 2 August
Becan, 1 October
Beccan, see Beagán
Bee, 17 August
Bega, see Bee
Begnet, 7 November
Beircheart, 5 December
Benen, 9 November
Benignus, see Benen
Beoadh, 9 May
Berach, 22 April
Berchan, see Mobhí
Berthold, 28 July
Bigseach, 28 June
Bithe, 11 November
Blathe, 21 September
Blathmac, 19 January
Bolcan, see Olcan
Breaca, 4 June
Brendan of Birr, 29 November
Brendan of Clonfert, 16 May
Bricin, 5 September
Briga of Annaghdown,
    21 January
Bride of Kilbride, 26 January
Brigid of Kilbready,
    30 September
Brigid of Kildare, 1 February

Brochan, 4 December
Bronach, 2 April
Brone, 18 June
Brynach, 24 May
Brunsecha, 19 May
Buite, 7 December
Buo, 5 February
Buryan, 29 May

Cadán, 15 December
Cadroe, 18 May
Caidoc, 1 April
Caillin, 13 November
Caimin, 25 March
Cainneach, see Canice
Canice, 11 October
Cannera, 28 January
Caoimhe, 1 November
Carantoc, 23 July
Carthage, 15 May
Cassan, 23 May
Cathal, 14 July
Cathan, 17 July
Cathbad, 19 November
Catherine McAuley, 10 November
Cele Chriost, see Christicola
Celestine, see Cellach
Cellach, 6 April
Cellach, 1 May
Cera, 6 May
Charles of St Andrew, 9 Dec
Christian, 12 June
Christicola, 3 March
Ciannan, 25 February
Ciara, 2 March
Ciarán of Clonmacnoise, 9 September

Ciarán of Saighir, 4 March
Cillian of Artois, 16 November
Cocca, 29 June
Cognat, 19 April
Colcu, 3 May
Colman of Austria, 13 October
Colman of Cloyne, 24 November
Colman of Cork, 27 June
Colman of Dromore, 7 June
Colman Elo, 26 September
Colman of Inishboffin, 18 February
Colman of Kilmacduagh, 29 October
Colman of Slanore, 20 August
Colm McCrimthann, 3 December
Colm of Terryglass, 13 December
Columba, 9 June
Columba Marmion, 30 January
Columban of Bobbio, see Columbanus of Bobbio
Columban of Ghent, 2 February
Columbanus of Bobbio, 23 November
Columbanus of Slanore, see Colman of Slanore
Colmcille, see Columba
Comgall, 10 May
Comghan, 1 December
Commaigh, 27 May
Conall Coel, 22 May
Conall of Lough Gill, 2 June
Concord, 22 June
Conleth, 4 May

Index of Saints 287

Connoc, 26 November
Corbán, 19 July
Cormac of Cashel, 14 September
Cormac of Durrow, 21 June
Cronan of Balla, 30 March
Cronan of Roscrea, 28 April
Crone, 16 July
Crumnathy, 9 August
Cuach, 11 June
Cuan of Ahascra, 15 October
Cuanna, 9 April
Cuman of Aharney, 22 January
Cummeen the Fair, 24 February
Cummian the Tall, 12 November

Dabeoc, 4 January
Dagan, 13 September
Daganus, see Dagan
Daig, 18 August
Dairbhile, see Dervilla
Dallan Forgaill, 29 January
Dallan of Glencar, 3 October
Darerca, 22 March
Dathai, see Tathan
Davnet, 14 May
Declan, 24 July
Dega, see Daig
Deganus, see Daig
Deicuil, 18 November
Diarmaid of Inis Clothrann, 10 January
Dervilla, 3 August
Dervla, see Dervilla
Diarmuid, 29 July

Dichu, 18 October
Dicuil of Bosham, 16 February
Dichull of Inis-mac-Nessa, 15 March
Dime, see Dimma
Dimma, 6 January
Dioma, see Dimma
Disibode, 18 September
Domaingert, see Dimma
Donagh, 22 October
Donán, 17 April
Donard, 2 October
Donatus, see Donagh
Doolagh, see Doulaigh
Doulaigh, 17 November
Drostan, 11 July
Dubhthach, 30 June
Dubhthach of Iona, 14 January
Duffy, see Dubhthach of Iona
Duig, see Daig
Dúileach, see Doulaigh
Dymphna, 20 July

Eché, 7 August
Edan, see Aedan of Ferns
Edel Mary Quinn, 12 May
Edmund Rice, 5 May
Efflam, 5 June
Eibbán, see Aedan of Ferns
Eigneach, 29 September
Eithne, 8 May
Eliph, 17 October
Eltin, see Multose
Elwyn, 13 April
Emer, 10 December
Emin, see Beagán
Enan, 22 November

Enda, 21 March
Erc, 2 November
Erenai, see Ergnat
Ergnat, 30 October
Erhard, 10 February
Erkenbode, 12 April
Ernan, 11 January
Espain, 13 July
Etchen, 16 April
Ethbin, 19 October
Ethna, 26 February
Eton, see Etto
Etto, 10 July
Eugene, 23 August
Eunan, see Adamnan
Eusebius of St Gall,
  16 March

Fachtna, 14 August
Faithlinn, 15 August
Fanchea, 1 January
Farnan, 15 February
Fergal, 27 November
Fechin, 20 January
Feidlimidh, 8 August
Felim, see Feidlimidh
Fiacc, 14 October
Fiacre, 30 August
Fidelma, 26 February
Fillan, 9 January
Finan Cam, 7 April
Finan Lobur, 10 March
Finbarr, 25 September
Fincheall, 25 January
Finchu, 25 November
Fingar, 23 February

Finnian of Clonard,
  12 December
Finnian of Moville,
  10 September
Fintan of Clonenagh,
  17 February
Fintan of Rheinau,
  15 November
Fionnlugh, 3 January
Flannan, 18 December
Foillan, 31 October
Forannan, 25 December
Francis Taylor, 26 October
Fraoch, 20 December
Fridian, 18 March
Fortchern, 24 April
Fursey, 16 January

Gall, 16 October
Garbhan, 18 July
Gedanus, see Cadán
Gelasius, 27 March
Gerald, 13 March
Gerardine, 8 November
Gerebern, 22 July
Germanus, 2 May
Gibrian, 2 July
Giolla Criost, see Christian
Goar, 4 August
Gobain, 30 July
Gobban, 6 December
Gobnait, 11 February
Grellan, 17 September
Grimonia, 24 September
Guasacht, 24 January
Gunifort, 24 August

Index of Saints 289

Herenat, see Ergnat
Hymelin, 29 April
Ibar, 23 April
Iberius, see Ibar
Íde, see Ita
Indract, 4 July
Iserninus, 7 May
Ita, 15 January
Ive, 23 March

Jarlath, 6 June
John Henry Newman,
   9 October
John Sullivan, 8 September

Keelin, 3 April
Kentigerna, 7 January
Kenneth, see Canice
Kessog, 13 January
Kevin, 3 June
Kilian of Würzburg, 8 July

Lachtain, 19 March
Landelin, 7 October
Lappan, 26 March
Laserian of Devenish,
   12 August
Laserian of Leighlin, 18 April
Lassair, 29 March
Lassar, 5 November
Lawrence, 14 November
Lelia, 11 August
Liadain, 10 August
Libhear, 26 May
Loichene the Silent, 12 January
Loman of Lough Gill,
   10 October

Loman of Lough Owel,
   7 February
Loman of Trim, 4 February
Lorcan, see Lawrence
Lua, 11 May
Lugaidh, 11 September
Lugdach, 6 October
Lughaidh, 9 March
Lupait, 2 September
Luran, 28 October

Macaille, 25 April
Macanisius, see Macnessa
Macartan, 24 March
Machalus, see Maughold
Macheanog, 20 May
Macnessa, 3 September
Maculin, 16 September
Mael-Brigid, 22 February
Maeldoid, 19 September
Maeldubh, 20 October
Maelduff, 17 May
Maelruain, 7 July
Maelrubha, 8 June
Maglorious, 23 October
Maghnend,
   see Maighnenn
Magnus, 6 September
Maighnenn, 16 December
Mailduff, see Maelduff
Maimbod, 23 January
Malachy, 3 November
Malchus, 25 May
Manchán of Mohill,
   14 February
Manchán of Lemanaghan,
   20 September

Mansuy, 1 September
Margaret Ball, 26 October

Marianus Scotus of Ratisbon,
    9 February
Marnock of Portmarnock,
    1 March
Mary Aikenhead, 19 February
Matt Talbot, 25 June
Maughold, 28 December
Maugille, 30 May
Mearnóg of Kilmarnock,
    25 October
Mel, 6 February
Melangell, 14 June
Melle, 31 March
Menou, 12 July
Michan, 17 December
Michean, see Michan
Michanus, see Michan
Mirren, 15 September
Moabba, see Abban
Mobeccoc, see Beagán
Mobhí, 12 October
Mochae, 23 June
Mochta, 19 August
Mochua, 24 December
Mochorogh, 23 December
Modomnoc, 13 February
Modwena of Polsworth, 5 July
Moengal, 27 September
Mogue of Clonmore, 11 April
Mogue of Ferns, see Aedan of
    Ferns
Molagga, 21 February
Molaise of Inishmurray,
    28 May

Moling, 17 June
Molua, see Lua
Moluag, 19 June
Monessan, 20 April
Moninna, 6 July
Mono, 12 February
Mothorian, 26 June
Muadhán Oilithir,
    20 September
Mudhnat, 29 December
Multose, 11 December
Munchin, 2 January
Munis, 4 October
Mura, 12 March
Muredach, 13 August

Naile, 7 March
Nano Nagle, 21 November
Nathi, 1 August
Ninnidh, 17 January
Nennid, 21 April
Nessan of Mungret, 25 July
Nessan of Lambay,
    22 December

Odhrán, 30 November
Olcan, 20 February
Oliver Plunkett, 1 July
Onchu, 8 February
Osmana, 25 August
Osnata, 31 December

Palladius, 14 December
Pappan, 22 September
Paternus, 10 April
Patrick, 17 March
Peacon, see Becan

Index of Saints 291

Pellegrinus, 30 April
Phelim, see Feidlimidh
Piran, 5 March
Priscianus, see Senan
Rioch, 6 August
Ronan of Locronan, 1 June
Ronan Finn, 27 July
Ronan of Kilronan,
  2 December
Ruadhan, 15 April
Rumold, 24 June

Safan, see Samthann
Samthann, 19 December
Sanctan, 10 June
Saran, 27 February
Schotin, see Scuthin
Scolan, see Scuthin
Scothinus, see Scuthin
Scuthin, 5 January
Seachnall, 28 November
Seadhna, 16 June
Secundinus, see Seachnall
Senach, 21 August
Sedna, 5 October
Senan, 8 March
Senell, 6 November
Sillao, 26 July
Sillaeus, see Sillao
Siollan, see Sillao
Sinach MacDara,
  28 September
Sinell, 31 May
Sinilis, see Senell
Silvester, 26 August
Sunniva, 3 July

Tacan, see Tegan
Tassach, see Assicus
Tathan, 26 December
Tatheus, see Tathan
Tegan, 28 August
Thaddeus MacCarthy,
  24 October
Tida, 7 September
Tigernach, 4 April
Tigernan, 8 April
Torannan, 27 October
Tressan, 14 April
Triduana, 8 October
Tuathal, 28 March
Tullala, 30 December

Ultan of Ardbraccan,
  4 September
Ultan of Fosses, 13 June
Ursanne, see Ursin
Ursicinus, see Ursin
Ursin, 21 December
Ursinus, see Ursin
Usaille, see Auxilius

Vindolinus, see Wendel
Virgilius, see Fergal
Volcanus, see Olcan
Vougay, 20 November

Waldolen, see Wendel
Wendelin, see Wendel
Wendel, 21 October
Winoc, 29 August
Wiro, 9 July

Ze, see Etto